Teacher Lore

Learning from Our Own Experience

Teacher Lore

Learning from Our Own Experience

edited by

William H. Schubert
and
William C. Ayers

 Educator's International Press, Inc.
Troy, NY

Schubert, William H. & Ayers, William C.
Teacher Lore: Learning from Our Own Experience

Published by Educator's International Press, Inc.
18 Colleen Road
Troy, N.Y. 12180

Previously published by Longman © 1992
(previous ISBN: 0-8013-0796-1)

Library of Congress Cataloging-in-Publication Data:
   Teacher lore: learning from our own experience
edited by William H. Schubert & William C. Ayers.
     p. 180 cm.
Includes bibliographic references and index
ISBN: 1-891928-03-1 (paper: alk. paper)

   1. Teaching.   2. Teachers--United States--Attitudes.
I. Schubert, William Henry.   II. Ayers, William, 1944-
LB1775.2.T43 1999   99-24191 (CIP)
371.102--dc21

ISBN 1-891928-03-1 (pbk.)

Manufactured in the United States of America

04 03 02 01 00 99   1 2 3 4 5 6

Contents

Prologue

Who understands the peculiar demands of teaching, the mind-wrecking and back-breaking moments of it, the forests of paperwork that surround it, the endless preparation for it, the invasiveness of it into every corner of a life? Who knows the ecstasies of it, its specific satisfactions, its dazzling transformative possibilities—and these are not merely for the learners, but, in an elusive and wonderfully interactive way, at least as powerfully for the teachers themselves? Who can say what teachers think they are up to, what they take to be the point of what they are doing, what it means for teachers to teach? Who, indeed. To say that teachers are the ones who understand, know, and can say seems so obvious that it is beneath reporting. But in the often odd, sometimes upside-down world of social research, the obvious news must be reported and repeated: The secret of teaching is to be found in the local detail and the everyday life of teachers; teachers can be the richest and most useful source of knowledge about teaching; those who hope to understand teaching must turn at some point to teachers themselves.

WILLIAM AYERS

Preface

TEACHER LORE: CONTEXT AND ORIGINS

Through this book we want to provide teachers with perspectives on teaching drawn from other teachers. We offer these perspectives to both experienced teachers and to those who aspire to become teachers. Perhaps the greatest potential of teacher lore resides in an oral tradition among teachers who exchange and reconstruct perspectives together. This reflection on experience, this reconceiving of the meaning and purpose of one's life and contribution as a teacher, is the essence of teacher lore.

Teachers tend to be taught by researchers, scholars, and teacher educators. The understandings, reflections, textbooks, and articles that these people offer can be useful, but our concern is with the necessary but neglected use of perspectives of experienced teachers themselves for teacher education. During the past ten years we have witnessed increased attention to teachers as sources of insight about teaching. This is an essential corrective, an important expansion of the knowledge considered "legitimate" in teacher education. A wide range of work is beginning to bring teachers' perspectives to the benefit of other teachers through research and teacher education.

The tradition of action research, which stems from the vast work of John Dewey, has been reinvigorated at different times since its heyday in the 1920s and 1930s. Revived in the 1940s and 1950s by Stephen Corey and Alice Miel, this approach conceived of teaching as intellectual experimental work, and recognized teachers as being in a position to inquire about teaching in ways not available to those outside of classrooms. Teachers can see nuance, subtlety, and complexity. They can raise questions that require sustained time to answer in the embeddedness of classrooms. While misguided attempts to do action research have had teachers mimic traditional researchers and have thereby missed the point of action research at its best, enlightened action research (such as the work of such action researchers as Ann Lieberman, Stephen Kemmis, and Robin McTaggart) has viewed teachers as having developed their own brand of inquiry worthwhile to school settings.

A second line of teacher-oriented research, known as the teacher-as-researcher movement, also provides the enlightened perspective described above. Initiated by Lawrence Stenhouse in England, the teacher-as-researcher idea started by pairing a university researcher/theorist with a classroom teacher. Teachers and researchers would thereby converse, address problems, and reflect on possibilities together. Teachers who participated in the teacher-as-researcher movement typically replicated their experiences by joining with other teachers in similar projects. Thus, the idea spread, leading to conferences and writings in which teachers formally shared ideas with other teachers.

A third approach implicitly respects teachers as people who reflect in action. Donald Schön has written much about how professionals in many careers reflect with great seriousness as they carry out their daily work. Ken Zeichner has focused on teachers' critical reflection in their work. Reflective practitioners are often too occupied to write about or otherwise preserve their insights and understandings. So, others have tried to do so in different ways.

Stemming from the work of Elliot Eisner and several of his former students, renditions known as educational criticism have been used in an attempt to capture or portray educational situations in their textured richness and complexity. Like critics in the arts, after which they are patterned, educational critics should be connoisseurs of that which they observe, describe, and interpret. These researchers typically offer their interpretations to the teachers about whom they write to gain their input for future renditions.

Educational psychologists, especially those predisposed to favor cognitive psychology, have tried to capture thinking processes of teachers. They sometimes compare the thinking of novices with that of veteran teachers. Some of this work is summarized in the 1986 *Handbook of Research on Teaching* edited by Merlin Wittrock.

Some researchers call for narrative or storylike renditions of teachers and teaching. Michael Connelly first investigated the "personal-practical knowledge" of teachers quite systematically. Today his approach and that of his colleagues praises the value of stories. In fact, Connelly and D. Jean Clandinin have recently begun to advocate the sharing of stories and ideas among teachers through a newsletter entitled *Among Teachers*.

Finally, others (such as William Pinar, Madeleine Grumet, and Richard Butt) advocate that biographies of teachers, especially autobiographical accounts, are the best sources for understanding teachers. Biographies and autobiographies of teachers have long been available in book form and more recently as films.

These streams of inquiry that flow into the larger notion of teacher lore are not exhaustive, but are, instead, illustrative of work in progress. This work is influencing teachers, supervisors, administrators, teacher educators, educational researchers and theorists, and educational policy makers of varied stripes.

This book fits within these streams or traditions, sometimes overlapping several of them, drawing insights from many, and hopefully contributing to each in some fashion. While additional references are presented at greater length in Chapter 9, it is enough for these prefatory remarks to mention the larger context of teacher lore in which The Teacher Lore Project, the main research source for this book, is situated. The Teacher Lore Project began at The University of Illinois at Chicago in 1985. It grew out of a desire of teachers to see their own experiential learnings and those of other teachers become acknowledged as worthwhile knowledge in the field of education. Interviews, observations, and reflections have served as a basis for researchers to produce this book.

In The Teacher Lore Project, we specifically wanted to know more about what reflective teachers have learned from their experiences. We are convinced that this should be a greater source of insight and understanding for those who seek to become teachers and for those who strive to become better teachers.

Seven years ago several of us, all experienced teachers, gathered to study topics of mutual interest. Our attention frequently turned to the lack of participation of teachers in research about teachers. We could all think of wonderful teachers, teachers who influenced our lives and the lives of others. We wondered: Why weren't these teachers and others like them given a chance to share what they learned from their years of service as teachers? Why do the great teachers of our generation (and from past generations as well) so frequently retire into a kind of obscurity where their work is considered done? Why are teachers so often invisible and silent even in their own worlds? We wondered, too: What gives meaning and direction to the lives of teachers? What advice might they offer to others who are teachers or want to be teachers? How could good teachers help us better understand how teaching can be improved?

We wanted to act on these and related questions—in short, we wanted to make our study group become active and engaged. We wanted to try to extend greater opportunity for teachers' experiential insights and perspectives to be better known. (See the Note of Acknowledgment at the end of this Preface.)

We remain convinced that conscientious teachers reflect seriously on their work. They think and feel carefully about what they do and why they do it. They use their experiences as a basis for fashioning responses to similar situations that they encounter daily. They imagine new possibilities and try to anticipate the consequences of acting on them. This involves a careful eye to subtle but powerful side effects, not just main or intended outcomes. Such teachers continuously monitor their underlying assumptions about teaching and learning, their personal philosophies of education, if you will. They tune in carefully to the way their assumptions both guide and are created by practice. They reflect on or about their experiences when they have the time, *and* they reflect and rebuild their orientation in the course of experience as well.

In this book, we want to give you a flavor of this kind of reflection as it is done by teachers, teacher educators, and instructional leaders. This will be done sometimes by using teachers' own words, sometimes by telling stories of teaching experience, and at other times by commenting on and interpreting teachers' perspectives. We see all three of these approaches as acknowledgment of the value of teachers' voices. In Part I, I begin by autobiographically remembering my own experience as a beginning teacher, how I drew upon a "teacher lore" of my own to create the teacher I was becoming, and how some of my experience can now serve as teacher lore for others. Janet Miller responds to the idea of teacher lore by drawing upon her considerable experience with teachers who reflect together on the meaning and purpose of their work, trying to find their voices and create spaces for their free expression. In Part II, Suzanne Millies helps us to see that teaching saturates the being of teachers, forging dimensions of personality, assumptions, and repertoire, and that it is not merely technique. Mari Koerner then portrays ways in which teachers see themselves and their work, spanning the range from the mundane to the ideal. Virginia Jagla examines what it means to be imaginative and intuitive as a teacher, while Carol Melnick shows that good teachers know their students as whole people and develop learning experiences based on lives of their students outside of school. Pat Hulsebosch examines how and why some teachers engage meaningfully with parents and others do not. Part III encourages other educators to learn from teacher lore and expand on it in their own ways, by discussing resources for doing teacher lore (Chapter 8), readings to make the idea of teacher lore more robust (Chapter 9), and perspectives on what kinds of research are in the spirit of teacher lore (Chapter 10). Finally, in Chapter 11, Bill Ayers enables us to journey through some of his experiences and perceive the necessary and neglected place of teacher lore in several realms of teaching that he has known.

Teacher lore is not an end in itself; instead, it is a basis for teacher reflection, and it is our contention that it is only reflective teachers (not those who teach by recipe, technique, or doctrine) who are able to grow continuously. They are the ones who genuinely have twenty or thirty years of experience, instead of one year of experience twenty or thirty times. Such teachers are the hope for enabling children and youth to fashion their own growth and to contribute to the improvement of the world around them.

NOTE OF ACKNOWLEDGMENT

We sought and received funding from the Chicago Area School Effectiveness Council (CASEC) at the University of Illinois at Chicago, started by Gary A. Griffin (then dean of the College of Education). We asked administrators, teachers, former students, teacher educators, and others to nominate good teachers for us to interview. Gary Sykes and Norman Weston, our first researchers whose initial interviews were exploratory, helped us define our purposes more clearly, and helped begin the process of building an eclectic methodology. Anne Isaacson and Mari Koerner spent considerable time and effort analyzing taped interviews, reviewing relevant literature, and making suggestions for next steps. Ideas from these explorations were shared with other members of the group (Pat Hulsebosch, Ginny Jagla, Carol Melnick, Suzanne Millies, Georgiana Zizzis, Joe Nelson, Tom Thomas, Bill Ayers, and Bill Schubert). Each of us played with these notions and our own pet concerns within the general topic. Ideas were explored with Ann Lopez, Joel Spring, Noreen Garman, Gail McCutcheon, Frances Klein, Nelson Haggerson, Louis Rubin, Jeff Cornett, Wayne Ross, Alan Tom, Ken Kantor, Dan Marshall, Sue Jungck, Anne Bennison, Jean Erdman, Shirley Kessler, Fred Klonsky, Grace Stanford, Larry Braskamp, Gary Griffin, George Olson, Judith Ponticell, James Henderson, Suzanne Lindsay, Geneva Haertel, and Danielle Raymond. All of these individuals and CASEC are thanked for their thoughtful contributions. Lisa Brendel, Linda Dale, and Marilyn Geron are thanked for their excellent contributions through word processing.

Heartfelt thanks are extended to Naomi Silverman, as Longman's editor, who has made invaluable suggestions and has supported the idea of this book from its early stages. Victoria Mifsud, our production editor, is thanked for her fine work. Anonymous reviewers selected by Longman are also acknowledged for their recommendations, criticisms, and encouragement.

WILLIAM H. SCHUBERT
WILLIAM AYERS

CONTRIBUTORS

William Ayers is Assistant Professor of Education at the University of Illinois at Chicago. He writes frequently about teaching, teacher education, and ethical and political issues in classrooms. Having served for a year as Assistant Deputy Mayor of Education for Chicago, Dr. Ayers is an active leader in Chicago's well-known projects of school reform. An early childhood educator for twelve years, he is the author of *The Good Preschool Teacher* and his numerous articles have appeared in such journals as the *Cambridge Journal of Education, Democracy and Education, Educational Forum, Teaching Education, Teachers College Record, Harvard Educational Review,* and the *Journal of Teacher Education.*

    Patricia Hulsebosch has been a teacher for twenty-one years. Her teaching experiences have included working with young children in public schools, children in an alternative school, and deaf adolescents in a residential setting. Her areas of interest include school-community relations, equity in education, and gay and lesbian studies. Currently, Dr. Hulsebosch is Assistant Professor and Director of the Preservice Education Program at the National-Louis University urban campus in Chicago.

    Virginia Jagla has been working in education for twenty-one years. She taught and was an administrator in the Chicago Public Schools at the elementary level, taught science and computer classes for the Museum of Science and Industry, and worked in arts education through Urban Gateways in Chicago. Dr. Jagla supervises student teachers and teaches methods classes for Barat College and previously worked for eight years as a student teaching supervisor at the University of Illinois at Chicago. Currently she is an administrator and consultant for the Waukegan Public Schools in Illinois, and is completing *Teachers' Everyday Use of Imagination and Intuition: In Pursuit of the Elusive Image.*

    Mari E. Koerner is Assistant Professor in the College of Education at Roosevelt University. Her experience includes teaching at the elementary and preschool levels in public schools in Chicago, where she continues to teach junior high and consult with schools. Dr. Koerner teaches in and chairs the Teacher Education Program Area for preservice and in-service undergraduate and graduate students. She is a contributor to the recently published book edited by James Henderson, *Reflective Teaching: Becoming an Inquiring Educator.*

    Carol R. Melnick is Chair of the Department of Special Education at National-Louis University. Her teaching experiences have included working with children in the Head Start program, with youngsters from birth to twenty-one as a speech-language pathologist, and with graduate students in her current position. Dr. Melnick is the guest editor of a special issue of the *International Journal of Educational Research* entitled "Parents and Teachers as Educative Partners," and has contributed a chapter to *Reflective Teaching: Becoming an Inquiring Educator.* Her interests include parent-student-teacher partnerships and early childhood special education.

    Janet L. Miller is Associate Professor of Education and Director of the Ph.D. Program in Curriculum and Teaching at Hofstra University. A former secondary school teacher of English, Dr. Miller specializes in curriculum studies, gender issues, and teachers' knowledge and development. She serves as Managing Editor of *JCT: An*

Interdisciplinary Journal of Curriculum Studies and has contributed to journals on feminist studies, curriculum theory, and teachers' lives. She recently completed *Creating Spaces and Finding Voices: Teachers Collaborating for Empowerment.*

Palma Suzanne George Millies is an educator with many years of teaching experience. She has taught French and Language Arts at the elementary level for five years and English at the high school level for almost twenty years. She has served as the District Coordinator of Gifted Education and the Assistant Principal for Instruction at Willowbrook High School. Dr. Millies is currently serving as the Assistant Superintendent for Instruction for Maine Township High School. She is coeditor (with Gary Griffin) of the book, *The First Years of Teaching: Background Papers and a Proposal,* and teaches courses at National-Louis University and Roosevelt University.

William H. Schubert, Director of The Teacher Lore Project, is Professor of Education and Chair of Curriculum, Instruction, and Evaluation at the University of Illinois at Chicago, where he was given the Distinguished Scholar-Teacher Award by collegues in the College of Education in 1988. A elementary school teacher for seven years, Dr. Schubert now develops in-service education with schools. His books include *Curriculum Books: The First Eighty Years* with Ann Lopez-Schubert, *Curriculum: Perspective, Paradigm, and Possibility* and *Reflections from the Heart of Educational Inquiry: Understanding Curriculum and Teaching through the Arts* with George Willis. Schubert serves on editorial boards of such journals as *Educational Theory, JCT, Teaching Education, Journal of Curriculum and Supervision,* and *Phenomenology and Pedagogy.* He is President of the John Dewey Society, former President of The Society for the Study of Curriculum History, and former Factotum of Professors of Curriculum. An outgrowth of the study of "teacher lore" is Schubert's initial work on "student lore," about which he has become a book series editor for SUNY Press; the series is entitled, *Student Lore: The Educational Experience of Students in School and Society.*

PART I

What Is Teacher Lore?

CHAPTER 1

Our Journeys into Teaching:

Remembering the Past

William H. Schubert

For over forty years I have been privileged to listen to and engage in the discourse of good teachers. As a child and youth, I vividly remember discussions about teachers and students at the supper table in our rural Indiana farmhouse. My mother was a high school social studies and mathematics teacher, and a frequent recipient of the "Favorite Teacher Award" in the nearby town. My father was a school administrator of another small town school, and in my early years I recall him simultaneously holding the posts of superintendent, elementary and secondary principal, industrial arts teacher, commercial teacher, and coach of all sports. My grandmother and great aunt, the twins, told stories of teaching in the one-room schoolhouses that dotted the Indiana countryside from 1912 to the 1950s. Down the road lived another great aunt who also taught in rural schools for many years. I heard stories of ways to reach students through their outside interests, of student achievements and frustrations, and even of several generations of students from the same families.

I was at home in school, because schooling was so thoroughly alive in my home life. Yet, for some time (during adolescent rebellion), being a teacher was not a high priority on the list of what I wanted to become. I wanted to be a great athlete, a sports writer, an architect, a psychologist, a minister, a biologist, a philosopher, and more.

At a small liberal arts college, however, I discovered the world of ideas and how much they could contribute to whatever is most fundamental to the guiding philosophy of a person. This seemed most important to me. No longer did I see literature, philosophy, mathematics, biology, chemistry, music, art, psychology, history, and other disciplines as independent entities. I had begun to perceive their interdependence as relevant to my own growth as a human being. As a person, I contributed and could intentionally contribute to what I became in the world. What I became had to be tied carefully to what I wanted to contribute. I wanted to help others see the value of these connections for their own lives. In short, I wanted to teach.

I thought back to my earlier experience as a cadet teacher in an elementary school classroom while I was a senior in high school, and as I concluded my senior year in college, I was moved by experiences as a student teacher. I began to reflect on the lives of children I had begun to influence. I knew somehow that there was something deeper, more wonderful, and mysterious than mere instructing and testing—something that resided in the personal encounter with each emerging life that made the real connection between teaching and what I wanted to do in life. This knowledge filled me with enthusiasm. I discovered that I aspired to help others create their lives. I wanted a high calling in life and could think of none higher than that of helping new generations meet the world.

I wanted to explore more about how to achieve this calling, and decided to study history and philosophy of education in a master's degree program before plunging into a classroom. I learned quickly that every generation stemming back to antiquity had great teachers who asked similar questions, and who perceived the education of subsequent generations as the highest calling. Like parenting, teaching was a way to help humanity remake itself.

While much of my journey to become a teacher involved deliberate philosophical reflection, more than I realized at the time was to happen serendipitously. I recall my initial quest to get a job teaching. The late 1960s was a good time to seek a teaching job, in part because, like today, there was a considerable supply of jobs and a need for more good teachers to fill them. As I concluded my master's degree program, recruiters came to Indiana University from many school districts to interview those who were about to graduate. I decided that I wanted to find a job in or near a major city. I must have had thirty interviews on campus and almost as many invitations to come to school districts for the more formal interview process, which often included the "wine and dine" experience that has long been prevalent in interviews for the business world. So I went on visits for several interviews.

One particular interview in a Chicago suburban school district with a fine reputation was most memorable. After visiting with an assistant superintendent over lunch and then meeting several other officials in the central administrative offices, I was ushered to the office of a principal of an elementary school. With all the interviewing practice I had at the university, I felt confident. In fact, I practically thought, "I challenge you to come up with a question that stumps me!" At just that point things stopped going so smoothly. The principal asked, "What do you think of a multitext approach, and how would you develop a program based on that approach?" I was taken aback. I had never heard of a multitext approach. Some fast thinking was necessary here. I knew that "multi" meant many and "text" referred to classroom books. So, groping at first, I somehow began to pull together an answer.

Surprising myself as I listened to what I made up, I heard something like this: "Well, in social studies or science, for example, I would not order one textbook for each of thirty students. Instead, I would survey existing textbooks and order, perhaps, six copies from five different publishers. Then I would look at the district curriculum guide and generate leading questions that would stimulate students (individually or in small groups) to seek information, draw inferences, pose problems, and reflect on the meaning of what they encountered. I would also try to find trade books and other sources of information to have available, coordinating available media (films, filmstrips, and the like) with topics studied as students pursued the leading questions. I could even go to garage sales, flea markets, and used bookstores to accumulate materials for the enriched learning environment that I would like to develop with the students. They, too, could be encouraged to contribute to the collection of classroom materials on any topic, so that they would feel a greater part of ownership in the classroom life."

I went on like that for a while, and then continued to respond to other questions, but my mind remained focused on the multitext approach. To this day, I do not know where that principal came up with the term. I did learn later that there was some use of it, and similar terms in the science education literature in the mid-1960s, and the principal's main area of interest was, indeed, science education. Nevertheless, the more important consideration at the time was that I was, in fact, hired.

Upon being hired, I asked to look at my classroom. Immediately, I noticed that on the bookshelf there were small numbers of textbooks from different publishers, rather than one for each student from only one publisher. I congratulated myself, "You guessed right, Schubert!" I knew what I had to do during the summer. I began to prepare leading questions and project ideas to stimulate the multitext approach. I did not want to be behind the other teachers in that regard; I did not want to be the young old fogey who was mired in traditional pedagogy.

By the time school opened in September, I was ready with my leading questions and project ideas. I knew that I must be right in assuming that everyone taught this way in this school when I learned that individualized reading was a district policy. Instead of reading basal readers, students were to read library books, both story and information, that they self-selected or selected with the guidance of the teacher or librarian. I was impressed with this approach. I was astonished to see most of the children carrying stacks of books around, even the most active and least stereotyped bookworms. Teachers would have conferences with students about what they had read. Sometimes students who read the same books would have discussions. Students would make book advertisements for the benefit of other students, and good reading materials became a subject of the student grapevine. If a conference revealed a need for some specific reading skill, teachers would have on hand a selection of worksheets to assist students, the end being the increased capacity to enjoy and learn from a higher level of reading material.

My plans for the multitext approach in other subjects seemed to be a logical extension of the individualized reading program. So, with considerable haste, I began to put it into practice. I was especially fond of the way it worked in social studies. My sixth graders responded well, and took considerable interest in the questions and projects.

As my second year of teaching got under way, I noticed that I was being observed by the district-level supervisors, and occasionally even the associate superintendent for curriculum and instruction. I thought that this must be a matter of course for new teachers. One spring day in my second year, the associate superintendent quietly informed me that he and his colleagues had been watching me with some interest in the area of social studies, and wondered what I called the approach I was using. I quickly responded, "Why, it's the multitext approach, of course," thinking that once again I might have said the "secret word." He looked at me in a rather puzzled fashion, and this was a man who knew the field and its literature quite well. The puzzled look was followed by a request to tell more. I did, in much the same fashion that I imagined aloud to the principal in the interview two years earlier. Now, however, I had concrete examples to back up my advocacy. The associate superintendent said that he had been impressed with this approach for some time and thought it would be a good idea to make other teachers aware of it. He asked that I consider receiving extra summer pay to develop the "multitext" approach so other teachers might use it as well. I was flattered. I spent the summer writing more than twenty learning packages and presented them to teachers in the fall preopening workshops in the district. Some of my "teacher lore" (assumptions and practices developed from my experience) was passed along for other teachers to interpret in their own ways according to the circumstances of their teaching situations.

As I reflect on my experience with the "multitext approach," I realize that it is but one of many instances in the seven years that I taught in elementary school that I was engaged in teacher lore. I was engaged in teacher lore in at least two main ways. First, ideas and approaches that I developed were influenced by the lore I had accumulated from teachers I had known and from my own developing experiences. Second, teaching situations that I developed and reflected upon constituted teacher lore that others might profit from sharing.

My "multitext approach" is a form of teacher lore that I have to offer other teachers. Similarly, in its development I drew upon the teaching of others. To illustrate, in trying to make a learning package (set of leading questions) come alive for the traditional social studies topic of prehistoric time, I modified an activity by Neal Merritt, a history professor from my undergraduate days at Manchester College. I asked students to devise a fifty-pound pack of items from contemporary society to take into a long-term visit to prehistoric times for purposes of survival. When the students collaborated in small groups for this project, they gave reasons for selections, critiqued the usefulness of items on one another's lists, tried to think of the taken-for-granted products of our culture that one would not want to be without, noticed greater connections among products (such as the senselessness of taking anything that needed to be plugged into an electrical socket), and worked together to create improved lists. I recall well the debates about the best items to help produce fire (flints, matches, lighters, a magnifying glass?). With eleven-year-olds, I always enjoyed the ways in which childhood clearly showed itself; for example, thirty pounds of seriously determined materials with twenty pounds of bubble gum added on. I shall never forget the perceptive eleven-year-old boy who wanted to bring the neighbor's three-year-old daughter (weighing in at twenty-eight pounds), claiming that when he was twenty-six and she was eighteen the age difference would not seem so great.

I could elaborate more than space provides on how, for six years, I directed a stage version of *A Christmas Carol* by Charles Dickens, and how seeing the students as actors and as characters helped me realize a greater potential for acting in my regular classes with them. I began to look for opportunities to "act things out" in all subjects. I vividly recall an incident in my fourth year of teaching when I began a favorite unit on prehistoric times. I had an opening "speech" and set of questions that encouraged students to think philosophically (my pet hope for people!). The speech took forty-five minutes, and I thought it raised important questions that got students to wonder about who, what, why, when, and where they were. I was surrounded by sixty-three sixth graders and had just announced that I was about to lead them on a journey into prehistoric times. Then, the principal entered the area and announced that he forgot to mention the assembly that was to occur for all students in about twenty minutes.

I knew that I could not do the planned lesson . . . but I had to do something. I desperately looked around for clues. I found none from the other teachers with whom I was team-teaching, and the students were ready for the journey into prehistory that I had promised. Somehow, the idea flashed through my mind that I always wanted to try acting as part of my teaching, harkening back to the Dickens performances, and how always before I had thought of excuses to cover up the fact that I was embarrassed to step into the actor's role as teacher. There was no alternative but to push myself off the diving board. A sure way to be innovative is to make public promises that cannot be broken.

I glanced at the chalkboard and noticed a list from the previous social studies unit, a reminder of the different types of social scientists: historians, geographers, archaeologists, anthropologists, sociologists, economists, political scientists, and so on. Quickly, without realizing what I was promising, I heard myself say, "We are going to introduce the new unit on prehistoric times *and* review the unit on social scientists at the same time. I will start this off by pretending that I am a prehistoric man doing something. Your job is to guess which social scientist would be most likely to study whatever it is that I am doing." At that point I had no idea how I would live up to this bizarre promise. In order to give myself a moment to plan my next step, I ruffled my hair, put my sport coat up over my head in a strange attempt to look prehistoric, and mumbled a rather loud sequence of nonsense syllables. Without pause, a student piped up, "Linguist!" We were off and running; the students even invented stories, such as a change in group leadership (to be studied by political scientists), finding a tool from earlier prehistoric tribes (archaeologist), and many more.

We went to the assembly that day. Although I cannot recall what it was about, I vividly marked the day as the beginning of acting as an approach to teaching that had lasting value for me. By popular demand from the students, we acted out other social studies situations—for example, space travelers looking at the earth and thinking how odd the customs were, people on a street corner discussing the value of learning to do different kinds of lessons in school (the kinds we were then learning), people commenting on the human and social value of different scientific and technological discoveries and inventions, and the techniques that advertisers use to dupe buyers. Students often spontaneously responded with group skits or one-person shows to illustrate a point or elaborate an issue in story form. In some way I knew that my desire to be an actor as a teacher was prompted by a philosophy professor who would come to class and role-play a different famous philosopher each day.

Another illustration of innovation derived from pushing myself into a corner comes from Charles Hampel's sixth grade, in which I spent a year as a cadet teacher in a future teachers' club, while a senior in high school. Mr. Hampel had a particular strength in science and technology. I did not, and do not today. He had his sixth graders bring in various broken devices to class: cameras, radios, tape recorders, toys, and many other items. He then would structure opportunities for children to work on exploring, repairing, reconstructing, and dissecting these "artifacts." A dozen years later as a sixth-grade teacher, I still remembered the enthusiasm, the discovery of scientific principles, and the group problem-solving of Mr. Hampel's students. I doubted that I could have the same results in my own class, because of my lack of ability to work successfully with technological devices or practical repairs. I was, however, quite comfortable in teaching about scientific ideas, the more abstract stuff. So, one day in my third year of teaching I decided to give it a whirl. I told the students to bring in anything they could find that did not work or that they would just like to take apart and put together. We were soon overflowing with gadgets of all sorts, even a power lawn mower (which frightened me a bit). I would wander through the class area and ask inquiry questions, genuine inquiry questions, not ones for which I had the answers (for I knew few answers in this domain). That, in itself, was a turnabout compared with the usual contrived inquiry teaching situation in which the teacher does some tricky maneuver or asks questions in order to get the response from students that was wanted from the start. So, I would throw in questions such as: Do you remember the six simple machines? Do you see any levers, inclined planes, screws, pulleys, and so forth, in there somewhere? They often did, even if I did not, and we learned that complex machines were made of simple ones, and much more.

The students were far ahead of me. They formed problem-solving groups and learned more sophisticated lessons about relationships among parts of a working device than I could have put in a lesson plan. In addition, I noticed new purveyors of expertise among the students. Students who were not recognized as talented on the intelligence and achievement tests or did not receive the highest grades were now being tapped as resources. Their intelligences were cultivated in different spheres. I wondered if schools were at fault for not emphasizing those intelligences and achievements. I resolved to keep in mind a new guiding maxim: Figure out a way to genuinely recognize the expertise of each student in every class. Though not always easy, it seemed a worthy goal, and it was easier than I expected. The results were indeed positive. Students could be recognized for their strengths, for example, the ability to put together my stapler, an artistic sense for what a classroom arrangement might look like, an ability to tell a good joke, the background to illuminate a different culture or way of life, the ability to help others feel better about something or learn a new skill, and so on. To be given the recognition of genuine expertise added much to those who had seldom before been recognized for achievements in school. Similarly, those who had a history of recognition in school for matters school traditionally valued began to see a wider range of worthy abilities through their classmates. I, too, came to understand the value of a community of learners, all of whom had something valuable to teach the others. My traditional notion of who is teacher and who is learner was challenged productively. I began to see all members of the classroom society as teachers and learners.

THE IMAGE OF TEACHER LORE

These illustrations are only a few of the many encounters I value greatly as I reflect on what I learned as an elementary school teacher. I continue to draw insights from my elementary teaching days. I can think of many teachers from elementary school through graduate school whose approach, manner, and personality have affected my own teaching. Teacher lore for me includes both what I have gained from other teachers for my own teaching and what I can offer other teachers from my experience.

I am quite content with a fluid image of teacher lore. I want to resist the usual expectation that academics should always develop a theoretical framework. I fear that such a framework would do to deep inquiry what a lesson plan too often does to teaching—namely, separate learning from spontaneity. It decreases the chance of being a reflective practitioner in the course of action. It kills the spontaneous and limits relationships. In the illustrations drawn above about some of the most influential experiences in my teaching career as an elementary teacher, spontaneity was a very big factor. The ways in which the multitext approach and teaching through acting developed are key examples. An attempt to devise a theoretical framework that defines or gives rules for exactly what teacher lore is (and is not) prevents teachers from saying what it is that they learned, from telling their stories in their own best ways. Bearing this in mind, what I am about to say is offered with great caution. I do not want to be vague, but even more I do not want to be rigid.

Teacher lore includes stories about and by teachers. It portrays and interprets ways in which teachers deliberate and reflect and it portrays teachers in action. Teacher lore refers to knowledge, ideas, insights, feelings, and understandings of teachers as they reveal their guiding beliefs, share approaches, relate consequences of their teaching, offer aspects of their philosophy of teaching, and provide recommendations for educational policy makers. Teacher lore can be presented through teachers' own words, and through the interpretations provided by experienced teacher/researchers who interview and observe teachers. Each of us who contributed to this book is an experienced teacher. Therefore, at one level we reveal our own stories and at the same time we report on and interpret stories of other teachers who have influenced our perspectives on teaching.

This image of teacher lore is quite thoroughly related to conceptions of teaching and learning in the work of John Dewey and others of the so-called progressive orientation (see Chapter 9). The main point here, however, is not to define teacher lore in terms of somebody's philosophy. It is to relate insights of teachers and to uncover teaching philosophies embedded in teaching practices. We offer particular interpretations of teachers' commentaries, as well as the words of teachers themselves. Distinctions between voice and interpretation pale, since what teachers say is already interpretation, and commentary by us is voice as well. Further, every quotation is an interpretation, since it is one of many possible selections, taken from a history and placed in a written context here. So this book provides an integration of several layers of teacher voice and interpretive commentary by teacher/researchers who share their voices as well. The authors have met and studied the words, the activities, and the ideas of teachers through The Teacher Lore Project. Thus, our own ideas and insights as teachers are shared as teacher lore. Our interpretations of teachers we have known are shared, along with illustrative passages from interviews with them. We hope that our portrayals of these teachers incorporate some of the context from which the teachers' words are fashioned, so that their words come more fully to life.

Our major hope for this book is not that teacher lore becomes what we say, but that it is a beginning of something larger. Something larger is dependent upon those who read this book. We hope it is a challenge to create a broader and deeper sense of what teaching is and can become. We hope that you will share your own teacher lore with others and help give rise to communities of teachers who learn more from each other through writing, reading, listening, talking, and most of all reflecting—which, in turn, improves and enriches teaching and learning for all of us and for our students, which is, after all, the point.

REFERENCES

Ross, E. Wayne, Cornett, Jeffrey, and McCutcheon, Gail (Eds.) (1992). *Teacher-personal theorizing*. Albany: State University of New York Press.

Schubert, William H. (1990). Acknowledging teachers' experiential knowledge: Reports from The Teacher Lore Project. *Kappa Delta Pi Record*, 26(4): 99–100. (This is a theme issue, edited by Gerald Ponder, on The Teacher Lore Project.)

Schubert, William H. (1991). Teacher lore: A basis for understanding praxis. In Carol Witherell and Nel Noddings (Eds.), *Stories lives tell: Narrative and dialogue in education*. New York: Teachers College Press.

Willis, George, and Schubert, William H. (Eds.) (1991). *Reflections from the heart of educational inquiry*. Albany: State University of New York Press.

CHAPTER 2

Teachers' Spaces:
A Personal Evolution of Teacher Lore

Janet L. Miller

Teacher lore. For me, this phrase conjures up memories of four colleagues and myself scrunched around a trapezoid-shaped laminated table in a teachers' workroom, sharing our third-period preparation time by drinking coffee and swapping ditto sheets as we updated the adventures of our early morning classes. Our conversations were ongoing, usually concentrating on particular students' antics or on questions of method and content. Our words flowed from previous mornings' debates or discussions. Our talk was seamless, fragmented only to those who did not share the synchronous rhythms of ringing bells, rotating students, and shuffling papers and texts.

Even other teachers, who were scheduled into different prep periods and who might have stopped by the room only to run off a last-minute ditto or to staple together a pop quiz for the fourth-period class, could easily slip into the banter of our particular assemblage. For, although we might not exchange the particulars that emerged from countless days of scheduled intimacy in our cramped third-period planning space, we shared similar concerns, questions, and frustrations about the ephemeral nature of our work as high school teachers. And we pondered that nature within the fifty-minute segments that marked off our teaching lives.

I valued those communal explorations with my colleagues, those conversations interspersed between the clatter of the hand-turned ditto machine and the faceless voice of the public address system that inevitably disrupted the constant dissections of our teaching experiences. I had not only a sense of common grappling with those experiences but also a sense of knowing that could only be easily communicated among those who worried and wondered each day about the often seemingly capricious processes of teaching and learning. That knowing did *not* reflect a certainty about the approaches and techniques to which our work as teachers was often reduced by others who watched us through the windows of our classrooms or evaluated us through the student achievement scores published in the town newspaper. Rather, that sense of knowing signified an awareness of the variety of our own and our students' experiences, backgrounds, and understandings that influenced, in complex and often hidden ways, the constantly evolving nature and forms of our interactions.

Thus, even as my colleagues and I debated the current research on the processes of teaching and learning, what always captured our attention during our third-period conversations were the examples of the variation, the uncharted, the exception in our classrooms. These constant anomalies often contradicted a tidy description of a successful teaching approach reported in a journal article that one of us had just read, or surefire combinations of methods and materials that we remembered from our teacher preparation programs. And, underlying our debates about these contradictions, were our constant wonderings. We especially wondered why we found elements of our particular disciplines to be fascinating in ways that many of our students did not, and how we might teach so that they could at least appreciate (although later we were told that "appreciate" was not an appropriate objective), if not love, what we cared about. We wondered how we could possibly do all this in the fifty-minute segments that fragmented into separate entities not only our disciplines but also our connections to students, to texts, and to one another.

INTRODUCTORY SPACES

One of my teacher friends referred to our truncated teaching attempts as "snippets"— little clipped versions of the processes of teaching and learning that we intuitively knew required time and spaces in which students and teachers might truly work together. As a new teacher, I quickly entered into our third-period discussions as a way of combatting the constant fragmentation that I felt as I tried to resist the numbing effects of those "snippets." Our talk was one way of creating a sense of continuity for me within a system that seemed to constantly cut off my attempts to develop that continuity with my students and with the content that I was expected to teach to high school juniors and seniors. I struggled to effect connections between my love of the literature that had filled my English major college life and the splintered versions of grammar, vocabulary, reading comprehension, and five-paragraph compositions about that literature that were billed as "the teaching of English." And I turned to my colleagues for advice, support, and consoling reassurance as I vented my frustrations and confusions about the contradictions that seemed to permeate my teaching ventures.

Often, not needing many details of my latest example of student resistance or my own teaching inertia, because they inevitably had experienced a similar glitch in their own teaching or in a student's lack of response, my colleagues could immediately jump into debates over the possible ways in which I might handle such a situation the next time. As I moved through my seven years of high school teaching, I also began to share the knowledge of the "next time," while accepting the fact that none of us was able to prescribe any one way of handling or approaching the inevitable trouble spots that contributed to the halting nature of our segmented work. But together, as we grew in our understandings of one another and of the very elusive processes of teaching, my colleagues and I could pose for each other a number of possibilities for redirecting the particular lesson, or kindling the apathetic student's interest, or including the quiet one who always sat alone in the back of the classroom.

These were kinds of shared knowledges that we now could describe in current research terms as part of "teacher knowledges" or "teacher lore" but that, in 1966, when I began teaching, had no formal label to distinguish them from the general conversations that teachers exchanged in countless planning periods, or in the halls between classes, or in parking lots after school. (The plural form, *knowledges*, is used here to emphasize the multiple perspectives that teachers bring to their work.)

We did not know that what we were sharing during our prep time together also could be considered a form of research; we could not have conceptualized our wonderings as such because they were a form of inquiry into our particular knowledges as teachers that had no specific boundaries, no definitive answers. We only knew about others' research then, only understood it to be something that others did to us or our students in order to prescribe certain behaviors, approaches, or techniques that we were to implement in our classrooms.

In contrast, ours was a form of inquiry spurred by our daily encounters with colleagues, administrators, parents, and students, and framed by the ringing of bells and the testing of students' understandings or at least memorizations of the "snippets" from our disciplines that we had presented in our classes. We could not name our questions to one another and to ourselves during those third-period planning sessions as a form of any research that we had been exposed to in our teacher preparation courses. Our kind of talk about teaching, because of its apparent meandering and wondering nature, seemed virtually impossible to categorize, to replicate, to control, or to even share with those who did not teach.

Thus, as my colleagues and I huddled together in our morning oasis, our questions and our common as well as unique experiences of the classroom coalesced as forms of knowledge about teaching that could be easily communicated only to one another. And we shared our evolving knowledges, not through sets of goals and objectives or measurable means or standardized checklists of our behaviors, but rather through the stories that we told to one another. Even as our individual experiences differed, we were bound together by the very processes of teaching—processes that we could not fully articulate in terms of cause and effect, for example, but that we could examine as well as convey to one another through the telling of our stories of classroom events and students' responses and our own wonderings about our daily work.

SPACES FOR TEACHER LORE

I believe that the shared yet largely unofficial, informal knowledges, revealed in the telling of our teaching sagas and lived and created in the spaces of our daily teaching, form the core of what the contributors to this text have developed as the concept of teacher lore. As I reflect on the accumulated stories of our third-period planning brigade, I know that I did have a sense of our shared confusions and questions and yet particular knowledges about the contradictions that we often experienced in our teaching attempts. However, I also now realize that what I did *not* have during the seven years that I taught high school English was a way of thinking about those third-period conversations that could illuminate them as forms of curriculum creation or research or teachers' knowledges.

Thus, the very word "lore" resonates for me now as a way of conceptualizing as well as honoring the intentions and knowledges of wondering, involved, caring teachers. The varieties of teacher lore presented here capture the spirit of the shared processes and quests of my third-period cohorts, even as they point to the multiple differences among teachers, their situations, and their questions.

Framing teachers' knowledges and evolving understandings as "lore" signifies the dailiness, the regularity of rhythms and schedules, the countless small details and the subtleties of interaction that characterize teachers' work. Over time, as we moved through the halls, caught up in the swirling patterns of students changing classes, or as we gathered each third period as colleagues, slamming the workroom door against the swell of shrieks that always accompany the class-change ritual, we accumulated the stories of each day's encounters, adding, often unconsciously, to our understandings of our work. By calling attention to those accumulated stories as "lore," as knowledges experienced and created in the spaces of teachers' daily lives, we now can acknowledge not only the concrete exemplifications of teacher knowledges as constantly evolving and changing, but also the abilities of teachers themselves to create as well as to share those knowledges with one another.

The term "lore" thus captures the intuitive, the informal, the spontaneous and subjective undersides of what, in recent years, have been codified as planned, predictable, controllable, and objective elements of "effective" teaching. Lore is what we know to be similar in our teaching experiences, even as we tell our stories in order to point to the differences among us. And, over time, the telling of our stories allows us to hear our own changing and evolving understandings of ourselves as teachers.

What the concept of teacher lore now provides for me, then, is a framework or a scaffolding upon which to build understandings of myself as an active creator of knowledges about teaching, curriculum, and research. The notion of teacher lore confirms and affirms the necessity of dialogue among teachers as a way of creating and revising our knowledges about teaching and learning. The sharing of teacher lore signifies the common threads that weave together the tapestry of teachers' experiences and knowledges, just as the sharing also enables us to examine the differences, the variations of composition and direction, among those weavings. The gathering of teacher lore emphasizes the ways that our knowledges often are provisional, given the shifting relationships and larger contexts that influence what and how we teach.

As a high school teacher, I had countless examples of those constantly changing conditions and situations in my own classroom, although I could not articulate, at that time, all the possible underlying reasons for the provisional nature of teachers' knowledges. All I could articulate then was the wish, echoed by numerous colleagues, that our particular knowledges about teaching *could* be codified and standardized, so as to appear valid and respectable to an outside world that responded most immediately to measured evidence of our teaching effectiveness. At the same time, my colleagues and I were able to admit, quite often with a sense of rebellious pride, that much about our work could not be captured in definitive evaluation checklists of "effective teacher characteristics" or in printouts of students' achievement scores. Even though the standardization of our work promised the ease of predictability in the classroom that we often longed for, we resisted those attempts to smooth out and hide our differences and our unique ways of approaching the daily surprises in our classrooms. And many times, because we wanted to preserve the spontaneity that marked our teaching as our own and not someone else's conception of effective pedagogy, we felt that we could discuss the nuances of our work only with those who also stood silently in front of waiting students, and who knew that fleeting moment of blankness that preceded every teaching episode.

However, had we the framing that teacher lore now provides for teachers' discussions, reflections, and questions about the provisional, changing, and elusive aspects of their work, my colleagues and I might have felt comfortable in attempting to expand the possible arenas in which we examined our work. We might have considered the possibility of continuing our discussions beyond the safety of the closed workroom door, in moving our questions into spaces that included supervisors, parents, administrators, and students. Rather than feeling that we were supposed to have mastered the right answers and the correct ways of teaching once we left the safety of our third-period discussions, we might have been more able to discuss our ambivalences and our hesitations with others. Teacher lore, because of its acknowledgment of the variety, breadth, and diversity of focus in teaching approaches and experiences as well as in research of teachers' knowledges, now encourages and enables those particular knowledges, which I once considered to be private and idiosyncratic, to be shared among all those who are interested and concerned about teaching and learning.

In retrospect, I wish that early in my teaching career or in my preparatory studies, I had been introduced to such a way of thinking about my own teaching. I wonder how I might have viewed differently my beginning experiences as a high school English teacher, had I read about and studied the wealth of teachers' perspectives and knowledges here presented as teacher lore. Perhaps, had I understood early on in those experiences that there were, as Patricia Hulsebosch notes in Chapter 7, "divergent visions of what it means to be a professional teacher," I might not have struggled quite so much with my own sense of disjuncture and fragmentation within prescribed versions of "good," or in today's terms, "effective" teaching.

I will not deny the importance, for me, of my own meandering and continuing attempts to make sense of my teaching life, but, at the same time, I regret that I had no formal, or in a sense, validated "divergent visions" from which to draw as I began to teach. Even given these examples of teacher lore, perhaps I would have asked the same questions, pursued the same search for support and collaboration, but I might have begun to formalize the asking and searching at a much earlier point in my career. I would have continued to huddle with my colleagues around our book-piled table, would have continued to share our stories and our questions and frustrations. But we all might have been able to see those daily encounters as a form of inquiry that honored our own changing and developing understandings of our work as teachers, had we the conceptual frames and rich descriptions that the examples of teacher lore here presented provide.

One powerful reason for framing teachers' experiences and knowledges as teacher lore, then, is the immediacy with which readers might relate these "divergent visions" and versions of teaching to their own experiences and expectations in that role. The detailing of particular teachers' experiences, assumptions, and questions provides new openings from which readers then might view their own potential or present teaching and researching practices. As well, these examples of teacher lore provide incentive for teachers themselves to engage in the kind of critical examination and reflection on their work that can place them at the center of current attempts to create a "knowledge base" for teaching.

Envisioning teachers as the fulcrum upon which theory and practice balance also highlights teachers' knowledges that, as Grumet (1988) notes, evolve in human relationships. Such knowledges, created between students and teachers, teachers and parents, veteran and novice teachers, teachers and community, emerge from the reciprocal movement of theory in practice and take shape in the variety of relationships that teachers forge in their daily work. Placing teachers' work at the heart of these evolving relationships disrupts attempts to construct knowledge bases for teaching that ignore such relationships in favor of technically oriented, skill-based conceptions of teaching. Teacher lore, focused on the stories that teachers tell about those relationships that constitute their purposes in teaching, disrupts versions of teacher knowledge that posit teachers only as technicians, compliant transmitters and managers of ideals and structures of knowledge into which they have had little officially sanctioned participation.

Disrupting static and mechanical conceptions of teachers' work, posing our own questions in order to make our own and not some others' sense of our classroom life—that is what my colleagues and I were doing in that constant prep period interaction, although at the time we could not have spoken of our encounters as such. We were not encouraged, in either our preparatory or in-service contexts, to articulate or to develop any conceptual frames in which to place those seemingly casual inquiries. Further, we had no official sanctions from our institution or the larger educational community that would acknowledge such inquiry as a form of research on our own knowledges and practices as teachers.

As Duckworth (1986) notes, it is only because teachers know how to do their job as practitioners that they are in a position to pursue their own questions as researchers. But, in 1966 when I began my teaching career, teachers were the focus of research conceived and conducted by others. My colleagues and I did not see ourselves as researchers as we sat around the cramped table, pondering the latest incident in our classes that had us stuck on what to do next.

Now, like Schubert, I argue that teachers are also researchers of the assumptions and expectations that underlie and thus frame and drive their practice. As well, I argue that teachers must be researchers of the particular historical, social, and cultural factors that contribute to and frame their constant creations and re-creations of those assumptions and expectations through their curricular and pedagogical choices and approaches. But then, I knew only that my colleagues and I drew support, advice, and understanding from one another in our attempts to figure out the best ways in which to reach our kids while we tried to cover the "required" content of the course and, at the same time, tried to convey our various degrees of passion about our students as well as the disciplines that we had chosen as major in our academic lives.

Thus, I believe that the notion of teacher lore as exemplified in this text points to one way of conceptualizing and sharing the constant dialogues, ponderings, and actions that reflect teachers' innate but often informal, and thus often unrecognized, research stance. As I now reflect on those third-period conversations, I can see ways in which our dialogues and dissections were a form of research on our teaching. I wonder, had we the conceptual lenses and frames that teacher lore now provides, if we would have formalized our wonderings into some more recognizable research patterns. I wonder, too, if we would have needed, or even welcomed, an "outsider" to help us reflect, frame, and further investigate our wonderings and our underlying assumptions. Thus, I am concerned about the relationship of researcher to researched, if, as in these examples of teacher lore, teachers' knowledges and research are mediated by the perspectives and intentions of those who share teachers' concerns but who are not, for example, third-period planning room colleagues.

As a university professor whose main research interests now center on teachers' lives and teachers' knowledges, this concern of course reflects my own struggles with the researcher-researched relationship. I worry about the possible impositional nature of this relationship if teachers' research is still set within the contexts of others' research on those processes. And, if that is the case, I want those "others" to engage in the same processes of reflection and excavation of underlying assumptions about teaching and research in which the teachers themselves are engaged. I worry about the impositional possibilities of the research relationship if the direction as well as the evolving interpretations of the particular research focus are not constructed as a form of *praxis* (Lather, 1986) and are not enacted as reciprocal, negotiated, and constantly evolving understandings.

Thus, in this text's examples of teacher lore, I am pleased to read each author's description of a particular biographical situation that has influenced the writer's research interests and perspectives. I will continue to encourage all of us who are engaged in various forms of constructing and sharing teacher lore to note the ways in which our own assumptions and those aspects of research process and topic have changed as a result of our interactions with those involved in our research.

Here, for example, although some authors note their sharing of interview transcripts or field notes with the teachers they studied, I wonder to what extent some of these accounts might be modified or changed by the addition of the teachers' responses to particular authors' interpretations. Contributor Carol Melnick does refer to the potential emancipatory aspects of such reciprocal reviewing (see Chapter 6), but I want to suggest that all teacher lore accounts could be enriched by such a reciprocal research stance.

Each author here approaches the study of teacher lore from a unique angle of interest and vision, and yet, in some ways, I see how all descriptions of teacher lore function as examples of Melnick's focus on out-of-school curriculum. Because each author attempts to get to the underside, the lore of teachers' work and practice, each study is informed by the particular intersections of historical, social, and cultural contexts that influence both the researchers' and the teachers' constructions of teaching and research. These intersections simultaneously influence the inside- and outside-of-school conceptions of curriculum and of relationships that emerge as images or forces in these teachers' and researchers' work. Patricia Hulsebosch's study, for example, of teachers' perspectives on relationships with parents (see Chapter 7), points to intersections of biographical as well as cultural influences from "outside" the class-room that intimately influence and frame teachers' and students' interactions while they are "within" the schooling context. Notions of in- and out-of-school curriculum begin to blur as we are able to examine these intersections in light of specific individuals' educative experiences.

In Chapter 4 Mari Koerner points to the sometimes contradictory images that teachers utilize in telling their teaching stories. I wonder to what extent those contra-dictions emerge out of the dissonance of unequal power relationships that exist in most schools, which these teachers too must acknowledge as framing their practice. I am interested in how we all personalize those points of dissonance, while sometimes neglecting to examine the influences of both inside- and outside-of-school political, economic, and social structures that guide and often determine what we do in class-rooms.

Suzanne Millies (see Chapter 3) too focuses on the mental lives of teachers in terms of personal conceptions of pedagogical personality, assumptions, and reper-toires. In Chapter 5 Virginia Jagla discusses these personal teaching constructs in terms of imagination and intuition. These framings of teachers' knowledges encourage teachers to consider the ways in which they ultimately can draw on their own understandings and enactments of their practice in order to construct teacher-centered versions of professional knowledges. If we combine these studies with those that develop applications for further examinations of the intersection of personal and cultural, political, historical, and social influences on teachers' work, we will be developing powerful accounts of the range of possibilities for our active contributions to the construction and reconstruction of the teaching profession. Combined with other examples of teacher lore, constructed and examined from a variety of perspectives and emphases, these accounts provide encouragement to all classroom and university teachers who are committed to including teachers' voices in current attempts to create knowledge bases for teaching as part of larger plans for educational reform and renewal.

These accounts of teacher lore, in all their variety and diversity of focus, have enabled me to consider my own versions of teacher lore. These versions first were spun through the stories of our third-period group, and now through my associations with teachers in graduate classrooms, in in-service settings, and in an ongoing teacher-researcher group. These versions also acknowledge the power of those associa-tions and those stories in shaping my current teaching and research interests.

CONNECTING SPACES

Clearly, then, those third-period discussions have influenced me in ways that, because of the reflective frames provided by the notion of teacher lore, I only have begun to reconstruct here. The repetitive themes that emerged from those constant interactions I saw then as reflecting only particular gripes or concerns or issues emanating from our corner of the teaching world in upstate New York. Of course, the passage of time and the experiences of teaching, both in the high school and the university classroom, and of working with other teachers in graduate and in-service contexts, have enabled me to understand that many of those concerns are aspects of all teachers' experiences and frustrations. At the same time, I have become aware, in ways not at all evident to me during the seven years that I taught high school English, that those same concerns are shaped differently for each of us, depending on the particular biographical, social, and historical configurations that mark our particular teaching worlds.

Those awarenesses first emerged most pointedly through my graduate studies in curriculum theory and humanities education. Like many women who taught during the late 1960s and early 1970s, I assumed that my teaching career would follow my primary commitments to home and family. After my marriage ended, I pursued my graduate degree out of necessity rather than choice, and I entered the master's program at the University of Rochester in 1973, intent only on earning the credentials that would guarantee me permanent certification in my teaching area and thus enable me to establish some economic as well as professional stability.

As I pursued my master's degree at the University of Rochester, I was mentored by William Pinar, who was in the initial phases of his explorations of autobiographical and psychoanalytic work as crucial perspectives in attempts to reconceptualize the field of curriculum studies. That entry year for me was also the one in which Pinar held the first conference of the reconceptualization at Rochester. Through no plan of my own, I was introduced to the thought and action of Maxine Greene, Dwayne Huebner, James Macdonald, Donald Bateman, and Paul Klohr, among others. In a few short semesters, my educational world was turned upside down, reframed by perspectives and critiques of schooling that addressed the deeply felt but largely unarticulated analyses of my third-period planning colleagues. Although the talk of "heightened consciousness, cultural revolution, and curriculum theory" (Pinar, 1974) was new and startling to me in its range of analyses and implications, I somehow felt that these educators were viewing educational problems and situations in ways that connected to our talk in the third-period planning room.

Those connections impelled me to further study the underlying sources of our frustrations and continual sense of fragmentation in the classroom. At The Ohio State University, I worked with Bateman and Klohr, who enabled me to pursue doctoral studies that combined my interests in English education and curriculum theory. Throughout those studies and the concurrent experiences in supervising student teachers and teaching undergraduate classes, what I now can trace is my constant search for connections and for that shared sense of questioning about the common and yet unique experiences of teaching that I first experienced in that crowded teachers' planning room. And now too, as I reflect on the nature and possible forms of teacher lore, the very notion of teacher lore allows me to clarify, in some ways, my decision to further explore teaching and curriculum theory as areas of study in my graduate work. And it helps to account for my continuing interest in collaborative, reciprocal, and negotiated forms of teacher/researcher inquiry.

My awareness of the broad influences on educational experience of one's biography, as situated within considerations of gender, race, class, and language, for example, continued to expand as I completed my doctoral studies and entered the world of academe as an assistant professor. Continuing to work, as I had begun with Pinar and then with Bateman and Klohr, in the autobiographical method, I struggled to make explicit the ways in which I had internalized others' expectations for myself as woman and teacher (Miller, 1983). These expectations had surfaced throughout my seven-year high school teaching career, but I had not considered the underlying assumptions of "women's work" in teaching, for example, or of the ways in which those assumptions accounted for my constant attempts to be the "good teacher–good girl." However, those unexamined assumptions about women's roles, in both professional and personal contexts, had in part enabled me to avoid confronting the ways in which I had tried to conform to others' expectations for myself as teacher, as wife, as woman.

Those passive and unconsciously complicit assumptions not only had shaped and affected my professional and personal life but also had reflected psychological, social, political, economic, and historical constructs which, heretofore, I had assumed as immutable and beyond question.

The developing perspectives of a variety of individuals involved in reconceptualizing the field of curriculum (Apple, 1986; Giroux, Penna, and Pinar, 1981; Pinar, 1975; Pinar, 1988; Pinar and Grumet, 1976) encouraged me in attempts to confront and to examine those underlying assumptions. My work as managing editor of *The Journal of Curriculum Theorizing* (*JCT*), a journal begun in 1978 in response to the move to reconceive curriculum as evolving from individuals' specific biographical, historical, political, and social contexts and as reflecting, responding to, and shaping the interactions of teachers and students, enabled me to begin discussions and analyses of these assumptions with a number of concerned educators. In the context of this reflection on teacher lore, I realize that these continuing discussions, shared in the contexts of the annual conferences sponsored by *JCT* as well as in a variety of other educational meetings and professional writings, replicate for me the ever-evolving conversations among my colleagues in that third-period planning room gathering.

A constant search for such connections also is reflected in my teaching and writing. I began to explore feminist perspectives and analyses as I grappled with excavations of assumptions that layered my work and the relationships that were at the heart of my inquiries. By continuing to focus on the depth and breadth of those assumptions about my necessarily nurturing role as woman and teacher, by confronting the self-alienation that such unexamined assumptions spawned, I attempted to preserve the nurturant capabilities that frame the generation of both identity and knowledge. At the same time, I wanted to develop an understanding of the forms that autonomous and critical perspectives might assume.

I was drawn into dialogue with other teachers, both women and men, in order to discuss and to examine the ways in which we perceived the same or differently our roles as teachers (Miller, 1986a; Miller, 1986b; Miller, 1987). Although my original emphasis in these conversations was on gender and that construct's relationship to individuals' perceptions and expectations of themselves as teachers, I heard in our dialogues the intertwined influences of cultural and biographical factors that included but were not limited to issues of gender. Thus, I began looking for ways to create spaces in which we might examine the myriad assumptions, generated by cultural contexts and biographical situations, that girded and framed our practice. In order to unravel these intertwined and often unexamined assumptions, I longed for the kinds of spaces represented by that third-period planning room, where we could tell our stories amid the bustle of daily teaching activities but also where, over time, we could examine the themes and patterns that merged from our constant storytelling.

In the summer of 1986, a group of five graduate students, who were themselves teachers in a variety of school settings, joined me in an attempt to create such spaces. We originally were drawn together by our questions about the possibilities of teachers becoming researchers of their own assumptions as well as of the historical, political, and cultural factors that framed those assumptions. As we continue to meet and to discuss explorations of our daily teaching practice, we attempt collaborative reflections, in both written and dialogical forms, on the contexts and assumptions that frame and influence that practice. Our work together thus has also become an exploration of the possibilities and dilemmas of collaborative inquiry and teacher empowerment. As we continue to question taken-for-granted contexts and assumptions, we also are exploring the constraints and potentials of defining and thus empowering ourselves as teacher/researchers. Throughout our deliberations, we constantly are confronted with issues of imposition and hierarchy, with structures of schooling and conceptions of teaching and learning that do not foster the kinds of interactive and reciprocal inquiry that we are attempting. We continue to meet as a group because we draw strength and encouragement from one another in our attempts to act upon our evolving understandings of ourselves as active creators in educative processes, even as we continue to uncover ways in which we approach our collective and individual work differently (Miller, 1990).

As our collaborative research group continues to meet, and as I reflect on our work together thus far within the context provided by the concept of teacher lore, what I can trace are my continuing attempts to replicate the exchange of ideas and concerns that I had shared so long ago with colleagues in that third-period planning room. For, as our collaborative group now continues to struggle with ways in which to transform our discussions and analyses into forms of action in our teaching contexts, I can see that we grapple with these attempts in ways similar to those of my workroom colleagues. We look for openings in our daily work, small spaces in which to transform the standard hierarchical and technical-rational approaches and interpretations of our roles as teachers into reciprocal, equitable, and collaborative forms. We realize that such attempts are not welcomed or encouraged in many educational settings, and we grapple with ways in which to talk about and enact our work that do not replicate reductionist versions of teacher empowerment. We reject the notion that empowerment is something that can be bestowed on individuals. We want not only to be able to engage in decision-making activities in our schooling contexts, which seems to be the current reductionist interpretation of teacher empowerment, but also to be able to examine educational situations and relationships that overtly or covertly oppress certain individuals or groups of people. We want to create spaces in which we might come together not only to analyze these situations and relationships but also to work together to change and transform that which we find to be oppressive or inequitable or silencing for any of us within our educational communities.

I think my high school teaching colleagues understood that the implicit commitment to one another and to our work as teachers was what connected our daily storytelling to the transformative possibilities contained within the fifty-minute segments of our daily teaching lives. So too does our collaborative research group continue to try to create those spaces for dialogue and action within our daily encounters with students, colleagues, parents, and administrators. We have begun to understand empowerment as an active process in which we must engage on a daily basis, even though many educational conditions and situations do not support or encourage such action. And we have begun to conceive of freedom

> . . . as an achievement within the concreteness of lived social situations, . . . as a distinctive way of orienting the self to the possible, of overcoming the determinate, of transcending or moving beyond in the full awareness that such overcoming can never be complete. (Greene, 1988, 4–5)

As we share our quest for those spaces as well as our accumulating experiences and examinations of that quest, we are developing our own form of teacher lore, our own chronicle of particular struggles and confrontations that might also contribute to this growing store of teachers' knowledges.

For I think that it is in the sharing of those wonderings, wonderings that for me began in that cramped teacher workroom back in 1966, that the full potential of the concept of teacher lore might be realized. The power to effect connections among the diversity of experiences and influences that mark all teachers' work is part of the potential of teacher lore, and the sharing of those connections requires that teachers' spaces be honored and cultivated. Teacher lore provides the context and motivation for such spaces to be created, nourished, and expanded, and it is to such spaces that this particular story is dedicated.

REFERENCES

Apple, M. W. (1986). *Teachers and texts: A political economy of class and gender relations in education*. New York and London: Routledge and Kegan Paul.

Duckworth, E. (1986). Teaching as research. *Harvard Educational Review, 56*: 481–495.

Giroux, H., Penna, A., and Pinar, W. F. (Eds.) (1981). *Curriculum and instruction*. Berkeley: McCutchan.

Greene, M. (1988). *The dialectic of freedom*. New York: Teachers College Press.

Grumet, M. R. (1988). *Bitter milk: Women and teaching*. Amherst: University of Massachusetts Press.

Lather, P. (1986). Research as praxis. *Harvard Educational Review, 56*: 257–277.

Miller, J. L. (1983). The resistance of women academics: An autobiographical account. *The Journal of Educational Equity and Leadership, 3* (summer).

Miller, J. L. (1986a). Marking papers and marking time: Issues of self-concept in women and men who teach. *Teaching and Learning: The Journal of Natural Inquiry, 1* (fall).

Miller, J. L. (1986b). Women as teachers: Enlarging conversations on gender and self-concept. *Journal of Curriculum and Supervision, 1*: 111–121.

Miller, J. L. (1987). Women as teacher/researchers: Gaining a sense of ourselves. *Teacher Education Quarterly, 14*: 52–58.

Miller, J. L. (1990). *Creating spaces and finding voices: Teachers collaborating for empowerment*. Albany: State University of New York Press.

Pinar, W. F. (Ed.) (1974). *Heightened consciousness, cultural revolution, and curriculum theory: The proceedings of the 1973 Rochester conference*. Berkeley: McCutchan.

Pinar, W. F. (Ed.) (1975). *Curriculum theorizing: The reconceptualists*. Berkeley: McCutchan.

Pinar, W. F. (Ed.) (1988). *Contemporary curriculum discourses*. Scottsdale, AZ: Gorsuch Scarisbrick, Publishers.

Pinar, W. F., and Grumet, M. R. (1976). *Toward a poor curriculum*. Dubuque, IA: Kendall/Hunt.

PART II
Teachers' Stories and Ideas

When teachers reflect on their experiences they take an essential first step toward transforming those experiences into a guiding philosophy, a set of personal beliefs, and a repertoire of actions to be drawn upon in the future. That is, through serious and sustained thought teachers begin to embody John Dewey's (1916) technical definition of education: "That reconstruction or reorganization of experience which adds to the meaning of experience, and which increases ability to direct the course of subsequent experience" (p. 76).*

In the following chapter Suzanne Millies draws a portrait of Alice, a sixty-one year old English teacher in a middle class suburban high school. Alice's story reminds us of the ways in which a teacher's school experience is inseparable from the rest of her life. A teacher's life outside of teaching contributes to the kind and quality of teacher she will become, and her personality, assumptions, and values impact her teaching directly and indirectly. Alice's story illustrates the importance of conscious awareness as a way to enrich and deepen the meaning of experiences, of reflection as a means of staying alive to the complexities and the demands of teaching.

---

*Dewey, John (1916). *Democracy and education.* New York: Macmillan.

CHAPTER 3

The Relationship between a Teacher's Life and Teaching

Palma Suzanne George Millies

Let us go then, you and I
When the evening is spread out against the sky
And the students wait—etherized at their desks
Passively waiting for their minds to be filled
    with disconnected, fragmented, useless knowledge;
The teacher, unthinking, wandering aimlessly to and fro
Reproduces wisdom from sterile texts
Never daring to ask the overwhelming question:
    What knowledge is most worthwhile?
Never daring to "touch" her students,
    Now distant and lost;
They echo with the hollowness of an empty pedagogy.

Let us go and make our visit.

This was my classroom and I was the teacher. The portrait, a parody of T. S. Eliot's opening lines from the "Lovesong of J. Alfred Prufrock," is of course overstated, but in retrospect from my position in the present, the past is like a portrait of the Dark Ages. My memory selectively paints a picture in dark, misty colors, which swirl in configurations blurred with a lack of awareness. The lack of awareness was simply caused by habits of nonreflection and nonanalysis. I never asked myself if what I was doing was meaningful. I never pondered why I did what I did. I mechanically went on with my teaching.

The metamorphosis occurred during my graduate studies. The irony was that I had read many of the great educators years before in my undergraduate courses, but their ideas had drifted in and out of my head with lazy indifference. Nothing connected. This was information that did not need to be filed away for future use—for, I felt at that time, it was totally useless. It would become useful only when I became reflective about my own teaching.

One of the catalysts that triggered my introspection was being assigned a low-track English class for the upcoming school year. These were difficult classes; the students were usually unmotivated, indifferent, and sometimes hostile. An English teacher with fifteen years of experience, I was apprehensive about the prospect of a year of confrontation.

Perhaps that unhappiness was strong enough to make me want to change the scenario I saw looming ahead of me. The ideas we were exploring in graduate school were intriguing enough, and some seemed to offer even promising possibilities. Two figures especially provided hope and inspiration.

The first was Joseph Schwab (1978). His concept of "eros" bridged the gap for me between the "intellectual" and "feeling and action." "Training of the intellect," stated Schwab, "must take place . . . in a milieu of feelings and must express itself in actions . . ." (p. 108). I resonated to Schwab's theory of Eros, for it confirmed what I already felt in my heart, that teaching, to be truly effective, had to begin with a teacher's love and concern for students. The problem was that some students were difficult to love. Schwab argued that if the teacher could establish an interpersonal relationship with the students, one in which students grew to love and respect the teacher, then they would be willing to follow the teacher through their studies and would be motivated to do well in their work in order to win the approbation of the teacher. Perhaps if I could look past the surface hostility of these students, if I could see the whole, complex individual each one was, I could find something to love.

The second figure who inspired me was John Dewey (1916) and his idea of the democratic classroom. In a democratic environment, students and teacher would share activities and even participate in the formation of the purposes that would direct learning. Students and teacher together would decide on what was important to learn and in what manner it was to be learned. This was difficult for me; I had always been the controlling force in my classroom, but I began to think that if I shared the decision making with my students, perhaps they would take greater responsibility for their own learning.

When the new school year began, I was determined to be positive and support-ive, and to allow the students to participate in determining their own learning activi-ties. On the first day of class I warmly welcomed them back to school. Whenever I met with hostility or negativism, I searched for underlying causes. Students and I decided together on how the class would be run. I briefly described the traditional classroom in which the teacher was the sole figure of authority; I then described the democratic classroom in which the students would share in the decision making. I encouraged the students to think about the advantages and disadvantages of each approach. They were quick to recognize that the self-directed classroom would place more responsibility on their shoulders, although I am certain that some saw it as an easy way out. After the discussion, the students voted to adopt the self-directed approach. This cooperative decision making would occur throughout the year when we had to deal with various problems in classroom management or units of study. Together we discussed and made decisions about seating in the classroom, setting up independent work contracts, establishing disciplinary procedures, improving class organization, selecting units of study, establishing and changing goals, and more.

The class often sat in a circle, selected a recorder, brainstormed ideas, discussed the pros and cons of an issue, and then came to a consensus on what we wanted to do. The range of topics was limited only by the parameters established by the nature of the course itself. For example, an American literature course was limited to the study of American writers, but the order in which we studied them and the strategies we used were subject to selection by the students. I was pleased with the maturity of the discussions and the consistent good sense that students exhibited.

Was the course successful? I think it was, and the students seemed to agree with me. Although I did not have any written goals, I knew I wanted them to read, discuss, and understand how good literature can affect their lives; I wanted them to think about and grapple with important ideas, concepts, and moral issues; I wanted them to become competent and confident in the use of their written language; and I wanted them to share decision making in a democratic classroom. I think in many cases they surpassed my expectations, and that as a group they accomplished all of this. Moreover, the students displayed a positive attitude, an eagerness toward the class, that I had not seen before. In this way, too, the class was a success.

My metamorphosis was a result of my own reflection on my practice. It marked the beginning of my fascination with the concept of teacher reflection as a possible key to teacher transformation. Teachers giving serious consideration to what gives meaning and direction to their lives and work could be an essential part of teachers growing and changing. My fascination with reflection led to an exploration of what reflection actually encompasses.

REFLECTION AND THE LIVES OF TEACHERS

Dewey's (1916) definition of reflection as "the reconstruction or reorganization of experience" requires a bending back of the mind (Morris and Pai, 1976) in order to focus on a past experience. It is a form of thorough inquiry (Dewey, 1933; Schwab, 1978) that asks questions of the experience in order to better understand it. By examining the past experience in a considered and focused way, one could learn and grow.

If reflection can be a way to learn and grow—a phenomenon that I validated in my own experience as a teacher—then, I reasoned, perhaps it could be used as a process by which to discover what gives meaning and direction to the lives and work of other teachers. The problem, of course, is that reflection is invisible. Although it is invisible, teacher educators (Feiman-Nemser, 1979; Clandinin, 1966; and Garman, 1986) have recognized that an invited discussion of past experience, through consideration of either an artificial or a real experience, can lead to increased understanding and professional growth. Conversations with teachers who are invited to walk back through their past professional experiences are a means by which we might enter teachers' minds and note their thoughts as they talk about their work and practice.

I wanted to learn more about the nature of the mental life of a teacher—to uncover the mind's contents through reflection. From preliminary interviews with teachers, I identified three domains that described the contents of a dimension of a teacher's mental life: the pedagogical personality, the pedagogical assumptions, and the pedagogical repertoire. "Pedagogical" differentiates the mental life of the teacher teaching from his or her mental life outside the classroom. The elements I identified are not, of course, a definitive list of everything that might exist within the mental life of a teacher, but they do provide a manageable and hopeful schema for understanding some aspects of a teacher's mental life. Through an exploration of this mental life, I hoped I would be better able to understand what gives meaning and direction to a teacher's practice.

The first domain, the pedagogical personality, is an embodiment of a range of qualities related to a teacher's practice. It consists of the individual's self-concept, motifs, uncertainties, ambivalence, concerns, biases, and so on.

The second domain is pedagogical assumptions; these are the suppositions guiding an individual's practice—they are the givens of one's cognitive world in regard to how one should function in one's practice. They consist of values, beliefs, principles, and strategies.

The third domain, the pedagogical repertoire, consists of the teacher's images, experiences, routines, and strategies. This repertoire consists of a collection of tactics from which the teacher may draw to facilitate learning in the classroom.

The teacher's identity (pedagogical personality), guiding suppositions (pedagogical assumptions), and reservoir of images, experiences, routines, and strategies (pedagogical repertoire) are part of the larger framework of teacher lore, for they attempt to highlight some of the factors that give meaning and direction to a teacher's work.

In my own attempt to better understand the mental lives of teachers, I used the conceptual framework of the three domains to explore the reflections of one teacher, whom I will call Alice, a veteran of thirty-one years of teaching. Alice was sixty-one years old, the chairperson of the English department, and she taught only two courses—both honors classes in American literature. Our conversation extended over seven months.

Pedagogical Personality

I asked Alice to walk back through the terrain of her teaching; I invited her to reflect on her life and her classroom. Her reflections on her life revealed many of the values that she would carry into her teaching. From her parents, who were first-generation Americans of German/Czech descent, she learned that work was noble. From her strong Lutheran background, she developed a love for Bible stories which eventually influenced her appreciation for literature. Upon graduation from high school, she entered Valparaiso University majoring in English and secondary education. After graduation, she married and began, or so she thought, the fulfillment of the American Dream. She stayed at home to raise her two daughters; however, "it was evident that everything was not working out the way it does in dime novels," and she was separated from her husband shortly thereafter.

At the age of thirty she began her career as a teacher in a third-grade class for which she felt "woefully unprepared." She would not have survived if it were not for a mentor who took her under her wing. Her mentor often taught her some method that she could use in the morning and then put into application that very afternoon. She stayed with the third grade for three years and then taught English in the seventh and eighth grades for another three years.

Because her financial obligations increased as her daughters grew older, she decided to get a master's degree and move into a high school position, one that paid a higher salary. In 1966 she received a position in English at a school in the western suburbs of Chicago. There she has been ever since. From the position as teacher, she moved for a time into a position as counselor and then as dean. Later she would return to the English department as the chairperson. This brings us to Alice's present:

> And now I'm sixty. With some regrets, I realize that I am probably at a stalemate in my career. I do not have the "paper" to go on. I do not look forward to retirement at all and am angered by the passage of time. Who I am is a teacher. What I will be after I retire is a mystery to me. But then, I've gutted it out before and I guess I will do it again. I have been a good mother and a superb grandmother . . . someone will give me a corner in which to live, I'll correct my grandson's theme, and teach the whole child again.

Alice, indeed, enjoys teaching: "I always enjoyed teaching . . . at any level. I've taught every grade from third on up and whenever anyone asks me that question I always have the same answer. I like what I'm doing. I don't think I've ever run from one thing to another because of dislike." She considers herself a traditional teacher— one whose class is "a read and write-an-answer kind of course." Students are expected to read their assignments and are held accountable for them: "Accountability's real strong with me for the kids. I don't consider myself a terribly creative teacher. And I have no way of judging whether or not I'm interesting or boring to the kids. I don't have a handle on that at all. Usually when I ask kids to evaluate me, they give a grade. Most all of them will say a B + or B − . . . ." She seems to feel confident that she is doing a good job from her own point of view as well as from the students'. However, she is not certain about whether or not her students find her class boring: "I think what I do, I do well. . . . I think when the kids are finished learning with me as a guide, that they have the skills that they didn't have before they were in my class. And those skills are skills that are self-directed." Alice's classroom is "teacher-centered"; she is in control of the body of knowledge to be learned, and she is careful to stay "on task."

Alice has a strong sense of what constitutes a perfect class. This conception is a significant part of her teacher lore, for it becomes the standard by which she judges her classes and becomes the norm to which she tries to mold her classes. If a class approaches her ideal, she feels "comfortable" with it and finds the students "delightful"; if it does not, she feels the class is "challenging." This year's students are "delightful" because they are a "very nice group of kids." They are "human" to each other, stable, friendly, and they don't "bite." "They're just nice human beings. Considerate, helpful, respectful."

Another characteristic of Alice's "ideal" classroom is mutual respect; she goes out of her way to establish it from the first day of class.

> I'd like the kids to respect me, and while the word affection is a pretty strong word, I want them to feel a kind of commitment toward me—that it is their responsibility to make

> the class go and it's my responsibility to make the class go. And that if they're unkind, they'll get unkindness back, because I can cut with the best of them. Or they can get kindness back.

To ensure this mutual respect, she purposefully practices such techniques as touching them, using nicknames for them, using some slang terms, calling them "kids," and admitting her mistakes. She dislikes confrontation; she finds it "not productive" and "wearing on the individual." In these so-called wars with kids, "there are never any winners": "Kids are destroyed; the class is destroyed. I don't like it, so I feel a part of me has been destroyed." Alice's "ideal" classroom is, then, one in which a spirit of cooperation and mutual respect exists.

For Alice, time is a central theme of her life:

> Time has always been a real thing with me. Some years ago, twenty years ago, I was assigned a task for a creative writing class of writing a utopia. In my utopia, man controlled time. Time was an essential figure of the entire story. Time went from segments of time when one was ready to move from that point in life. When all that was done, then you could say you were ready for the next segment of life. It was a central theme of that and I guess it was always a central theme.

Because of her preoccupation with time, "special moments" in life become important to her, and she often points these "moments" out in literature, especially poetry. At every opportunity she brings her class's attention to these moments because, as she says, "I feel sincerely that life is made up of beautiful moments. But not majestic events. Waiting for that in life, you're going to wait a long time. But if you can find little pauses . . . just something to bolster you up for the next day, then you always have the wherewithal to deal with whatever is coming."

Time seems to have a life of its own. In the beginning of the year, Alice is deceived into thinking she has "all the time in the world" and can walk slowly through the literature and "savor the moments." But by the end of the year time speeds up and she feels that she now has to race through the material: "In September . . . it's very, very different. I take the time to do everything in detail, so maybe it's OK now that we just skim over the top." In the beginning of the year, for example, she is willing to have the students watch a three-day video on James Fenimore Cooper because she feels the tapes are well done, the students like them, and they present valuable information. However, by the end of the school year, she is unwilling to allow students time to view videotapes of *The Great Gatsby* even though this work, too, is well done. She feels the end of the year sweeping down on her, and she is conscious of all that remains to be done: "There's always a push at the end of the year and I hate it. I don't know that it's . . . well maybe it's some bad planning, I suppose to a degree it's that, but I seem to always find one more thing to do with something and I do go into considerable depth with what I teach. I could teach more quantity in a more cursory fashion, but I tend not to like to do that." Because of the problem of time and her desire to teach "in depth," she struggles with trying to teach as she would like (a personal objective) and at the same time to get "into the twentieth century" (a district objective). She feels constrained by time as she is pushed to "come out even at the end of the year."

Alice feels that time has been elusive for her:

> Time cheats us of savoring things; we can experience it but we can't savor it. An experience of a child or of young womanhood or your maturity. You can't savor anything; it's gone before you even knew you had it. And you know it was there in retrospect, but at the time it was just all happening too quickly and you just sort of churned through it. To go back and savor, to really enjoy it, I think that's a common resentment of a lot of women, but I don't know about men. Women have all those pressures; we keep hearing them say, "I need some time for myself; some quality time." There just aren't enough minutes in a day for that quality time.

Family is important to Alice. Even though at times she experiences a conflict between the demands of her career and the demands of home, she admits, "The family has always taken precedence over things." She brings her mothering into her teaching, and she says she wants to "nurture" her students. When a student tells her she reminds him of his "grandma," she responds:

> They need as many grandmas as they can have in life. I do a lot of touching, too. Like when I walk up and down I'll very often put a hand on a shoulder, purposely. Kids don't even notice it any more, but when I stand near somebody, if I have an opportunity to do so, I'll always touch. . . . I think it's the thing to do. If it makes me more human to them, then it makes them more human to me.

Her consciousness of herself as a woman also causes her to focus more on the female characters in the literature assignments. When students were comparing Edith Wharton's *Ethan Frome* and Willa Cather's "The Sculptor's Funeral," she pointed out how the sterile settings were especially hard on women. When students were exploring the appeal of the frontier in O. E. Rölvaag's *Giants in the Earth*, she went on to focus on the role of women. She spoke of a scene in Arthur Miller's *The Crucible* when John Proctor asked his wife to bring in flowers to civilize the environment.

Alice's classroom is nurturing and protective. When students form a circle for a discussion, she checks to see that no student is excluded from the circle. She is especially sensitive to unkind remarks among the students and will not tolerate them. She even carries her nurturing tendencies over to the people in her department whom she tries to protect from others and worries over them when they are ill.

Making connections is another theme in her life; this theme especially has a tremendous impact on the curriculum, "the lived experience" in the classroom. Alice connects topics within a class period and from one class to another. Ideas run throughout the course and are stitched together so that students have a sense of coherence. Connections are also made to experiences in Alice's life as well as to the life experiences of students. On one occasion Alice tied the literature assignment to an experience some students had had at the Model UN the day before: "I don't try to tie in main events; I don't consciously try. But I guess subconsciously I will take advantage of an occurrence if I can, to make what we're doing in class a part of a whole-life experience. . . ."

Literature in the course is organized according to certain connecting themes, themes Alice feels are important. For example, she has taught William Faulkner's

"The Bear" with John Steinbeck's "Flight" for over three years because she feels they are "companion stories." She focuses on the "bear" as a symbol of what individuals want out of life, and uses it to contrast with the main character in "Flight" who does not have any goals. She creates a further link with Robert Frost's poem "After Apple Picking," using the symbol of picking apples as moments in life. These three literary works are rich with possibilities, but who she is and what she values determine the focus of her interpretation and the thrust of her lesson. She calls these works "ladders to life." How do these connections come about? Alice is not certain. "We were just working on the poem and it just sort of fits in. It was thought through as of last night, but it wasn't any great long planning. . . . Maybe I stretch to make things fit or maybe because it's great literature, it does fit. I can't answer that."

One vivid and dramatic example of her ability to create meaningful connections occurred on the last day of class. Students had prepared Thornton Wilder's *Our Town* for discussion. "Literature," Alice explains, "gives us a window to experiences that we cannot have in any other way. . . . We are oblivious to each other as we pass through life. Most of our lives are not filled with Anne Frank's diaries. Most is filled with small things." She then reads from the play: "Life should be 'awe-ful.' We are links in a long line of links because our lives are interwoven." She then makes a connection with Thomas Wolfe's *Look Homeward Angel*, a passage alluded to earlier in the discussion of her love of the dramatic. In this "moment" Alice has linked a theme she had found in literature with a belief of her own and then connected it to her desire to make this last day of class a special "moment" for the students and for herself. She chose a moment that was very special to her; it was her first reading of Thomas Wolfe.

Responsibility or accountability is another theme deeply enmeshed in Alice's pedagogical life. She has a strong sense of responsibility to her students. On the whole she feels that she does a good job in accomplishing her goals: "I think when the kids are finished learning with me as a guide, that they have skills that they didn't have before they were in my class. And those skills are skills that are self-directed." If she feels that she has not covered all that she wished, then she feels guilty. And the guilt essentially stems from her sense that she has not fulfilled her responsibility to her students.

Just as she feels responsible for her own actions, so, too, does she feel that students should be responsible for their own learning. Thus, a personal value is translated into an objective for her students. "I've always felt that students should be responsible for their own work, for getting their own information." She devises strategies to assure their accountability. Often she gives quizzes on the assigned readings:

> Years ago when I taught honors kids I made a mistake in my first year of thinking that honors kids were honorable and that they were beyond reading checks and those kinds of things and it really took me about a half a year to figure out what was wrong with that class. They had figured out that they could come into class unprepared and I would talk whether they were prepared or not. I would fill in the time and they wouldn't have to fill in the time. It was a very unsuccessful class for me and it gave me a real bad feeling about honors kids for a long time. Then the next time I taught them I had decided that they were just as dishonorable as any other kids and that they needed to be held

accountable and although some of it might appear to be mickey-mouse and I suppose some of it is, it's just surface checks on whether or not they did the task that I asked them to do.

Despite Alice's many years as a teacher, she still has moments of uncertainty and ambivalence. Although she has a strong sense of responsibility to her students and believes that she can "pretty well defend" what she does, she admits that nobody really knows if she is doing what she is supposed to because no one has really been in her room to observe her. Because of this lack of feedback, she is uncertain whether her perception of herself is always accurate. She perceives herself conducting a teacher-centered classroom in which she is in control "of what's going on" in the classroom. She feels this is necessary because there is so much material to cover and she must make certain that time is not wasted. ". . . I need to be aware of how much time things are going to take. And whenever we go off into one of these tangent kind of things, it always takes more time than I anticipate it's going to take. And then I get very resentful about all of this." She then wonders if she really is in control of the events in the classroom.

Another uncertainty concerns the amount of work she assigns: "I think the focus in an honors class is how kids learn, not really in the quantity of materials they can list on a page." When she compares her syllabus with those of other honors classes she sometimes feels guilty because she does not cover as much content as they do, but then she explains that she teaches them to think, or at least she hopes she does: "I don't know if I do it or not. I try to make them come up with things rather than my standing up there and doing a lecture. . . . Maybe I think I do it better than I do."

Alice admits that sometimes students criticize her for "my opinion being the right opinion," implying that she doesn't always allow them to express their opinions fully. She is sensitive to that criticism, even defensive about it. "I don't think I do that," she explains, "but evidently they perceive that I do that." She wonders about her role in the discussions: "Do I really allow them to do their own interpretations or am I too intrusive?" She hopes she is encouraging free discussion of ideas, but she worries that she might dominate the class with her own ideas.

Alice has tried many techniques to encourage students to participate, but her efforts don't seem to be enough. She feels that it is artificial to call on students and yet she wants a free and wide exchange of ideas. She advocates a student-centered discussion, yet she herself states that her class is teacher-centered. She wants self-directed participation, and she wants control: "I would like to be a little more creative and open it up for the kids, [to have them] do some more creative projects and things on their own. But then I seem to lose what I think is control over what they're doing. And then I get uncomfortable." She struggles with an ambivalence between a desire for control and a desire for creativity.

Uncertainty and ambivalence disturb the otherwise calm outward serenity of Alice's pedagogical personality. Underneath her tranquil surface lurks a nagging uncertainty about whether she is who she thinks she is in the classroom: Does she give her students sufficient work? Does she really allow for the free exchange of ideas? Are her connections real or artificial? Does she encourage or discourage student involvement?

Coupled with her uncertainty is vacillation between competing desires: Should her classroom be teacher-centered or student-centered? Should she retain control in the classroom or allow students more autonomy? Should she insist on the "right answer" or give more credibility to student answers? And finally, should she follow her curriculum or the district's?

Alice's "lore" is not fixed in concrete, apparently, for although she has a conception of what she wants to do in the classroom, she is not always certain that she is really doing it.

Alice's own preferences affect her curriculum. For example, she loves to teach Hawthorne and Twain, but doesn't enjoy teaching poetry very much. Because she likes Hawthorne, she spends a lot of time on him. On the other hand, her dislike of Hemingway causes her to treat his work rather casually. Her own bias toward poetry also causes her not to teach it very often: "I don't enjoy teaching poetry very much. We don't do a lot of poetry. Poetry is such a private kind of thing. And as soon as you have to explicate it, it seems to ruin it for everybody. Poetry should just be there to enjoy. Not to be taught. I've never been able to teach poetry."

Alice has proclivities toward particular students and antipathies against others. David is one boy who has "interested" her all year long. He is what she calls a "nontraditional" kid who is very able and "keeps her honest." "He strips me of façade. He doesn't let you pontificate too much." She feels so close to David that she "plays off him" in class some days. Another student, Bill, on the other hand, is a student she does not favor because he is "such an apple-polisher." A third student whom she likes is Alex, a student with whom she identifies. "I was an Alex. If I knew it, the whole world knew I knew it. I'm a rather shy person, too; I'm not a forward one, but I do feel that one has a responsibility to make the class go and there was nothing that bothered me more than the suffering teacher who was out there throwing out questions and not getting anything back. You could always trust me to say something. Alex always has something to say in class, even if it isn't very profound." Just as Alice likes Alex because he resembles her in many ways, so she has difficulty with students who are quiet in class and do not contribute. "I don't understand them. It's hard for me to understand why a kid would know something and not show that they know it. It's a mystery to me."

She readily admits that she has negative feelings toward a boy in her class whom she feels does not share many of her values.

> He has probably been the most negative student in the class. He doesn't like a lot of the things I ask him to do. He doesn't like the humanistic things; he really doesn't like them. Doesn't like the journals, doesn't like any of these things that make him feel anything other than . . . vocabulary. . . . He'll challenge me to do a lot of interpretation. He's very literal. And he probably is the one I feel most negative feelings about myself.

Alice's personality affects the classroom. Her enjoyment of teaching is communicated in a positive environment in which mutual respect and cooperation reign. She is the center of the classroom and all activities are under her control. The strength of her personality is, at times, so strong that she resembles an actress on a stage declaiming before a captive audience.

Pedagogical Assumptions

The pedagogical self is who the teacher is; the pedagogical assumptions are the translation of that self into rules of practice that will guide the teacher in the classroom. Values and beliefs are two important elements in this domain. Values—what the individual perceives to be of worth, merit, or importance—influence to some extent beliefs and mental convictions of the truth or actuality of something. These values and beliefs act as structuring guides in the determination of principles, accepted rules of conduct that can guide practice. These principles can be translated into strategies and techniques employed by the teacher that affect the way the curriculum is presented, how it is interpreted, what is emphasized, and even the amount of time that is spent on particular topics.

As has been shown, Alice values family. She often tries to parent, or in her case, grandparent her students. She makes regular references to her family. This belief is translated into a principle in which her classroom becomes an extension of her family. She uses several strategies to create a familial environment, such as walking around the classroom and touching students: "I think it's the thing to do. If it makes me more human to them, then it makes them more human to me."

Alice is a confidante to the students when they are having personal problems. They come to her as they would to a sympathetic parent and tell her their problems. She becomes an "oasis" for them where they can "dump their feelings without feeling any judgment against them. . . ." She recognizes that many times she cannot solve their problems, but at least she is there for them to talk to.

Alice tries to re-create an idealized family environment in her classroom, one in which students respect one another, are pleasant and kind, preserve their innate dignity as human beings, and function as a cohesive unit. The classroom she prefers is one in which students are "animated" and "react to each other." They are a "cohesive" group: "They work well together. There are no outsiders, and if there are kids on the fringe no one is unkind to each other. They are very quiet and very respectful to one another." In many ways Alice seeks to promote this positive environment: She makes certain no one is excluded in the circle discussion, she guards against unkind remarks, she doesn't raise her voice or scream, and she avoids confrontation.

Alice also wants her classroom to be "fun." This value translates into a belief that her class should not be high-pressured: "My class is not a high-pressured class. I try in many ways for it not to be a high-pressured class. Sometimes I feel guilty that I don't pressure them to the degree that they are pressured in other classes." The principle that guides her practice is to cater to their interests whenever possible. One strategy that she employs is to assign simple stories in order to take some of the pressure off. On other occasions she allows students to watch a video of a story or novel. She hopes to have student interests determine, to some degree, the course of study:

> I let the kids' interests dictate where I'm going to go next . . . if something is going well, often really going well, we'll do two more stories, but if something's dying on the vine we'll just not stay with something too long because there's no point in forcing the kids to read material that doesn't at least relate to their interests. And again, I'm not saying that

everything has to be like a primary interest to them. I wouldn't force-feed something when it's obviously not something that's to their benefit. It's not a contest of wills.

Just as Alice values her own sense of dignity, so, too, does she believe in the dignity of each individual. As a result of this she believes in such principles as preserving the dignity of students and respecting their points of view. For example, a strategy she used on one occasion followed a long weekend when she suspected that students were not very well prepared. She purposefully did not "hold them to a lot of detail"; as she put it, she "allowed them some preservation of their own integrity." When she asked them to find examples, she allowed them to use their books, so she "wasn't really backing them into a corner."

A key motif in Alice's pedagogical personality and one that is also basic to her instruction is responsibility or accountability. "I do feel that one has a responsibility to make the class go. . . ." But "it's not just the responsibility of one—it's the responsibility of everybody." An image that crystallizes this conception is the "lead mountain climber" who has the responsibility of leading the others but at the same time is attached to all the others and, therefore, dependent on them for success. The principle is that students have a responsibility to acquire their own learning. Over and over Alice reiterates this principle. She gives students

> lots of opportunities to show me that they are indeed prepared. . . . I have lots of daily grades. Everything is always read through. And I've done that since I began teaching. . . . I don't get around to all the kids to recite verbally; it's not just oral expression that indicates they know; there are lots of opportunities for written expression, so I touch every student every other day through some kind of written accountability and they can't hide in my classes. . . .

She works at establishing this sense of responsibility from the very beginning of the school year. One of the strategies she uses is to give students more reading quizzes at the beginning. Another strategy is to stop a discussion when she realizes that the students have not read the material.

Alice believes in dealing with material in depth. This translates into the principles of teaching for concepts or "big ideas" and having students read beneath the surface:

> I do go into considerable depth with what I teach. I could teach more quantity in a more cursory fashion, but I tend not to like to do that. . . . They can just read surface on their own. They're all good readers. Just to get a familiarity with things, you could give them tons of work to do, just tick off titles of novels. You could make them read one every other week if you really wanted to, but I tend not to want to do that. I think they need to understand what it means to read aggressively and have their thoughts provoked by what it is that author is saying. As in the last paragraph of "The Open Boat," which is so easy to miss. Because they're glad they're finished they just zap over that last paragraph and really it's the theme of the whole story. And it's also a wonderful example of style, but I don't know that I saw that the first time I read the story either.

Alice is concerned not with students remembering the "details" of a literary work, but with the wisdom and universal ideas implicit within great works of literature.

Another value is Alice's own love of literature. This translates into a belief that students should learn to recognize what literature can give them. She does not believe in teaching literature for its own sake; rather, she believes that literature offers students some "ladders to life or some rungs on that ladder to life." Teaching, then, focuses on the large ideas or concepts implicit within the work.

Pedagogical Repertoire

The pedagogical repertoire contains the reservoir of images, experiences, routines, and strategies that provide the teacher with a vast array of resources for use in the classroom. These resources, as opposed to textbooks, handouts, and other materials, exist principally in the mind of the teacher.

Images are symbols representing concepts; in many ways they present a concrete manifestation of an abstract and complex idea in a manner that is a shorthand notation. A teacher can access the concept simply through this single term or short phrase.

For example, "grandma" signifies Alice's conception of herself as a nurturer, one who tends to the needs of the students. Related to this nurturing image of "grandma" is the image of "oasis"—the concept that her classroom can be a place where students can come to "dump their feelings without feeling any judgment"—a home away from home. Both of these images convey her belief that the classroom must be a nurturing and supportive environment for students, one that meets at least some of their emotional needs.

Feeling comfortable is another concept that is important to her, and when she feels uncomfortable she uses the image "false feel" to describe this sense of unnaturalness or artificiality. She speaks of creating an artificial way of student involvement by going up and down the rows and calling on students. She says that this sets up a "false feel"—one in which her students don't act normally.

The demands of teaching are described by Alice through images such as "riding a horse" or "driving a car." The "horseback riding" image is used to convey the stressful nature of teaching: "I think that's why teaching is so stressful—it's sort of like riding a horse. The horse has its own will and so does the kid—they're not machines. It's not like driving an automobile; an automobile is easy to drive. A horse is not so easy to ride. Kids have their own will." And, of course, when the will of the students does not coincide with the will of the teacher, the ride becomes extremely bumpy.

Another image she uses to describe her role is "the lead mountain climber." This image describes her belief that learning should be a shared experience. At the beginning of the school year she shares an article with her students that describes all the things that a teacher is not, as well as what a teacher is—a "lead mountain climber." "This lead mountain climber has explored the mountain before and knows the pitfalls, but somehow is tied together with all the other mountain climbers. So the success of one is linked to the success of others and the failure of one means perhaps the failure of all the others. . . . I like that image so well," she explains, "that I keep it in mind." In keeping with this concept, then, she feels that all students have a responsibility to help to make the class work. This is the kind of student that she was. She always raised her hand out of a sense of obligation to contribute to the class. "I think that's why I like that figure so much about the mountaineer—people working together to make something work. It's not just the responsibility of one—it's the responsibility of everybody." This image of student–teacher interdependence is one of Alice's expectations in the classroom.

Her conception of time and her conception of "moments" also partially explain another image that she is frequently attracted to—that literature is a treasure house of special moments. There are passages in literature of "enriched experience" that are "windows to the world" or "ladders to life." With these images she represents her concept of the value of literature—that literature touches the great themes of humankind, ideas that all people of all times can recognize as common to their own experiences. These passages are especially "teachable" to her—that is, they are pregnant with possibilities for learning. These are moments that students can "internalize"—another image signifying the process of assimilation by which students actually "take in" the idea that the teacher is sharing with them so that it becomes part of their being.

Alice's own experiences as a student dictates to some extent what kind of class she wishes to conduct. In an anecdote that she related about two professors she had in college, she reveals her own learning style. Apparently she and her husband took an American literature course in college. The teachers' tests were "very detailed, all objective, a lot of line quote references." One professor would often give them complex outlines which her husband could commit to memory "at practically one glance," but "I never could." Her husband received an A in that course and she only a C. But she had the professor for another course that was totally different: "It was all discussion, all interpretation, all evaluation. . . . I got so much out of that, it was a wonderful experience. And I think it's my learning style that dictated my success and the way I appreciated the one and hated the other. . . ."

Her acknowledgment of her learning style is reflective of the kind of class that she thinks she runs: one that concentrates on the "big ideas" versus the trivial details, and one in which students are encouraged to do a lot of thinking versus regurgitation of information.

Her experience as a mother who had to raise two girls in a single-parent home also caused her to share with her students that she was able to raise her daughters successfully and that a "broken" home should not be used as an alibi for failure. Instead, she encouraged them with her own personal philosophy to bring out the best in themselves. As a parent of adolescents, she was also aware of how sensitive adolescents are to being judged. This sensitized her to judging and thus she was able to listen to the problems of her students without evaluating them, thereby providing them with an oasis for relieving themselves of some of their problems.

Even the church, which is an important part of her daily life, provides her with "tools" for her pedagogical repertoire. One Sunday her pastor had spoken about the number of American prisoners of war who did not survive because they had no system of values to sustain them through the long ordeal of prison. She took the idea and used it to examine the values of famous Americans and then encouraged students to examine their own values: "Literature is supposed to allow kids to examine their own value structure. We need to make them aware that they have one. . . ." The sermon then was incorporated into a lesson and served to confirm Alice in her own interpretation of the value of literature.

Alice's many years of experience as a teacher provide her with a vast amount of material for her repertoire. Each experience is filed away for future use. These experiences provide her with principles to guide her practice. Some offer her strategies that have proved to work; others provide her with things to avoid—for she has learned, the hard way, that they are not productive.

Alice began her years of teaching in the primary grades, and even though she is now teaching high school students, some of the principles that she learned in the elementary school are equally effective in the high school:

> When I taught primary grades, I used to do something that I've taught so many primary teachers, and it seems so natural for me. Primary kids are little, but they love to finish tasks; they are very task-oriented. They love to check things off that they've done. And I used to have spots in the room where when they finished something, they could get up out of their seat, walk over there, and mark it down. Or they could pick up another sheet and when they finished that they could walk someplace else and put it in another tray. But that gave kids this real good feeling that this is done. . . . And I used to have pretty well-behaved third grade kids. And I often thought that this was one of the reasons for this very simple task. Well, as we grow older, I like to have a list of things that I have done—this pile is done—and I don't really think that the high school kids are much different from that either. They like to have a sense of accomplishing something, finishing something, going from one task to another task.

Using this principle, she provides many opportunities for high school students as well to have a sense of finishing something. Experience is an important part of Alice's teacher lore. She has distilled from her life experiences and her classroom experiences, bits and pieces of information that direct her future interaction in the classroom.

Many of the routines and strategies that can be found in Alice's pedagogical repertoire have also come from her experiences in the classroom. The routines are, in many cases, consciously established patterns of behavior that she thinks facilitate learning and classroom management. Some of these routines are seasonal in that they depend upon the time of year; others are daily, regular patterns of behavior.

The seasonal routines differ from the beginning of the school year to the end. In the beginning, the instructor works hard to establish certain practices so that they become automatic. In September Alice takes time to do everything in detail. For example, in the analysis of literature, she painfully works through activities designed to help her students learn the techniques for reading beneath the surface; by the end of the school year she moves more quickly through the material because her students already have mastered the technique for close analysis of literature. This subtle realization on Alice's part is a strategy that was not found in a textbook but rather was acquired through her years of experience in the classroom. Another routine that she uses is to assign more quizzes in the beginning of the year in order to establish a habit of reading the assignment. In addition, she establishes terms that symbolize certain types of behavior. They become the "jargon" of the class, so automatic that students know what to do and how to do things without having to be told.

For example, the term "circle round" means that students are to move their desks into a huge circle. Other routines include vocabulary quizzes every Monday; no homework over the weekend; storing writing assignments in a composition folder; placing assignments for the next day on the chalkboard; always reviewing before a test; giving quizzes on daily reading assignments; and assigning periodic open-note quizzes.

WHAT DOES THIS ALL MEAN?

Teaching is an enigmatic and complex phenomenon. As Alice reorganized her experiences and walked back through her thoughts about her classes, she helped me illuminate some of the mystery of teaching. Through Alice I saw a strong connection between a teacher's mental life and the curriculum. Bussis, Chittenden, and Amarel (1976) speak of how educational research has "gradually sapped curriculum of its content meaning and injected in its place a 'methods' and 'form' emphasis. This metamorphosis has been achieved by persistent preoccupation with questions about the formulation and use of educational objectives, the form and organization of curricular materials, and the methods of presenting material" (p. 10). Alice's experience embodies a sense of curriculum as the "lived experience of the classroom." Curriculum is much more than content and materials. It is influenced by the teacher, for the identity of the teacher is a lens through which the curriculum is filtered. The teacher interprets content, selects materials, establishes parameters, and creates a classroom environment that is often consistent with his or her pedagogical assumptions. For example, Alice, because of her valuing of family and her own femininity, would often emphasize the female characters in literary works, would establish a nurturing environment, and would expect courteous and respectful behavior from her students.

Perhaps a broader interpretation of the term "curriculum" might help educators to realize that prepackaged recipes, since they are filtered through the complex mental lives of teachers, cannot protect the content from the teacher. Changing curriculum might be linked to changing teacher behavior, and changing teacher behavior, in turn, might mean changing that teacher's pedagogical personality, pedagogical assumptions, and pedagogical repertoire.

Reflection is a means for teachers to participate consciously and creatively in their own development. Alice spoke of the teacher as the "lead mountain climber." An outgrowth of that belief was the strategy of turning the class into circles. This, she indicated, students did "many, many times." "We talk to each other," she explained, "not to backs of heads, but to faces. I guess that, although I never realized it, the concept of group is really very important to me." Alice noted that this was the first time she had ever verbalized that assumption. On another occasion she acknowledged that the invited reflection "raised your consciousness of what you do." Invited reflection might be helpful in enabling teachers to make sense of their own worlds.

Another outgrowth of invited reflection is the stimulus for self-analysis. Although

Alice admitted that in the beginning of the interviews she was aware of my presence, she eventually lost that self-consciousness and concentrated on what she was doing. She stated that she found the interviews to be "enjoyable" and "informative" because she was forced to analyze what she was doing. The invited reflection forced her to go back through the observed period and to tease out those aspects that were of most concern to her.

Invited reflection, then, might also have implications for teacher educators and staff development. Although educators have come to acknowledge the importance of teacher reflection, there is still not much agreement about what teacher reflection actually is. Garman (1986) concedes that reflection is a "misunderstood, and rarely practiced aspect of the educational process" (p. 14). Howey and Zimpher (1967) hold that substantial attention to reflection is long overdue. Acknowledging the multiple perspectives on reflection, they ask how we might "increase our understanding of reflection and how such reflection might be facilitated in an inductive program" (p. 52).

Inductive programs using reflection have been instituted by Donald Cruickshank and Kenneth Zeichner. Cruickshank (1987) has stated that an educational professional who is mindful of his or her teaching skills and continually strives to enhance those skills should in fact be a more effective teacher than someone who does not engage in similar contemplation. The underlying belief in Cruickshank's reflective teaching program is that teachers who are able to learn reflective teaching skills acquire a powerful strategy for the careful consideration of their teaching—and they become more thoughtful and alert students of teaching.

Zeichner (1981–1982) has developed a campus-based seminar for student teachers to help them think critically about their field experiences in the public schools. One of the strategies that Zeichner believes is critical to the process of reflective teaching is to expose students to diverse and conflicting positions on any topic that is considered.

Alice embodies the complex relationship between a teacher's personal and professional life. Through her generous sharing of her life experiences and her thoughts, she is able to delineate the links between thought and action in the classroom. The depth of her reflection illuminates for us the complexity of teaching and the importance of the personality of the individual who teaches. And for Alice, it acknowledges a truly reflective and humane practitioner who embodies Schwab's concept of "eros."

REFERENCES

Bussis, M., Chittenden, E. A., and Amarel, M. (1976). *Beyond surface curriculum: An interview study of teachers' understandings.* Boulder, CO: Westview.

Clandinin, D. J. (1986). *Classroom practice: Teacher images in action.* London: Falmer.

Cruickshank, D. (1987). *Reflective teaching: The preparation of student teachers.* Reston, VA: Association of Teacher Educators.

Dewey, J. (1916). *Democracy and education.* New York: Macmillan.

Dewey, J. (1933). *How we think: A restatement of the relation of thinking to the educative process.* Lexington, MA: D. C. Heath.

Feiman-Nemser, S. (1979). *Growth and reflection as aims in teacher education: Directions for research*. Paper presented at the conference "Exploring Issues in Teacher Education: Questions for Future Research," Research and Development Center for Teacher Education, University of Texas at Austin.

Garman, N. B. (1986). Reflection, the heart of clinical supervision: A modern rationale for professional practice. *Journal of Curriculum and Supervison, 2*(1): 1–24.

Greene, M. (1987). *From the predictable to the possible: Recapturing a vision.* Keynote address at the CASEC Spring Forum, Chicago.

Howey, K. R., and Zimpher, N. L. (1987). The role of higher education in initial year of teaching programs. In G. A. Griffin and S. Millie (Eds.), *The first years of teaching: Background papers and a proposal.* Chicago: University of Illinois.

Morris, V. C., and Pai, Y. (1976). *Philosophy and the American school: An introduction to the philosophy of education* (2nd ed.). Boston: Houghton Mifflin.

Schwab, J. (1978). Eros and education: A discussion of one aspect of discussion. In I. Westbury and N. J. Wilkof (Eds.), *Science, curriculum, and liberal education: Selected essays.* Chicago: University of Chicago Press.

Zeichner, K. M. (1982). Reflective teaching and field-based experience in teacher education. *Interchange, 12*(4): 1–22.

Teacher reflection is enabled and constrained by a range of factors: Is there time and space in school for the personal and collective thoughts of teachers? Are teachers expected to critically examine their practice? Do teachers have colleagues and mentors who are able to challenge and nurture their particular vision?

Perhaps nothing has a greater impact on teacher reflection than the images teachers have of their work and themselves. In the next chapter Mari Koerner leads us on a journey through the varied images teachers have of their work. The journey is necessarily long and winding, for the images are contradictory and complex. The images explored here—partly formed through self-reflection, and partly formed as the result of media and public attitudes toward teaching and teachers—are gleaned from interviews with nineteen active elementary school teachers, each with between five and twenty-five years of teaching experience. These teachers describe both positive and negative images of teaching.

John Dewey (1929) argues: "The sources of an educational science are any portion of ascertained knowledge that enter into the heart, head, and hands of educators, and which by entering in, render the performance of the educational function more enlightened, more humane, more truly educational than it was before" (p. 76).* If an educational science, in Dewey's sense, is a hopeful goal, serious attention must be paid to the images teachers have of teaching. These images have a powerful, sometimes devastating, sometimes empowering impact on life in classrooms.

---

* Dewey, John (1929). *The sources of a science of education*. New York: Liveright.

CHAPTER 4

Teachers' Images:
Reflections of Themselves

Mari E. Koerner

I was the first woman in my family to graduate from college. I majored in English literature because I liked to read and talk about what I read. But, like many women coming of age in the 1960s, I didn't think past graduation to a career or even a job. Even though I taught, owned a business, married, and had a family, I don't ever remember making a conscious decision about a career. Actually, I didn't think about planning for a career until I decided to enter a Ph.D. program in my late thirties. In any case, there I was, twenty-one years old, in possession of a B.A. in English literature and no job. I heard a radio advertisement one day for classroom teachers for the Chicago public schools. The only requirements were that the applicant have a college degree and be breathing. I met the requirements. So I went down to the Chicago Board of Education and applied for a teaching position. I had to agree to take education courses beginning that fall. Two weeks later I was standing in front of a second-grade classroom, my first experience in an elementary school classroom since I graduated from a Chicago public school in 1959. That was the beginning of my life as a teacher.

I started to work in a school on the west side of Chicago, a poor neighborhood, entirely African-American. I started teaching in one of four mobile trailers, situated in the playground of an elementary school. It was here that I began to think about what teachers do and don't do, what kids learn, what you can't teach them, and what they can teach you. I found the preservice education courses I was forced to take in the evening—the credentialing ordeal—irrelevant to the real world of the classroom I inhabited during the day. It seemed no one in that college could tell me what to do with twenty-five kids who couldn't read, whom I couldn't even begin to figure out how to teach to read, who were often out of control (I counted twenty-five fights in my room in one morning—before recess), and who spent their days in an alien place, totally out of sync with the rest of their lives.

No one prepared me for the poverty or the hopelessness or the fear that was a part of that neighborhood and school, things that had never been a part of my life. It was there I came to find my most important resource in learning how to be a good teacher: the other teachers in the school who were struggling to do something of value. Although many of the young faculty lacked formal preparation to be teachers, they often made up for it in zeal and good will. There were basically three groups of teachers: the experienced men and women who didn't care about the children or education; the experienced men and women who were responsible and took their work as teachers quite seriously; and the inexperienced young women and men (most of whom were trying to avoid being drafted into the Vietnam War) who were sincere and caring, but woefully lacking in knowledge about children and the ways in which the young grow and learn. There were loud and lively discussions at lunch about the politics and policies that created neighborhoods and schools like the one in which we found ourselves.

The Martin Luther King riots happened during the second year I taught, and the young teachers were not surprised to see the anger and resentment that permeated the community erupt into violence. Afterward, the physical condition of the neighborhood became even worse, with burned-out structures and abandoned buildings as permanent testaments to the policies of racism and classism. I began to define myself as a professional who needed to think seriously about the tasks at hand. I began to see that it was necessary to be reflective and inquiring in order to teach. That core belief has lasted throughout all my years of teaching, and today it is that belief that I hope to carry to my adult students who are struggling to become teachers.

I taught in the Chicago public school system from 1967 to 1975, and that is where I learned how to be a teacher. It is there I discovered that I generally like people who decide to teach children, that I share values and views of the world with them. I even married one of them. For me, my life inside and outside the classroom merged in my relationship with my husband, and with the friendships I developed during those years. My life experiences became embedded in my teaching experiences, and my work with children in classrooms was influenced by my life outside of school. This was the real beginning of my interest in finding out what teachers think about themselves, their work, and their relationships with children.

That interest lay dormant for the many years I worked outside of the classroom. It was renewed when, as a requirement in my graduate studies, I interned in an early childhood center. I began to think more deeply about teachers and their perspectives. When I had to think more seriously about what I wanted to learn more about through formal research, I immediately turned toward teachers and their own ideas. Specifically, I was curious to know how teachers saw themselves and what could be learned from their own self-described images. If I were to hold a mirror up to them, what images would emerge in that reflection? That is how I came to investigate the images teachers have of their work, and the images of themselves as defined by that work.

To better understand the phenomenon of image, it is helpful to look at every person as an activist who is constantly making constructs in his or her life. These constructs are ways of integrating and labeling what has happened and what is happening. They also can "predict and anticipate events as forerunners of action" (Bussis, Chittenden, and Amarel, 1976, p. 17). To me, "images" are mental constructs through which people shape and define their lives. They are dynamic: The world influences and changes those images even as images give shape and definition to the world.

From the very beginning of my work as a teacher, I learned from other teachers. To this day I love to "talk shop" with teachers who have students of any age. We exchange stories, discuss events of the day, try to figure out what works in the classroom and why, and share ideas. From my own experiences of teaching at the elementary, preschool, and university levels, I knew experienced teachers had powerful ideas about themselves and what they do. These ideas were sometimes clear, sometimes muddy, but they were always interesting and informative. I was curious about the common threads in the images of experienced elementary school teachers. I wanted to find out, as well, how teachers perceived the images of teaching that they saw reflected in the larger society. So I talked to teachers. I asked them to describe what they do, what a "good day" in school is like, and how they perceived other people's images of them. I hoped that in the pursuit of these perspectives, these images, further understanding of the nature of what it means to be a teacher might be uncovered.

I tried to capture these teachers' descriptions, the mental images they had constructed, and I tried to develop a framework for organizing common images. Throughout this inquiry I returned repeatedly to my organizing question: What are the images that experienced elementary school teachers have of their work in the classroom? I asked three related questions: What are the personal images teachers have in relationship to their work? How do these images fit into the larger frame of teachers' lives? How do they fit into a still larger picture of society? I looked for common ideas.

TEACHERS' IMAGES

As I talked with teachers and recorded their stories, ten themes emerged as congruent pictures. These themes reflect, I think, the complexities, tensions and dilemmas familiar in the everyday life of teachers. The themes are teachers as (1) hard workers, (2) guides, (3) professionals, (4) personalities, (5) subordinates, (6) creators of the body electric, (7) curriculum makers, (8) ciphers, (9) collaborators, and (10) perquisitors.

"Hard workers" means simply that teachers repeatedly refer to teaching as difficult for many different reasons. Teaching is physically exhausting and mentally draining; it demands work beyond the classroom and beyond the hours of the school day. Teaching is also endless—there is always something more to teach. "Guides" describes teachers as people who lead children to knowledge or enable children to grow and learn. "Professionals" defines teachers as intentionally participating in activities important to ongoing growth and development. "Personalities" are important to success in the classroom; effective personality traits include empathy, sympathy, ability to communicate, flexibility, love of children, nurturing, and patience. "Subordinates" is a somewhat surprising theme with negative undertones; it describes teachers' feelings about the opinions of people outside of education.

As "creators of the body electric," teachers are makers of a new entity, a unified whole, from the individual children in their charge. Teachers establish a unique community in their classrooms. "Curriculum makers" means that teachers decide what should be taught and how it should be taught. "Ciphers" implies that teachers are nonentities with no special or unique characterisitcs. Ciphers is an image of teachers as merely generic place holders, totally interchangeable with one another. Whereas "curriculum makers" is an image of powerful people, "ciphers" is an image of people with no value. Finally, teachers see themselves as "collaborators" having important relationships with parents, colleagues, and students, and as "perquisitors" who receive a range of critical, tangible, and intangible rewards. Teachers see teaching as exciting, stimulating, intellectually challenging, and just plain fun.

These themes are my own construction. They are my way of organizing and making sense of the complex, detailed, and often contradictory information teachers shared with me. Each choice, while thought out carefully and supported by the teachers' own words and ideas, could have been another. The themes, then, do not merely represent the words of the teachers I spoke with for this project. They also reflect my own experiences and the experiences of the many teachers I have known and shared ideas with over the years.

I will explore three of the themes in more detail here in order to show the interrelatedness and tensions that exist for teachers, as well as the complexity in my own deliberations to understand teaching as these teachers understand it. Each sheds some light, I believe, on what gives meaning to teachers' work and lives.

Creators of the Body Electric

In my experience as a teacher, and in my role as parent/teacher to my own children, I know what it feels like to get to that special "teachable moment." I know what it is like to tell a story when people are listening with rapt attention. More than listening; they are understanding and are on the same wavelength with you. There is a feeling of being caught up in the moment, of being a part of a single experience that culminates in a light bulb turning on, a click sounding, a bell ringing—what some teachers describe as the "uh-huh" moment. The teachers I talked with had these feelings too. Call this theme "creators of the body electric."

In *Leaves of Grass* Walt Whitman writes of singing the body electric. He describes an individual body, while I refer here to the collective body of the classroom society. Like Whitman, I too am talking about feelings of intensity, depth, and possibility. The metaphor of the body electric captures both the idea of the collective body of students and teacher and the rapport and communication that can flow among them.

The teachers I talked with see themselves as creators or builders of minisocieties in their classrooms. They describe what it takes to make the individual children in their charge merge into united groups. If they successfully create these new entities, they use energy words, such as "flow" and "in sync," to describe the relationship between them and the children. The purpose of establishing these societies, and of developing a "sharing" feeling in the classroom, is to get to the "teachable moment." That is what the teachers I interviewed described as "a good day of teaching."

In contrast, "a bad day of teaching" is a day filled with interruptions that prevent the development of the body electric: Interferences from outside the classroom and beyond the teacher's control cause serious frustrations and setbacks. Those destructive events—that absence of the body electric—are equally real in the world of teaching and can be caused by children, administrators, teachers themselves, or mundane, everyday school occurrences like fire drills and public address announcements.

In a classroom where learning and teaching are going on together, there is a communion, a close relationship that teachers work hard to establish. One teacher named Sophie, describing the community of her classroom, explained that what is best about teaching is

> interacting in a classroom and receiving interest, excitement, communication back. Everybody's comfortable, everybody's happy to be there. Nobody's intimidated. Nobody's acting . . . quiet almost like being phoney because they're scared to death of you. It's not the other extreme of being too loose where everybody's talking out and running around. It's somewhere in between there, where we can have a mutual respect. They respect me . . . I respect them. We have a good healthy communication. They know they're there to learn. They know I'm there to teach—it's like that. That's when it's good.

Sophie made it clear that teachers and students are all there for the purpose of teaching and learning. They are all working together toward a particular and important goal. She includes herself as a member of the group and as someone who is instrumental to the communication and relationships that must exist in the classroom. She uses the word "excitement" to describe the setting. Other teachers spoke in similar terms about the relationships that develop between them and the children. There is nothing static about the body electric.

These kinds of relationships do not develop accidentally. The teachers work at them and plan for them. For example, one teacher named Abe says he spends the first two or three weeks of school establishing a "sense of community . . . a sense of my classroom as a place where you're going to succeed if you put in the effort." Another, Marge, focuses on the care she thinks the members of her classroom must have for one another. She introduces the idea that the lines between home and school are arbitrary in terms of the real education of children—especially young children:

> And I work very hard to make our classroom their school family, and to develop a love between them and myself and between the children, among the children. So that, they have a caring for one another, so that by the end of the year, or hopefully well before the end of the year, they really care what's happened to someone else and that they will help someone else without my having to point it out.

The care for one another causes the bonding that teachers both hope for and see as a consequence of that special kind of relationship: As a teacher named Pat describes it: "You get real close to them then. I like that. That's really the best part about it."

I recognize these kinds of feelings in my own teaching. I too know happy and lighthearted moments when I leave for home. This is one of the rewards, one of the perquisites, that is an integral part of teaching. Teachers find satisfaction in their work when they are effective, when they make a difference in children's lives, and when they are successful. By contrast, when these important events do not occur, demoralization and burnout begin.

On a good day, everything goes smoothly. There are no distractions. There's a flow. Everything is on track. Judy describes this kind of day:

> A good day is a day when you can go in and don't have a lot of extra paperwork to do. Your lessons are all planned. You have your material and supplies. You can have your reading groups and everybody's calm and cooperative and working hard. And you go through your math lessons and the children learn, and reading lessons . . . and everybody's working, cooperating. You don't have a lot of distractions. To me that's a good day. And you feel at the end of the day that the children have learned. And then at end of the day, you make homework assignments and the children bring their homework in and follow through and then they ask for more: "Mrs. Smith, give me some more" a little boy asked me today. "May I do an extra science project?" Those are good days to me when I feel that they have learned.

There are feelings of moving, of going toward a goal, of changing, running smoothly, affecting and being affected. Here is Toni's description of "flow" in the classroom:

> So it's a job that I think is kind of exciting because I can go in there and when I'm really down, and when I don't feel like teaching, and there are those days, I walk in there [and when] I have to psych myself up. . . . Those are the days that I get pleasantly surprised because all a sudden there's a flow. You and the children are moving together toward the common vision. I don't even like to say goal, it's like a vision. We're just all on the same mind set and the whole day is going along on the kind of mind set, all flowing together. There's just a sense of collaboration. And that's the neatest feeling every time. I love that sense of flow, that just everything pulls together that day.

Toni describes the sense of unity that can happen in a classroom—the idea that everyone is working together. Sophie says it is "thrilling" when it happens, because the children are enthusiastic and "take it a notch farther." She says everyone is "bouncing off one another" in this action-packed experience. All this movement leads to the moment that teachers wait for, the moment when, as Clara says, "Their eyes open and they have discovered something or they have learned something or they have experienced something they're going to take with them." Stephanie describes the atmosphere of the body electric during an anthropology lesson: "It's charged. You can see the moment. You can—it's not just passing information along. You can see the eyes wide open and the—you can see a heightened response." This is the connection, the bond, the tie that links them all together—the common purpose. It gives meaning and direction to their work.

There are ways to get the group to that moment. One is to create situations in which children can share ideas and feelings. Another is the routine and discipline the teacher sets up to ensure group cohesiveness. Communication is an essential ingredient to the body electric. It is the sharing of experiences and the ability to communicate on a significant personal level. As Joanne puts it:

> It's the sharing that's important as far as talking about your families, about yourself, your pets, your community and not just when we have shared time. But when we talk social studies . . . things that are more personal, those are always the easiest.

One of the most wonderful experiences of teaching is when there is a sharing of ideas and experiences in the classroom. It is when the personal and "school" identities merge and everyone becomes invested in the discussion, the interaction—when learning becomes a natually occurring event.

Teachers talk about the importance of the rhythms and routines of their classrooms. These routines add to a sense of unity; they guard against the interruption of or disruption to the body electric: Clara finds "comfort in the routine. . . . And then at a certain time [students] know they do this or at a certain time they do that. They don't want it to be boring. They need the structure and therein lies the discipline."

Beginning teachers with little experience in classrooms see discipline and management as major issues. This was certainly true of me in my mobile unit back in 1967. But these veteran teachers tend to talk about discipline in terms of creating the body electric, not as a separate entity. Classroom control is not an end in itself, but rather a means to an end, and an interactive part of vision and goals. Discipline is essential in order to move together toward common goals to keep the minisociety intact. With the order that comes from discipline, there is a sense of safety and security, necessary for the creation of any community. Teachers talk about discipline, but almost never about punishment. They describe themselves as models of behavior, setting up rules and structures, maintaining an air of authority, and conceptualizing discipline as mutual respect and caring. They do not see discipline as being in conflict with creating and participating in the body electric. Meg says that she sees herself "as the person who's in charge," and that she and the children establish a rule system together.

Many of the teachers experience this order-keeping role as one built upon mutual respect. Toni:

> I hope that I get the discipline that I desire because I show respect for them. I really feel that you have to model [behavior]. If you want the children to show you, as a teacher, respect, then I have to model that I'm somebody who respects them as well, and that what they say is something that is worth listening to. Just like—I would hope that whatever I'm saying they feel it's worth listening to because I've modeled that. So I see myself as somebody who tries to model the appropriate kinds of behavior in the classroom. But there are definite limits in my room. I don't want to say I'm strict, because that's not true either. I'm just very firm in my commitment that there has to be some control in the classroom—and the kids, I think, know that very well because we talk about it, because we talk about the kinds of things that would help our classroom be a place to learn in and what those things are—and I do try to give the kids the opportunities to say . . . to bring out what they feel they want in that classroom, and what kinds of things they respect.

Teachers talk about "bad days" in teaching as disruptions to the body electric. These include administrators giving them additional tasks and just generally getting in the way, paperwork, disruptive children, being disorganized and unprepared, and the myriad interruptions that happen in every elementary school. For Bob

> there are a lot of . . . extraneous things that can make it a bad day . . . like fire drills. People pull the fire alarm, or things happen. You try to get started. But the buses are

late. The kids are coming in and then . . . there's a crisis in the next class, kid comes in, sprains his ankle, somebody's drugged out. You get ready to do something great and ten kids are at Science Fair. So it's kind of like you never get out of low gear. It's kind of like you never get going. I think that a bad day is when situations arise that prohibit that something wonderful from happening, something good from happening.

Administrators are often seen as hindrances rather than aids. Liz notes that administrators are always "giving me extra things to do. They are always thinking of other things to add to the curriculum, and sometimes they don't give you the benefit of your expertise since you're the person out there in the trenches."

Sometimes it is not the children but rather the teachers themselves who cause disruptions. Teachers admit that if they come to school tired or distracted, they can prevent the flow, the coming together with the students. Sophie refers to this when she admits that "maybe I didn't get my whole thing together and so I'm hassled and hustling around in the beginning of the day trying to do this, that, and the other thing for various reasons. Sometimes I never recover from it—for the whole rest of the day."

What happens when the teacher and the students don't "click"? When there isn't chemistry or rapport? Carol describes that experience with a class that

didn't want to learn, they didn't get along chemistry-wise. Any time you came in and said, "We're going to do a new project," they would look at you strangely; they didn't want to do projects. They barely wanted to work, let alone do anything creative. So, it was a real strange year, and many times I would come home and say . . . I don't think I ever wanted to quit, I must admit that, but I would come home and say, "Oh, I'm counting the days for this year to end," and I was, till the very end.

Carol did not mean that these children had behavior problems or were actively disruptive to the class. She had a difficult time because she could never excite them or affect them. She was frustrated because she wasn't able to create a body electric.

The image of teachers as builders of the body electric is a positive and constructive one for present and future teachers. It represents teachers as active participants in the learning process and in the community of the school. It illustrates the importance of community and shared visions. The body electric is certainly elusive and complex; positing its creation as a goal puts teachers in situations without road maps, recipes, or instant answers. It demands that teachers be thinking, inquiring professionals in order to establish communities in their classrooms. But the payoff is at the very heart of teaching and it is a major organizing theme for teachers.

Subordinates

Teachers are suspicious of anyone asking them about teaching. They are familiar, of course, with being ignored and their opinions disregarded; that is more natural for them than being seen as sources of important knowledge or information. There are a range of reasons for this feeling. Some of them are captured in the image of teachers as subordinates.

Teachers see themselves as special people who are creators of the body electric. This gives meaning and direction to their work. Because that work spills over into their lives, teaching is an important part of their personal identities. But they don't think the larger society understands or cares about their work. Teachers question whether what gives meaning to their work and their lives is recognized as valuable by anyone else. So while they think they are important in some critical ways, they also believe that the rest of the world sees them as subordinates, members of an inferior class.

Teachers are affected by these conflicting views. The contradiction creates confusion and resentment. There was strong agreement on this point in my survey: Teachers have low status in society, teaching is treated as low-priority work, teachers are thought to have easy jobs in which they are merely children's custodians, and teachers hardly work at all. Teachers believe that they and their work are misunderstood and receive little respect, and that society has confused and contradictory role expectations for them. Still, teachers think what they do is critical and important.

I asked "If you had a child who was considering being a teacher, what would you tell that child about what it's *like* to be a teacher?" Many teachers responded that they would not recommend teaching as a career for their children because the job is not regarded as important in society.

One teacher spoke at length about the low esteem of teaching. Carol believes teachers are partly at fault, yet she is resentful of the treatment she and her teacher husband receive. Her frustration is apparent:

> I think too often, a lot of people, look at it and say, "It's an easy profession, it's an easy out." And that's what gives us a bad name. I get so frustrated when I hear people down teachers. And I think, "Damn it, how did you get through school?" But I just think that we need to change the whole profession, the whole outlook of why we're teachers . . . perhaps—and you've probably heard this fifty thousand times, but—maybe if we got on a level with other professions, like lawyers, and engineers, maybe not so much surgeons, because I can understand their training, and I can understand the time they spend, and the importance of their job. But I just feel that we're kind of pushed out all the time. I'm tired of it. I mean, even when—I don't know if you've ever had this—but even when I talk to people and they'll say to me, "Oh, what does your husband do?"—"He's a teacher."—"Oh (flattest voice possible)." Like . . . that goes right through me. "He couldn't make it in any other job?" He was in accounting, and could not stand it. He loves to teach. Just like he loves to coach, with his baseball. And I think that makes him a very special person. And I think that so many people can't understand that. So right away, "He can't make it in something else?" And that, that irritates me. I can't help it.

Teachers are often defensive when it comes to describing their positions to other people. For Pat, anger, resentment and hurt feelings prevail.

> But when you're told, by everyone, that you're worthless. . . . "You only work nine months of the year, you don't really do anything important," that's very . . . disheartening. So I just assume that everybody feels like that.

There are at least two factors involved in why teachers are seen as subordinates. First, their work is "women's work" and is defined by children. Second, teachers don't work regular business hours. As Pat put it: "You only work nine months of the year."

Teachers worry that people outside of education think they "babysit all day," that teaching is mainly custodial. They believe they are seen as people who do mindless tasks to simply keep children busy. Bill notes that teachers are "the cheapest daycare available. . . . [We are expected] to do daycare and teach when it's possible. I'm overstating it a little bit, but that's pretty much where it's at." Jolene shares this view:

> I think people think [teachers] only work nine months a year, they only work part of a day, they don't work eight hours. They just sit there and babysit these children. I don't think [people] have any comprehension of what it's all about.

To Jolene, seeing teaching as babysitting children is a way of devaluing her responsibilities. Bill relates this to the devaluation of children and what that means for the image of teachers:

> First place, you're dealing with society's devaluation of childhood, that little children are cute, number one. And number two, they grow up automatically. They kind of intuitively learn what they need to learn. . . . Now the downside of that is that anybody who works with kids is also devalued. So, number one, only women will do it. It's women's work. And number two, mothers are paid nothing. The next group up are childcare workers, who are paid next to nothing. And then the next group up are teachers. Because kids kind of spontaneously do all this, all you're doing is containing them all day. It's really not hard, you know.

Bill points out that teachers are held in low regard because they are doing low-priority work, because of the devaluation of children and women. Many teachers see education as an area whose importance is given "lip service" but little else, and that there is no sustained effort to improve the education of children. After working as a teacher for twenty-five years, Judy reluctantly admits that education is not a top priority in our country:

> We don't get the money to fund materials that we should get. We don't get the money to fund education like we should. I feel that the people in the United States know enough to have one of the best school systems . . . in the world. But we do more to hurt the children. It took me a long time to realize that educating children was not number one. Sometimes, maybe education is number two, or number three, or number four.

Because teachers are perceived as doing low-priority work, it comes as no surprise to them that they are treated with little respect. They accept it in a way, but they are hurt by it nonetheless. Liz:

> People don't say, "Oh. This is a great profession." Sometimes they make you almost feel ashamed that you're a teacher compared to something else. An engineer. "Oh. You're an engineer. That's great. What do you do?"—"I'm a teacher."—"Oh." Not so much that, but the fact that I don't think parents push respect for the teachers as when I was a child. This whole society, I think, is upside down because it's very unfair that you could pay somebody a lot of money to hit a ball with a stick and sit out in the sun for hours, which

is a dumb thing to do because you could become ill out there. And they pay grown people to hit a ball with a little stick and they pay millions and millions of dollars. The only thing they're interacting with is a crowd of people who are pleasure seeking. I guess there's a skill involved. But they get a lot of money. And then you have teachers who are preparing your children. We as teachers, we could do a lot of damage. But then we're paid so little.

Liz brought up salary as proof of the low status teachers have in society. Teachers see themselves as having to fight for every increase they have ever received, and still their salaries are not comparable with those of other professions. One teacher spoke bitterly about her nephew, who was entering another profession at the same amount of money a veteran teacher with a master's degree would be receiving. It is maddening and demoralizing to these experienced teachers.

Teachers in large urban districts are especially cynical about salary increases. Chicago teachers had experienced nine strikes in twenty years, and they felt that they had to be forever vigilant even to maintain the status quo. All of this took a toll on their sense of value and self-esteem. These teachers, especially, felt they were regarded as generic—faceless and nameless employees of a system that neither values nor rewards them and a public that demeans them. As Sophie put it:

What this society thinks in general of Chicago public school teachers is that they are . . . uneducated, sometimes crude, sometimes indifferent, mostly kind of incapable. That they produce a negative product in the classroom . . . I've never heard anything other than that.

Some of the teachers talked about social situations, outside of school, where they were treated badly because they were teachers. Carol feels that people minimize her husband's value because he is a teacher. Marge says "at times I think it's hard when someone hears you're a teacher. They want to jump on you." Marge's "general impression is that most people don't think too much of teachers. They think they're stupid and they're there because they can't get any other kind of job."

Teachers are stung by these notions, which go directly against the image that teachers have of themselves as competent, caring, hardworking professionals. Teachers believe that most people don't really understand their work, because if they did, people wouldn't have such negative views. There would be more respect, higher status, and better pay. Bob rather defensively echoes these sentiments but, interestingly, excludes himself from the larger group of teachers:

People just don't understand what it's like. And I don't care. That's their problem and I don't get real down because of what people think of teachers because they eventually have to deal with me personally. I don't think I'm typical. I take a lot of pride in what I do. I try to do it very, very well.

In the identification of himself as different, Bob seems to agree with the widely held notion that he so objects to: Most teachers must not "do it very, very well." Teachers are influenced by these commonly held negative images, and they wrestle with their own more positive images. It is part of the struggle of being a teacher.

But there appears to be no clear definition of what it is that teachers should do. What are the expectations society has for education, and what is the role of the teacher in that process? Teachers aren't sure themselves and are confused by the mixed messages they receive from the media, from parents, from school boards, and from legislatures. Karen captures this ambivalence:

> I get very confused when I read different articles and everything from *U.S. News* to the *Reader's Digest* of exactly what our society does expect teachers to do. One article will list a whole bunch of facts that kids don't know. Who was Walt Whitman? Then another article says we're not teaching them to think critically. So I don't even really know if society as a whole knows what they want from education. I think certain people have this image and this and this. I think probably certain people think that we should be teaching [kids] not to cheat and not to do this or that. I find that extremely frustrating because their parents don't mind cheating on their income tax if they can. I mean our society has values and ethics that are so fluid right now that how do you teach it to children— without a standard? What is the standard? But I think that probably there are people who expect us to be teaching values, not think about the implications of that. But I think they would expect us to think that.

Teachers feel themselves to be in precarious positions. Only in the classroom roles they define for themselves in relation to the children are teachers really comfortable. Teachers focus on their own definitions in order to combat the pervasive view imposed from outside.

Elementary school teachers experience devaluation of their work even more acutely. Bill says that the younger the child taught, the less value placed on the teacher. Pat is even more explicit as she lists the hierarchy of teaching positions:

> But I don't think teachers are valued at all. I think professors are valued more than especially elementary school teachers. In my experience, the elementary school teacher looks down on the preschool teacher and it's all the way up the hierarchy through junior high and high school, and I think the high school teachers have the easiest job. I really feel the older the child gets, the less responsibility the teacher has or blame the teacher will have. So I mean I can't say the high school teachers are bad, there are wonderful ones that work their heads off. But the onus is on elementary school teachers and that's just not valued. They never have been. I don't think that anyone has ever thought of them as being valuable. . . . My own family, they don't have any idea—my parents, my husband, and my brother doesn't know what kind of a teacher I am. Just like they tell you, you can't step on the kids for ten years and expect [them] to feel wonderful about themselves. It's the same thing with teachers. They're human beings. I don't know too many of them who feel good.

Having been an elementary, preschool, and university teacher, I have experienced firsthand the effects of this hierarchy. I know I have higher status because I now teach adult students rather than preschoolers. Pat touched upon the intense, negative feelings of many veteran teachers. They receive a lot of criticism, not many rewards, and after a while it takes a toll.

The lore of teachers, then, includes stories and anecdotes about how they are regarded and treated. They are affected by others' views of them as teachers. They see themselves as subordinates and must reconcile that view with their images of themselves as creators of something good, the body electric. What gives meaning to their work is not regarded as important by people outside their classrooms. Teachers get constant and clear messages that they contribute little that is worthwhile. This is an area where the professional and personal identities mix; teachers struggle to reconcile what they do in school with how they are treated and regarded in their lives outside school. The struggle highlights the need for teachers to make sense of their personal images: Teachers need to sort out these opposing views and feelings in order to move forward.

Perquisitors

Teachers have images of themselves as creators of the body electric and as subordinates. What makes the work they do worthwhile? Why do they continue to teach? I had to answer these questions when I decided to return to teaching after a ten-year hiatus. The answers came from the nature of the work and the heartfelt belief that I, as a teacher, could positively affect other people. Anyone who has successfully taught someone knows the intense, positive feelings attached to this accomplishment. It is a common reward or a perquisite teachers feel. They are perquisitors because they are the recipients of all the benefits, many intangible, that come via the classroom.

Teaching is fulfilling and rewarding work. Teachers see a wide range of opportunities for their work to be exciting, even thrilling, stimulating, intellectually challenging, and fun. They value the relationships they have with children in their classrooms, and they think they play a significant role in those children's lives. Teachers have a sense of accomplishment when they reach goals that they think are important, and those successes encourage them to see their work as meaningful. Finally, they like the time off from the job that teaching allows.

Abe articulates the feelings of many of the teachers when he says of teaching, "It's very exciting. It's a lot of fun. I learn all the time. I'm very excited about that." Sophie expressed the same feelings: "The only reason I [teach] is because it is invigorating. It's exciting! It's unique!" Joe describes teaching this way:

> I find it exciting. I find the pace is good for me . . . always something going on. Never, never ever look at my clock and say, "Oh no. Three hours left?" I like learning myself. So teaching gives me an excuse to pursue topics myself.

Not only is teaching exciting; some teachers describe it as being plain old fun. The bottom line is that they enjoy their work. Sophie says, "I just mainly do it because I like it and it's fun." Pat, who asks herself aloud, "Am I that cynical" about teaching? also says:

> I like it! I like it when they do well, and I like the kids. I have a good time with them. And I especially like to get into social issues with them. That's really fun, and they're, they're always right on the cusp of that when they're going into junior high. They're asking all those neat questions about AIDS and drugs and stuff, and I love to get into that with them. I think I make a difference with that. And I teach them, and I like that. And I like the teachers. I just like the job, I could never—I couldn't see a nine-to-five regular job.

As Joe says, there is also an intellectual element to teaching, not only in the subject areas but also in the process of teaching itself. It is a complex task that calls for a lot of decision making, reflection, and problem solving. Teachers who are interested in being educated themselves often find the mental stimulation—deciding what to teach and how to teach it—positive to their own intellectual growth. It is exhausting, but positive. The job is hard work for many of the reasons it is exciting work. Teachers derive pleasure from the fact that their work is different all the time. It is seldom boring and there are changes with every new class, every new child, with every new day, and perhaps with every new hour.

Teachers like the feeling of control they have in their own classrooms, the minisocieties they have created. Bob talks about how he has changed the courses he teaches every year because then it becomes an opportunity for him to learn more about history. Thus he is constantly stimulated by learning more about his specialized content area. Although there is a necessary routine, a "dailiness" about Bob's classroom, the day-to-day life in that classroom is what is appealing:

> What I do, day to day, is wonderful. It's exciting. It's always different. I make it change. I like it to be considerably different each year. I enjoy being on my feet, being forced to be imaginative. . . . I find that environment to be very exhilarating.

Perhaps because teachers feel they can and do affect young people's lives, and therefore perceive their work as having high human stakes, the job is inherently thrilling and electrifying for them. When the body electric takes form and the teachable moment happens, there is a true sense of accomplishment for the teacher. Ethel found this in working on a science project:

> I didn't believe it very much at the beginning and the end result [was] that . . . the science project was the best in the whole school. You see things like that, or . . . see the results of the students. "Today we're going to take the unit test," and everybody passes with 90 percent or 100 percent. So I then am very, very, very happy.

Liz, who wonders aloud why she has stayed in teaching for so many years with too few financial rewards, also talks about the rewards of getting to that teachable moment:

> Teaching is very difficult. But very rewarding. The rewards—I think the rewards, people say there are few, but I see them in small ways. So if you're waiting for big things you may not ever see them—the rewards. You could sometimes see when you're trying to explain something and you see a child say, "Oh. I got it." That kind of little thing. So there are many, many of those.

When teachers talk bitterly about the lack of recognition and positive feedback from outside their classrooms, they acknowledge that they retreat to their classrooms for the rewards that make the entire endeavor worthwhile. Meg says, "I think it's hard work and yet it's the kind of thing that you can see the rewards daily." It is the relationships they have with children that allow teachers to see themselves as successful.

Teachers often say they like, even love children. They make it clear that this is an essential quality for outstanding teachers. In a classroom they have the opportunity to be with children. As Karen says, "I like kids. I mean that is the bottom line. I love kids."

Joe tells a story his father had told him when Joe decided to go into teaching:

> Well if you're going to be a teacher, you're never going to be rich. But you'll never starve. If teaching is what you like to do then there's no other career that you'd be satisfied doing. But if you don't like teaching, there's no amount of money that will make it worth doing.

Teachers remain in teaching if, for them, it provides more dividends than drawbacks. Here again, the personal and the professional merge. Teachers are rewarded by the positive human interactions that take place in classrooms. Teachers have an image of themselves as doing work that is personally and professionally valuable.

THE NATURE OF BEING A TEACHER

My career as a teacher has influenced the way I see the world. My perceptions of myself and my identity include my images of my professional self—my images of teaching and teachers. Images are elusive in that they cannot be seen, but certainly they influence teachers' behavior. Unlocking teachers' minds and revealing their images makes it possible to learn more about what it means to be a teacher.

I tried to develop common themes in the images teachers have constructed from their personal and professional experiences, and then to use teachers' words to describe these shared images. I wanted to come to a deeper understanding of teaching by recognizing teachers as sources of knowledge about the practical reality of teaching and learning in schools. In uncovering these images, I hoped that a fuller picture of what it means to teach might be reached, and the question of what gives meaning and direction to teachers' work and lives might be more fully explored.

Certain assumptions were made about teachers: They are thinking, inquiring people; they are complex human beings who inhabit the complicated community of the classroom. The themes as a whole present a picture of complex interactions between and among human beings. Instead of providing a clearly defined vision of a teacher or teaching, the images are sometimes contradictory and often reveal the ironies and dilemmas in teachers' work.

For students who want to become teachers, these images may provide information about how to prepare, and what it means to be a teacher from the insider's perspective. These images provide a framework beyond learning how to do a lesson plan or how to teach mathematics to first graders. While it may not be possible to anticipate every experience every student will encounter as a teacher, it is perhaps realistic to provide a fuller view of what teaching means to teachers—of what the work itself encompasses—and to prepare students to be the active problem solvers they will have to be in order to be effective in the classroom. Inexperienced future teachers may learn a good deal about the profession from the images that experienced teachers have developed.

These images remind teachers and would-be teachers that perceptions change and actions, based on the perceived world, change accordingly. It is not possible to prepare for every situation, to be ready for any incident. It is possible to set realistic expectations and to struggle against the prevailing images of teaching. Part of becoming a teacher is to forever be a learner, to keep on becoming a teacher.

The common image of teachers as creators of the body electric presents teachers as active forces in the formation and continued life of the classroom community. It creates a picture of combined efforts and shared visions. Instead of presenting teachers as isolated workers, pulling unwilling students down the road toward education, this image views teachers as partners in children's education. Teachers need, then, the kinds of leadership skills necessary to establish vibrant classroom communities. Leaders don't rely on cookbook recipes to solve problems; they develop their abilities to make sense of the world and implement their ideas.

The image of the teacher as a subordinate is difficult, yet this too is an integral part of teaching. Teacher education programs tend to ignore the impact of these perceptions, and teachers' organizations rarely take up the subordinate concept in a proactive way. It is important that teachers find ways to grapple with this image, perhaps to resist it. Teachers are not regarded as leaders, as people with vision who should have control and be in decision-making positions. Respect is not awarded outside of the classroom society.

With all the problems and difficulties teachers report, there is still a strong sense that teaching is work that can be exciting and fulfilling. Teachers take pride in being educators and think they are needed by society whether society knows it or not. People who are thinking about joining the teaching profession need to be made aware of this sense of pride—and all teachers need to be reminded of it. In an age where role models have been sent to jail because of greed and ambition and where being self-centered and cynical has been touted as virtuous, teaching remains one of the few professions that fosters empathy and concern for others. Teachers see themselves as people who have important choices to make within a value-laden context, and those choices have direct, immediate impact on other people.

What are your images of yourself as a teacher or a student, and what are your images of other teachers? Think about your perception of teaching and how it is reflected in your image of being a future or present teacher. How do you prepare yourself to fit or resist that image? What do you need to learn, or how do you have to change and develop? What was important in your past experiences to get you to this point, and what kinds of knowledge and experiences will you have to acquire? Because you are responsible for your professional self, what kind of map are you making now? What are your metaphors for teaching? Teachers need to become aware of their own thoughts and perceptions, their own images of teaching, as well as of images others hold about teachers, if they are to shape a future more whole and more hopeful than today.

REFERENCES

Bussis, A. M., Chittenden, E. A., and Amarel, M. (1976). *Beyond the surface curriculum.* Boulder, CO: Westview.

Koerner, M. (1989). Teachers' images of their work: A descriptive study. Unpublished doctoral dissertation. Chicago: University of Illinois.

The imaginative and aesthetic dimensions of teaching can be critically important in a teacher's life. Generally devalued and dismissed in a time when technology is king, these dimensions remain vital for outstanding teaching. For generations teachers have developed expressive ways of knowing, and have rendered their experiences in patterns and images that have enhanced their understanding and their practice.

In the following chapter Virginia Jagla pursues the question of imagination and intuition with eight outstanding teachers. Their experiences range from early elementary to college teaching, and each is recognized by his or her peers as an exemplary teacher. Jagla develops a dialogue on the value and uses of imagination and intuitive knowledge in the daily lives of teachers, and provides a way to consider the power of imagination in teaching.

Real teaching is never quite as straightforward as textbooks and research papers would have it. It is always more complex, more confused, and more idiosyncratic than anticipated. Curriculum guides, lesson plans, scope-and-sequence charts have important limitations in regard to planning and actually teaching. Imagination, thoughtfully developed and employed, can provide the power for a kind of deep planning and serious reconsideration of teaching.

CHAPTER 5

Teachers' Everyday Imagination and Intuition

Virginia M. Jagla

Imagine. Picture this: You have the opportunity to design your own school. A dream? Sure, go ahead. Do you use a big building or a small one? Do you use a building? How many classrooms do you have? What do they look like? Do you have classrooms? How many students are in each classroom? How many teachers? How do you group students? Do you group students? What? How? When? Where? Who?

These are the types of questions I posed to student teachers as I proposed to "teach" them to be teachers. "Think of your 'ideal' classroom," I advised, and then had them draw the physical facilities: ". . . and this is the door that leads out to the forest . . ." ". . . and here is where the swimming pool would be . . ." ". . . I'd put the desks here and . . ." The responses ranged from the mundane placement of desks to the less routine placement of trees. But all students were imagining, picturing this classroom-to-be.

Where did my intense interest with the imagination come from? My two brothers and I were imaginative and creative with our play as kids. We made up characters on a mythical neighborhood block and would while away the hours play-acting our different parts as we went along. "But we were *all* imaginative as kids," you say. "Why does a grown woman concern herself with how adults, how teachers use their imagination?" I answer with the question "Why not?"

I have experienced firsthand the importance of using one's intuitive and imaginative abilities as a teacher. I employed my own imagination in daily planning and evaluation throughout more than twenty years of teaching in elementary, junior high, college, and museum settings. Within the classroom I relied on intuitive insights to guide and shape lessons with my students. Later, working with student teachers in elementary settings, I was struck with the necessity of being able to articulate what the teacher's daily use of imagination and intuition means. I observed student teachers who were comfortable with these concepts, and others who might have benefited from more experience with them.

It has been suggested that "teacher lore" implies the straight rendering of teachers' stories on topics of their own choosing. I asked teachers to consider the question of their use of imagination and intuition and steered them in that direction, but within that framework their stories were allowed to blossom. The final interpretation is mine, but any storyteller is the instrument of interpretation for the parable. Just as folklore is altered slightly in different countries and by different groups, so teacher lore should be told by individuals who are interpreting the stories in meaningful ways. It is certainly true that another storyteller might interpret the stories in a different manner. Someone else might not choose to tell certain stories at all. Countless stories exist, whether verbalized or not. Only when written, however, are the renditions subject to sustained scrutiny. In the oral or written tradition, teacher lore has many facets, for it can inspire, instruct, recall, question, answer, entertain, persuade, expose, or describe.

> Lead me from darkness to light!
> —*Brihadaranyaka Upanishad*

> I shall light a candle of understanding in thine heart, which shall not be put out.
> —*The Apocrypha*

To educate: The Latin *educare* means to lead out—specifically to lead from darkness into light. The Sanskrit word for teacher, *guru,* means the one who shows the way from darkness into light. For me, enlightenment is sparked by imaginative and intuitive teachers. There are teachers who tirelessly invest themselves with their classes year after year to make learning exciting and meaningful. Such teachers know the joy of learning and clearly understand the need for inspirational teaching or "leading." This concept implies the need for teachers to use their own imaginative capacities while interacting with students to engage them in learning.

The teachers I talked with and observed as I pursued my interest in imagination and intuition ranged from elementary teachers through college professors. Kathryn, Leticia, and Erica are primary teachers. Erica is a veteran teacher with over twenty years of experience. Kathryn has been teaching for a little over a decade, and Leticia is a second-year teacher. Nan is an intermediate teacher who has been teaching more than twenty-five years. Dominic teaches in a junior high school and has been teaching for just under a decade. James and Rebecca are high school teachers. James is a communications and history teacher with fifteen years of experience. Rebecca is a thirty-some-year veteran math teacher. Alicia is a college professor, presently teaching philosophy courses. I have been teaching for more than twenty years. Presently I am a district-level administrator, but I have taught most elementary and junior high grades as well as college. Together we have over 150 years of experience to draw upon.

EXPRESSIONS OF IMAGINATION AND INTUITION

> And as imagination bodies forth
> The forms of things unknown, the poet's pen
> Turns them to shapes, and gives to airy nothing
> A local habitation and a name.
> —*Shakespeare, A Midsummer Night's Dream*

So, just what do we mean by the terms "imagination" and "intuition"? The terms are complex, their definitions neither easily apprehended nor succinct. As we attempt to talk about various meanings and the range of ways imagination and intuition are embodied in classrooms, we gain some insights.

Imagination—What Is It?

The word "imagination" is used habitually in diverse contexts. As with many such frequently used terms, the word has taken on varied meanings. Gilbert Ryle, in *The Concept of Mind* (1949), calls attention to the fact that the word refers to a wide variety of activities, including pretending, acting, impersonating, fancying, and imaging. Sutherland (1971, p. 1) warns that imagination "is in fact one of those useful but misleading words which can fit without any perceptible jarring into a good many contexts." *Webster's Ninth New Collegiate Dictionary* (1987) defines imagination as

> the act or power of forming a mental image of something not present to the senses or never before wholly perceived in reality; creative ability; ability to confront and deal with a problem: resourcefulness; the thinking or active mind: interest; a creation of the mind, especially: an idealized or poetic creation; fanciful or empty assumption.

"Imagination" is derived from the Latin word *imago*, which means an image, or representation. Typically when we use the verb "to imagine," we are referring to this root meaning of conjuring up an image, visualizing. Likewise "imagination" often refers to conception or visualization of something. However, the noun "imagination" and the adjective "imaginative" have come to have many more meanings than that of simple representation. Robin Barrow (1988, p. 81) has considered some of the colloquial uses of the word "imaginative": "Some people appear to use the word as a synonym for 'sensitive,' others for 'creative,' 'inventive,' 'reflective,' and so on."

Perhaps "playing with ideas" is at the heart of the creative process. "It reflects the basic relationship between science and imagination, and more importantly, between imagination and all human ways of knowing and doing" (Barell, 1980, p. 3). Barell claims that playful imaginative activity is what Einstein was doing at age sixteen when he visualized himself riding along a ray of light to study its properties. Leticia concurs that "imagination is something that you can visualize in your mind. It is something that you can see but nobody else can." Jacob Bronowski, in *The Identity of Man* (1971, p. 58), claims that the "invention of these ideas and their interplay in language is imagination—the making of images inside our heads. In this sense science is as much a play of the imagination as poetry is."

I remember times when I would picture my class in my mind. The image was not still; it was a moving picture with constantly changing action. Typically I would see the class from my usual perspective, through my own eyes. But every now and again I would picture myself in the scene, looking in from a "God's eye view" at what was taking place. Some of this imaging had to do with planning.

Kathryn's definition of imagination includes thinking of the various possibilities of a certain situation—"the things that are possible and the things that aren't possible and the things that you would like to be possible, given the situation. For example, if you want to make an invention, you have to know scientifically what will work. You also have to go after what has never been done before; you don't even know if it could work, so it's not in the realm of reality—you don't know if it's possible. You have to be a little bit of the dreamer and not always practical." Schubert (1975, p. 4) defines imaginative projection (IMPRO) as:

> A curriculum decision-making strategy that enables curriculum planners and implementers to generate possibilities, project probable consequences, formulate and entertain hypotheses in action, and assess the consonance of hypotheses with aims and principles. It refers to a process of inventing solutions to problematic curriculum situations, a process which is simultaneously based upon defensible ethical principles. It is a situation analysis.

Karen Hansen (1988, p. 138) also considers imagination in terms of possibilities: "Imagination is what allows us to envision possibilities in or beyond the actualities in which we are immersed." The imagination has the ability to dispense with boundaries, but often when particular limits are set the imagination soars within the confines—a seeming paradox, but one that artists recognize quite well. The painter selects oils, acrylics, or watercolors; he or she limits the size of the canvas or paper. The poet selects a particular subject and pentameter. Within these limitations the imagination takes shape.

Erica pictures things in this way, looking at the possibilities and seeing the constrictions under which she is placed. She also points out how individual the idea of imagination is:

> Imagination is picturing in your mind what will transpire or is likely to take place. I think teachers do that when they're planning ahead, making lesson plans. As I mentioned to you, since we've met I'm more conscious about it. I actually picture more images in my mind than I used to and I think that's helpful. I image when making the plans and then when evaluating them afterwards. I think that imagination is a very individual thing too. Some people don't visualize at all. I usually have a dialogue with myself. I have a conversation about the possibilities of what could happen.

Dominic, similarly, looks at many possibilities when imagining:

> If I use my imagination I have to put it into an action. When I use my imagination I take an idea and then I attach as many meanings to that idea as possible. I take the idea and then I have to imagine a variety of ways that I can present that concept to the students so that my ideas get across. Some of the ideas are very dry if we're using a prepackaged worksheet. Some of the ideas are very dramatic. But my imagination would be a cluster of ideas around a concept. When I actively imagine I take the same concept and try to think of it, exhaust it with as many situations as possible.

Nan and Rebecca speak of imagination in teaching as implying creativity. Nan initially had a hard time calling herself "imaginative" because she does not regard herself as an artistic person. Nan considers teaching an art, however, and certainly considers herself a good teacher. So as our dialogue progressed, she began to consider ways imagination might be applied to her teaching.

Rebecca says:

> Imagination is the name I'd give to the ability to think creatively. Imaginative teaching would imply instruction that is creative. Imagination and creativity probably are very close. What can be called creativity? Probably conjuring up something that is either new to you or new to you and others. Whatever it may be. Whether it's music or technique or a drawing. A sentence.

This idea of newness or discovery is inherent in Rugg's (1963) definition of imagination, which involves discovery. Barrow (1988, p. 84) suggests that to conceive of the new or "unusual" is one of the criteria for imagination: "The criteria of imagination are, I, suggest, unusualness and effectiveness. To be imaginative is to have the inclination and ability consciously to conceive of the unusual and effective in particular contexts."

Rebecca adds a strong link between imagination and intelligence: "I think one of the things teachers have to be able to teach is intelligence. I really have not met many people who are intelligent who are not imaginative. There's a uniqueness of thought that comes with it." Again, this is in line with Barrow's view of an imaginative person. Barrow (1988, p. 89) uses the word "educated" rather than "intelligent": "I would argue that an educated person, as distinct from a well-trained person or an indoctrinated person, must necessarily possess imagination."

Rebecca also sees love of subject matter as an important factor in being imaginative in teaching. James speaks of love when defining imagination:

> Imagination is letting your love be translated into your classroom. Because imagination really comes from love through loving something, through loving what you do, through loving your subject matter, through loving your students, or loving your profession. So many of us are so afraid to be passionate about what we teach or how we feel about it. There are times when schools become so loveless and pale that students just feel like there's no need for them to be there, that they can be replaced by a computer monitor, that the teacher could be replaced by a monitor and it wouldn't make any difference. So I see imagination as being a passionate activity, because it is a loving thing to do. Anybody can prepare a lesson plan and go in and teach a subject. But I often say, "I don't teach subjects, I teach students." There is a big difference.

To Alicia, imagination is "pure and simply completely crucial. There is no education without it. Period." Alicia feels that imagination provides us with the ability to place knowledge into context:

> The imagination is what enables us to connect and without connection we don't know anything. Without the imagination there is no such thing as a whole, there are only a whole bunch of disassociated parts which are completely without meaning. It's tricky because connecting goes in so many different ways at once. It goes backward to what one already knows. It reaches forward to the thing that one is learning. It comprehends intuitively the whole into which those things that one's learning fit. It stretches in all different directions at once.

Alicia sees the teacher's use of imagination as making things "come alive" for students. This is similar to Coleridge's (1817) idea of the "secondary imagination," which unifies disparate images and ideas, thereby creating and re-creating and putting life to thoughts.

Egan and Nadaner (1988, p. ix) view the use of the imagination as indispensable in teaching and learning:

> Imagination . . . is the heart of any truly educational experience; it is not something split off from "the basics" or disciplined thought or rational inquiry, but is the quality that can give them life and meaning; it is not something belonging properly to the arts, but is central to all areas of the curriculum; it is not something to ornament our recreational hours, but is the hard pragmatic center of all effective human thinking. . . . Stimulating the imagination is not an alternative educational activity to be argued for in competition with other claims; it is a prerequisite to making any activity educational.

What Is Intuition?

The word "intuition" similarly is fraught with confusion and ambiguity. Colloquially, intuitions are "hunches," "instincts," "gut feelings," or "guesses." As a form of action, to intuit is "to see," "to know," "to sense," "to perceive," or "to feel." Often these words are preceded by the word "just." "I just knew," "it just felt right," "I just sensed that"—thus meaning, "it is nothing more than that," or "I cannot explain it any further." The sensations or feelings related to intuition are often perceived to be within one's body. Therefore, we have idioms like "I feel it in my bones," "I know it in my heart," "It was a gut reaction." Intuition, then, is beyond the grasp of systematic rational analysis, and difficult to define with words. It is something felt from within, instinctually, something that defies logical explanation.

Intuition is derived from the Latin verb *intueri*, meaning "to look upon." Thus, some element of looking or seeing is inherent in the roots of the word. *Webster's Ninth New Collegiate Dictionary* (1987) defines intuition as "immediate apprehension or cognition; knowledge or conviction gained by intuition; the power or faculty of attaining to direct knowledge or cognition without evident rational thought and inference; quick and ready insight." Spontaneity is embedded in intuition.

In their book *Awakening the Inner Eye: Intuition in Education,* Nel Noddings and Paul Shore (1984, p. 57) offer the following definition: "Intuition is that function that connects objects directly in phenomena. This direct contact yields something we might call 'knowledge.' " Noddings and Shore see intuition as an act involving the will in which the analytical process is speeded up. They view this as a conscious process, unlike most others who think of it as taking place in the unconscious. Many writers have used the term "intuition" to mean a spontaneous understanding or perception that is not consciously evoked.

For me, intuition is a grasp at knowledge that connects the subconscious and the conscious mind—pulling prior knowledge synthesized in the subconscious to the conscious level at an opportune moment for immediate insight.

Rebecca says "intuition is the name I'd apply to an action or reaction that is felt or sensed, often not resulting from any identifiable thought process." James defines intuition as "listening to the song in the heart rather than the song in the head. Following the gut, allowing the gut to lead you sometimes." Besides "just going with the hunch," James views intuition in a more studied manner:

> With intuition, I tend to be a little more scientific about it than many people. I think that it really is built on observable factors, but we can't always verbalize what they were. What was it that you saw that told you to do that? Now where are we going to go with this? How far are we going to get with it? Sometimes the intuition comes in with answering the question for yourself. Is this class going to go better if I tell it where to go or if the students tell it where to go?

To Erica intuition involves "thinking on the spot *and* reacting to those thoughts by acting accordingly." Dominic refers to picking up cues from the students: "Intuition is a process where one would make a multisensory observation and formulate some type of a judgment." This is similar to the way Rubin (1985, p. 61) describes the teacher's use of intuition in the classroom: "The teacher makes a rapid assessment, assimilates the available cues, and forms a conclusion."

Erica associates intuition with confidence: "It's the feeling of confidence to go with something that just occurs to you spontaneously." Nan is also convinced that these "feelings" are linked with confidence. And just as confidence increases with experience, so does intuitive ability. Nan says:

> I don't know if it's intuition. Maybe it's just confidence. It's the same thing that everything else is. It's looking at [the students] and seeing that they have listened to me, that they have worked hard and it's not going anywhere. To me it just seems obvious. Now, is that intuition? I don't know. That takes confidence, because I don't consider myself a failure and I don't consider them a failure. Whereas earlier on [referring to her beginning years of teaching] it probably would have been all their fault.

Links between Imagination and Intuition

> Imaginative play is a key that opens the door of intuition, and its practical value is readily visible.
>
> *—Frances E. Vaughan (1979, p. 153)*

Alicia says: "Intuition is what we use that enables us to trust what our imagination dishes up for us. Intuition is the enabler. Imagination is what is enabled." She feels that

> it's intuition as well as imagination that guides you through the darkness, that helps you stay alive to a heuristic struggle. It's the intuition that this will be over. That this will give way. I'm not sure if that's intuitive or not. It is hard often to distinguish between intuition and imagination. Imagination deals in more concrete terms. One can have intuitions that thus and so will occur. But the actual occurrence comes about through the imagination.

Erica sees imagination as preparation for intuitions: "I think if you imagined all kinds of possibilities beforehand, then you're open to go with one that comes up at the moment. So imagination has prepared you to feel free to act intuitively."

To Rebecca, intuition causes the imagination to be activated, and she does not feel that imagination is a deliberate, cognitive function:

> Imagination in teaching is often the response caused by intuition. Imagination is not, however, a cognitive process planned to be an awakening fantasy. There are things that set off the imagination that sometimes you are not aware of. Prior to a presentation, I often try to develop a learning experience that evokes unique, fresh, and enjoyable responses. The liaison is *always* directed to evolve from familiar ground to that ground embellished with new material.

Dominic regards imagination and intuition as complementary and necessary components of the teaching day: "Intuition is part of my diagnosis. I do formal diagnosing, but intuition constitutes my informal diagnosing. Imagination builds my fund of knowledge and activities of what I can do for my objective of the day. I've got to put the two together to come up with my day."

James sees a relationship between imagination and intuition in the planning process:

> I use intuition in lesson planning quite a bit. It ties in closely with your imagination. Will this work? With this class, yes. With this class, maybe not. There was one time, I can't even remember exactly what the lesson was. I had spent a lot of time preparing this lesson. Just as I walked in the class I said this isn't going to work. It just won't, the kids are going to get upset by this and I didn't do it. I alluded to it in the course of a lesson and I saw by their reaction it just wasn't going to work.

James also refers to moments when he reacts intuitively to a student's imagination: "Every once in a while a student will come up with an idea, or a way of looking at something that hadn't occurred to me." He tells a story of a girl in a remedial English class who asks "What if it wasn't a dream? What if Dorothy really went to Oz?" James did some research and found out more of what Lyman F. Baum, creator of Oz stories, had in mind: "One day's worth of research convinced me that he believed she went to Oz. The movie doesn't depict that, but the book does. That she actually went there, and went back several times, and that she was eventually able to go back and forth quite often." His intuition led him to research the girl's imaginings and this led James to a further use of his own imagination in planning a lesson.

THEMATIC THREADS UNRAVELED

> I have here only made a nosegay of culled flowers, and have brought nothing of my own but the thread that ties them together.
>
> — *Michel Eyquem de Montaigne, Essays, Book III, Chapter 11.*

Similar themes appeared in separate conversations with teachers. Themes are integral to any storytelling venture. I have unwoven a few of these thematic threads and reworked them here.

Connections and Context

> Each time new resonances are awakened, new connections disclosed, I am made aware of
> the uses of imagination and its place in helping me penetrate the "world."
> *—Maxine Greene (1988, p. 54)*

Connection is an inherent part of Alicia's definition of imagination. Alicia has pointed out that the "fullness" of things, looking at "wholes" instead of "disassociated parts," putting things into context for students, are all dynamic aspects of imaginative teaching. Bringing about "imaginative fullness" is what provides meaning. Putting things in context means connecting with the past, present, and future: "Part of the imagination is a sense of things always in context—the passing of time . . . reaching backward and reaching forward and being part of a thread of history—which is the only thing that makes any *body* meaningful, leave alone any *thing*." Not only must there be a connection within the content, but there should be a connection between teacher and student—among students and among teachers—in a school setting.

Using the word "image," Connelly and Clandinin (1985, p. 198) paint a similar picture of connection in time:

> Image is here conceptualized as a kind of knowledge embodied in a person and connected with the individual's past, present and future. Image draws both the past and the future into a personally meaningful nexus of experience focused on the immediate situation that called it forth. It reaches into the past, gathering up experiential threads meaningfully connected to the present. And it reaches intentionally into the future and creates new meaningfully connected threads as situations are experienced and new situations anticipated from the perspective of the image. Image emerges from the imaginative processes by which meaningful and useful patterns are generated in minded practice.

It is creating connections and finding the appropriate context that makes learning "come alive" and become relevant. Without that the meaning is lost.

Some of this connection making and awareness of relevant context begins in imaginative planning. The teacher anticipates those connections and personalizes them. Connections are made through evaluation and reflection too. The teacher needs to help students reinforce what they've learned so that it stays with them. Much evaluating and reflecting happen spontaneously during classroom activity. Some connections are initiated by the teacher through intuitive responses. At other times the student's own self-intuition and the material provoke relevant connections and enliven the contextual base.

Erica feels strongly that the best way to teach is by connecting subject areas so that they are not perceived in isolation from one another: "The interrelatedness of the language modes is important. I think traditionally everything has been isolated. . . . If activities in the classroom can be natural, like real life, they are more effective. I resent having to segment the day. It's always so exciting when everything comes together."

Erica feels that making connections apparent for students and helping to create a context for them is an imaginative process: "To be imaginative enough to put concepts in terms that will make connections for kids so they'll take off in their own minds is a real gift. We learn best what we can relate to. Things put into the context of our lives and what's important to us help us to see the whole rather than isolated parts."

Nan places importance on the idea of helping students make connections and ascertain appropriate contexts: "Figuring out what the context is for the kids, that's an important thing to do and it's not easy. If they don't understand it you give them some of the "around words" [ideas that clarify context] to put it into their experience so they can understand it." Nan feels that it is imperative for the teacher to discover the students' own contextual framework—where they are "coming from."

Rebecca believes that the ability to facilitate these connections for students comes from a thorough understanding of the subject matter involved: "If you have something to hang a topic on, and you put it in a place in your lesson that would be receptive to the students. That comes from knowledge of subject. If a person is able to make liaisons within his major field as well as among others, then this person has the tools for imaginative presentation."

Dominic thinks that the main way teachers use their imaginations to provide students with a context for ideas and to facilitate the making of connections is by planning meaningful experiential activities in the classroom: "As a teacher I needed to provide the conceptual base. So I needed to take a concept and put it into an activity that could be experienced in the classroom."

James, like Alicia, teaches in a way to "make it come alive" for students, so that they can make their own connections. James provides students with a context through his stories and dramatizations. He makes connections from history to students' everyday lives in the present. James accomplishes this by having a good understanding of his students and by remembering what it was like to be in high school himself. He creates a warm, open climate in his classes so that students are comfortable enough to explore their own possible connections to topics. This non-threatening environment set up by James facilitates exploration on the part the students. Students are not afraid to speak out and question or raise an issue that they feel is pertinent or helps them connect. Role playing and simulations provide a context that can give meaning to many concepts.

An intuitive understanding, then, stems in part from making connections—for example, linking a present situation to one from the past for immediate insight, or linking an imagined response to the actual reaction of the moment for further comprehension.

Spontaneity and Openness

Spontaneity is inherent in intuition. During imaginative teaching and learning much of what occurs is spur of the moment. The connections that students make and that teachers facilitate are often happening spontaneously. When speaking about intuition, some of the teachers referred to spontaneous evaluation of lessons needed to take a different tack. Some educational research (Elbaz, 1983; Haley-Oliphant, 1987) alludes to the spontaneous nature of reflection in action. Kathryn and Leticia mention that they often go with their feelings. Erica speaks of being outside oneself while one is teaching: "You're the one conducting the lesson, but then you're also the one observing it all." Spontaneous decisions are constantly necessary in any classroom setting. So there is need for continual reflection and monitoring of the situation by the adult in charge.

Dominic refers to reflection as "editing" or making "split-second decisions." This is an expected mode of behavior for good teachers. Nan says that on-the-spot evaluation is her main method of assessment: "If I don't know right then, while it's happening, I won't know later. I have to be open to see [cues] so I can know what to do."

Schon (1983) views this spontaneous nature of dealing with situations as an inherent part of the work of reflective professionals. Practitioners are constantly reflecting, reevaluating, and conducting "on-the-spot-experiment[s]" (Schon, 1983, p. 62). Schon refers to the "intermittent zones of practice" or situations of uncertainty as a swamp that practitioners need to wade through to glean the relevance lurking there. Spontaneously pulling from this intermittent zone gives an element of certainty to a particular aspect from that which is unsure. In terms of education, the teacher needs to be open to the possibilities that lie in the realm of uncertainty, and flexible enough to spontaneously flow within the swamp and yet not be sucked down.

Noddings and Shore (1984, p. 53) refer to "the clarity and certainty with which intuitive knowledge affects us." Here we find the threads of "spontaneity" and "confidence" entangled. It is the spontaneous certainty and clarity of direction from which confidence springs. One could also argue that it is confidence that gives one the feeling of spontaneous clarity and certainty. This aspect of certainty is often inexplicable in the spur of the moment, and many times cannot be put into words even after time and reflection have aided the endeavor. It may have been "just a gut feeling."

Spontaneity is a central attribute of intuition. In a simplistic way, intuition or perception is a spontaneous happening. It is something that sparks the imagination. The imagination is needed in order to work at igniting that spark to build a fire. The intuition is like the unveiling of something, and an active imagination is needed to give life to the idea, to put it into action. James feels that "just going with the hunch, and saying this is going to go right now," is often the most important thing that a teacher can do.

Interwoven with spontaneity is the idea of opening up (or freeing) on the part of the teacher, and subsequently on the part of the students in the classroom. To James, being open with students is critical to all other aspects of teaching. It paves the way for sharing, trust, caring, and all meaningful interaction: "I think openness to yourself and to your students is the key part of it."

Openness is the basis for the give-and-take in the continuing "conversation" of teaching. Nan feels that she has "to be open" to see the cues that let her know how a student is reacting. Openness allows her to "read" the student, to obtain the necessary feedback to know how to proceed. She says, "You can feel if somebody opens up toward you." It is, therefore, important to keep the lines of communication open within the classroom. Nan refers to being open enough to pick up on the "vibes" from the students. Dominic and Rebecca also speak of cueing in to the energy level of their classes as an intuitive way of understanding where to go.

Openness implies a type of freedom. Sutherland (1971) reminds us that it is necessary for teachers to provide students with "freedom to think" in order to encourage the use of the imagination. Leticia and Kathryn believe that in order to provide opportunities that foster children's imaginations, the teacher must feel free to proceed. The locus of this feeling of freedom is partially within the teacher, but it is also external. The administration, then, needs to encourage imaginative teaching. Kathryn points out that some students may not feel free enough to be different from the rest of the class. She also suggests that veteran teachers need to open up more to fresh ideas and to explore other ways of teaching.

Confidence and Experience

> The mutual confidence on which all else depends can be maintained only by an open mind and a brave reliance upon free discussion.
> —*Learned Hand, Speech to the Board of Regents, University of the State of New York (1952).*

Confidence is an important issue in imaginative teaching. It is equally important to the teacher's use of intuition in daily classroom activities. In order to utilize an insight, teachers need confidence in that intuitive feeling and in themselves. It is an aspect of confidence in the self that promotes the freedom of "openness" to ideas and allows for "spontaneity" of thought and action.

Referring to a mental planning "checklist," Alicia notes that "the more confidence I get as a teacher, the more the checklist is in my unconscious," thus leading to a freer, more spontaneous performance. Alicia also believes that when confidence is lacking, the teacher is governed by fear—and unimaginative teaching results. She speaks of such sterile teaching resulting from "a complete lack of ego," a time of apprehension when confidence is shaken. At this time communication with self is lacking or buried, "like snow drifting over": "The ego is the important thing. I've lost self, I've lost trust, I've lost what we're all about." When one is not in conversation with oneself, if one has "lost touch" with the "I," there can be no creativity and imagination. A teacher's lack of confidence is related to a lack of connection with the "fullness" to which Alicia refers.

The idea of confidence and intuition go together. Erica defines intuition as linked with confidence and spontaneity: "It's the feeling of confidence to go with something that just occurs to you spontaneously. It probably isn't as spontaneous as it might appear. I don't really think you can be intuitive until you've had some experience, felt some confidence. So you feel safe enough to take a risk and just do something spontaneously."

Confidence plays a key role in this intuitive manner of working. Subtle impressions may guide you, because you have encountered similar situations, because you know the people involved so well, and because you have reflected on these aspects. Knowing that you have made sound decisions in the past on the spur of the moment gives you confidence to make more such decisions and to act according to your feelings at any given instant.

Intuition has a lot to do with past knowledge of facts, feelings, situations, people, routines, interactions, and responses. The insights or subtle intuitions that constantly occur to guide us as we teach rely heavily on a large storehouse of experiences and information. The more information and experiences that we have in our reservoir, the more accurate our spontaneous insights will be. As we gain experience in teaching and continue to assess the accuracy of these intuitive guides, we tend to have more and more confidence in them and in ourselves. It is a vitalizing circle.

Rubin (1985) urges teachers to have confidence in their intuitions. He claims that these intuitions are readily attainable through experience. He tells us that as teachers gain experience they can "sharpen their intuitive faculties and use them more fully. After a few years in the classroom, sophistication increases, there is a greater sensitivity to the problems of pedagogy, and the subtleties of the art gradually become more clear" (Rubin, 1985, p. 62).

It is our becoming as human beings that spawns our becoming as teachers. The more comfortable and confident we are with ourselves and our lives, the better we will be able to affect the lives of others. Being in tune with one's insights, building a capacity for a trustworthy intuition and being willing to act upon it—all are part of a philosophy of life that can lead to better teaching.

Alicia feels that becoming a good teacher is being able "to make the shift . . . from one who knows addressing those who don't to two people on a path together, the kid and the teacher." This shift comes with experience. But sometimes when the self-confidence is shaken or the feeling of openness is lost, even an experienced teacher may resort to playing "God."

Openness is directly linked to confidence. Teachers are more likely to rely on their intuitions when they have greater confidence through experience. Nan says that she was not as confident as a beginning teacher but "I've been able to open up to the interaction." Kathryn suggests that confidence in students is essential: "For kids to express their imagination, they have to be fairly confident that it's going to be accepted." It is the responsibility of the teacher, then, to create an environment where students feel confident in using their imaginations and in taking risks.

Rebecca speaks of the increase in intuitive ability that comes with greater experience and confidence:

> You get much better at improvising on the spot and thinking of examples and counterexamples and bringing people in and going away from your lesson plan and coming back to it and moving in another direction. It is fantastic! It can put you on a high you can't believe, when you have finally achieved the ability to roam all over and pick up on things as they come. I think it takes a very secure person in the classroom and I don't think new teachers are ever that secure when they first start.

Having trust in oneself and one's abilities is another necessary ingredient for good teaching. Also important are the trust and confidence students place in the teacher. Rebecca feels strongly that teaching cannot occur without them: "I don't think you can do anything with classes if you don't have trust. . . ."

James builds the climate for trust by creating a caring atmosphere. He warns against being intimidating to students: "The power that teachers have to be threatening is enormous, much more so than many realize." He takes great care in making things comfortable for students. The openness he espouses allows for trust to occur. This climate often leads James into socioemotional realms of his students' personal lives. He becomes the adult whose shoulder they can cry on or whose advice they seek. He reports that on several occasions he has positively helped students in crisis, including preventing possible suicides, through this bond of trust and confidence. Because they trust him, his students are anxious to get involved with the activities he plans.

Variation and Possibilities

Variety is the mother of enjoyment.
—*Benjamin Disraeli, in Vivian Grey (1826), Book V, Chapter 1*

A common theme within the field of imagination is being able to picture something in many different ways, to look at possibilities. This thread is entwined with another, the theme of "resourcefulness." The teacher utilizes resources to add variety to teaching. Resources can be thought of as possibilities themselves. Inherent to the idea of creativity is a sense of newness or uniqueness. The invention of variations of presentation, the creation of novel approaches, and innovativeness in general are all elements of the use of imagination. Teachers use their imaginations to invent new and varied ways to present material in order to keep students engaged and interested and to promote understanding.

Rebecca refers to variation as part of the art of teaching—"being able to say the same thing in different ways, whether it be different media or different words."

Often a limitation, such as a single object or a particular theme, stretches the imagination as the teacher conjures up various uses for the object or the theme. Alicia speaks of imaginative teaching in reference to using a common object to teach various concepts: "You could take an orange. You could teach everything you needed to teach just through an orange." She believes that being able to see variation is inherent to imagination. It is the belief that there is only one correct way to do something that leads to unimaginative teaching and a lack of learning and understanding: "The kind of focus on tests, multiple-choice tests, is destroying teaching kids to think for themselves. If you're teaching always to a test, then there's no room for any real learning to occur whatsoever. Because there's only the right answer."

James stretches his students' imaginations by having them look at things in a variety of different ways to see other possibilities:

> I will occasionally have my history students write histories from the points of view they don't agree with. Assume for a moment that Germany won the Second World War. Write the history of the war, or part of it. Give them a specific assignment. Justify what you've done. If you're Japanese, write the history of the war, assume you've won. Justify Pearl Harbor. Let's look at this. Be a Tory. Why did they do that? There is more than one way to look at history. You begin to see all sides which to students tends to be very interesting.

Emotion—Excitement, Love, and Caring

Imagination may be called the reflection of the emotional life.
— *Ruth Griffiths (1935, p. 187)*

Imagination is an emotional issue. Most often in classrooms when imagination is evoked there is an air of excitement. There is excitement inherent in making connections. Lessons that "come alive" through storytelling, dramatization, role playing, or whatever means, are exciting and engaging. Egan (1988, p. 117) discusses bringing characters, events, and situations to life as in oral cultures "because they created powerful images. These were not simply imagined events or characters charged with binding ties of emotional attachment. These techniques stimulated—in a sense brought into being—the imagination, that ability to be moved by, to behave as though one perceives and is affected by, what is actually not present or real."

When an imaginative connection is made by a student, Nan thinks that "it's exciting and real and alive. The excitement of learning something new and how wonderful how all these pieces fit together and it makes sense. There's an order to it. Those are the things that are exciting." She views the excitement as something that is addictive and spreads throughout a class:

> The excitement comes from two places: the subject and the children. You have to think what you're teaching is valuable for the children to know. When you teach it and they learn it, to me, how can that help but be exciting? That excitement . . . makes me want to be imaginative, because you want to get that high and do it again. It keeps you going. The other thing is you have a nice group atmosphere. They are happy that somebody else got it. Everybody's pulling together in this exciting process.

Dominic had similar reactions to moments in the classroom when imagination is at a peak: "The times when I have felt most imaginative, I have felt incredibly emotionally charged. Sometimes even to the point where you want to cry. It's like winning an athletic event. You just feel charged."

Intuition is deeply embedded in the making of connections, the bringing to life of subject matter, and the general environment in which such things take place. Intuition can spark excitement in the classroom. The word "feeling" is often used when referring to intuition. Much of the emotion, excitement, love, and caring that is felt in classrooms stems from the teacher's everyday use of intuition.

Imaginative teachers tend to show genuine care and concern for their students. They listen to their students, and their dialogues with students are characterized by sharing and caring. Noddings (1984) views genuine dialogue and intent listening as caring things to do in the classroom. She sees the "talking and listening, sharing and responding to each other . . . [as] vital in every aspect of education" (Noddings, 1984, p. 186). It is through careful listening that teachers gain the familiarity necessary for their intuitive responses. We are reminded of Nan's important lesson from her courses with Bruno Bettleheim: "Listen to children, they have something to tell you." Obviously, caring involves much more than merely listening to children's words.

There is a distinct excitement and energy level that can be felt in the classrooms of imaginative teachers. Students are engaged in activities they enjoy. These teachers all love teaching. Their enjoyment sparks the students' delight in and love of learning. James says: "The single most important factor in any classroom is the teacher's feeling about what they are doing. My students know that I genuinely enjoy what I'm doing. My classes really respond to that. They have fun. They enjoy it. They know that I'm there because I want to be there. I'm passionate about teaching. I love what I do." Noddings and Shore (1984, p. 168) view love of teaching and learning as pivotal to all of education—"there is the love of teaching and learning, a love that is at the center of the entire educational enterprise. Without a love of teaching in the broadest sense, teachers can do little that is useful. . . ."

Besides sharing a love of teaching, each of the teachers in the study displays a love of learning. Some would say these "go hand in hand." Rebecca notes: "There is something in common with loving to learn. Most teachers that I have ever met who are good teachers do enjoy learning themselves. You could be a professional student. It's a difference between somebody being stagnant as opposed to alive and alert."

Alicia believes it is important to foster the idea of love of learning in new teachers, and to rekindle the liberal arts notion of love of subject matter:

> It used to be that people taught stuff that they loved. There weren't education departments which taught people how to teach things. When we educate students to teach, it's our job to make them love learning. They need to be able to love learning while they're being students. The young teacher's heart and soul really needs to be in the knowing of the things and the loving of the communicating of the things. All the teachers I ever had who really taught me, were people who loved what they were teaching and then also loved sharing it with somebody else.

Rebecca and James agree that love of subject is important. Students are aware of the existence of this love. If teachers truly love the domain of knowledge that they are teaching, there is automatic excitement to engage and interest the learners. Noddings and Shore (1984, p. 166) agree that "love of subject" is "something that either students or teachers can feel." They feel that a teacher's intuition comes into play in order to communicate this passion of a particular field to students. Students' subtle intuitions, of course, enter in as well:

> In order for this communication to happen, several things must be present: a fascination with the particular subject, an intuitive sense of some (but not necessarily all) of its relationships and concepts, a desire to give this knowledge to others, and the ability to communicate effectively and engagingly. Intuition figures importantly in each of these factors, for the teacher needs to draw upon instantaneous impressions of students' interests and aptitudes, the atmosphere of the classroom on any given day, and many other factors that cannot be analyzed rationally in the fluid, dynamic setting of the schoolroom. Intuition needs to be cultivated and trusted as the teacher decides how, when, and in what amount information about the subject should be communicated. But we must keep in mind that not only factual information but *love* of the subject area can be communicated, and for the latter we have no simple procedures, no foolproof strategies. The most specific statement we can make is that a caring teacher who is genuinely excited about a subject or approach will convey this excitement to some of the students. . . . (Noddings and Shore, 1984, p. 168)

Love of teaching, love of learning, and genuine love and concern for students is evident among these imaginative teachers. James' definition of imagination includes the idea of love: "Imagination is letting your love be translated into your classroom. . . . So I see imagination as being a passionate activity, because it is a loving thing to do." James uses the word "care" in his definition of both imagination and intuition. Once, when trying to clarify his idea, I asked James if imagination means caring passionately about your subject matter, and intuition is caring about your students. He agreed that it was "something along that line." But that "really caring, though, is the bottom line to it. It's the common silk that weaves through the whole experience of teaching."

> I tell you there is no such thing as creative hate!
> —*Willa Cather, The Song of the Lark (1915), Part 1*

INFERENCES

These teachers all view the use of imagination and intuition as essential aspects of daily teaching. The teachers' use of imagination and intuition is essential for meaningful curricular decision making and planning. Teachers use imagination and intuition when matching instruction to content and to individual students in day-to-day practice. Imagination and intuition are highly valued by the teachers themselves. Indeed, education is nonexistent without the use of imagination and intuition.

Egan and Nadaner (1988) concur that there is no education without the use of imagination. They view imagination as an essential element for any teaching/learning situation. They are convinced

> that imagination is not some desirable but dispensable frill, but that it is the heart of any truly educational experience; it is not something split off from "the basics" or disciplined thought or rational inquiry, but is the quality that can give them life and meaning; it is not something belonging properly to the arts, but is central to all areas of the curriculum; it is not something to ornament our recreational hours, but it is the pragmatic center of all effective human thinking. Our concern is not to promote imagination at the expense of something else—say, rational inquiry or the foundational "3 Rs"; rather it is to show that any conception of rational inquiry or the foundations of education that depreciates imagination is impoverished and sure to be a practical failure. Stimulating the imagination is not an alternative educational activity to be argued for in competition with other claims; it is a prerequisite to making any activity educational. (Egan and Nadaner, 1988, p. ix)

The teachers' use of imagination and intuition gives life to curricular content. Imaginative teaching makes the subject matter "come alive" to be further lived and experienced by the students. It is during the living and reliving of the content at hand that teachers need to rely on their intuitive receptivity to help guide and facilitate students' acquisition of meaningful understanding and knowledge. Good teachers need to be able to think intuitively at a moment's notice. The teachers' use of imagination and intuition is a valued, *essential* aspect of educational endeavors.

It is heartening to have worked with teachers who truly value the use of imagination and intuition in teaching—who, in fact, cannot understand teaching without these qualities. However, these teachers are also quick to realize that imagination and intuition are not universally valued in schools.

Maxine Greene (1978, 1981, 1988) has expressed the necessity for imagination and intuition throughout education. However, she is recently troubled that the educational reform reports of the late 1980s have neglected to mention the value of imagination. She says that the use of imagination, the noncognitive and the intuitive, is affiliated "with the merely playful; and none of these are granted relevance for serious learning or for mastery" (Greene, 1988, p. 45). This lack of openness to "alternative possibilities" is troubling. It makes teaching subservient to routinization and boredom. This is a backward trek into darkness, into the abyss of ignorance. Greene (1988, p. 48) champions the cause of imagination as she looks toward "a kind of education that recognizes imagination as fundamental to learning to learn, essential to the feeling that life is more than a futile, repetitive, consuming exercise."

We need to rethink our idea of school to allow for the use of the imagination and intuition in classrooms. Environments need to be arranged to promote interaction, spontaneity, and openness. It is not necessary to shy away from the element of randomness in the school setting. A more natural balance between structure and randomness needs to be acquired. Teachers need to be open to variation and possibilities. Imaginative conceptions are essential if students are to connect with material, one another, and the teacher. The teacher must strive for "imaginative fullness" to clarify the context for true understanding, knowing that students will intuitively achieve their own enlightenment.

Commitment, time, and effort are necessary ingredients for imaginative, intuitive teaching. The emotional commitment involved with teaching in an imaginative and intuitive way is both tiring and exhilarating, but always fulfilling. As James noted, "caring is the bottom line." In my work in elementary schools, I came to similar conclusions—student understanding does not hinge on particular approaches to teaching. All that really matters for an exemplary classroom is a concerned, caring teacher. As Noddings and Shore (1984, p. 175) remind us:

> A caring, concerned teacher should be aware of the intuitive factors shaping student perceptions of subject matter. Likewise, as educators become more aware of the role of intuition in interpersonal relations, they will come to value caring and educational caritas even more than before. If we remain open to the possibility of expanding and strengthening the use of intuition and the expression of caring, then education can be a more meaningful experience for both student and teacher. Beyond this, the legitimization by schools of such generally deemphasized topics as love and intuition will aid their more widespread acceptance by the public and will earn these human capabilities a greater place in our conception of the functioning, thinking, feeling human being.

It is only through emotional involvement with students, subject matter, and the environment that we are able to formulate ideal teaching. Teachers' everyday use of imagination and intuition is necessary for *educare*, authentic teaching. Genuine education, leading from darkness to light, is accomplished with the brilliant flame of intuition, the passionate blaze of imagination, the luminous kindling of caring, and the radiant glow of love.

REFERENCES

Barell, J. (1980). *Playgrounds of our minds*. New York: Teachers College Press.
Bronowski, J. (1971). *The identity of man*. New York: Natural History Press.
Clandinin, D. J. (1986). *Classroom practice: Teacher images in action*. London: Falmer.

Coleridge, S. T. (1817). *Biographia literaria*. J. Shawcross (Ed.). Oxford: Oxford University Press, 1907.

Connelly, F. M., and Ben-Peretz, M. (1980). Teachers' roles in the using and doing of research and curriculum development. *Journal of Curriculum Studies, 12: 95–107.*

Dewey, J. (1900). *The school and society*. Chicago: University of Chicago Press.

Dewey, J. (1902). *The child and the curriculum*. Chicago: University of Chicago Press.

Dewey, J. (1938). *Experience and education*. New York: Macmillan.

Egan, K. (1988). The origins of the imagination and the curriculum. In K. Egan and D. Nadaner (Eds.), *Imagination and education*. New York: Teachers College Press, pp. 91–127.

Egan, K., and Nadaner, D. (Eds.) (1988). *Imagination and education*. New York: Teachers College Press.

Elbaz, F. L. (1983). *Teacher thinking: A study of practical knowledge*. London: Croom Helm.

Greene, M. (1978). *Landscapes of learning*. New York: Teachers College Press.

Greene, M. (1981). Educational research and the arts: A dialogue with Elliot Eisner and Maxine Greene. Symposium presented at the 1981 Annual Meeting of the American Educational Research Association. Los Angeles.

Greene, M. (1988). What happened to imagination? In K. Egan and D. Nadaner (Eds.) *Imagination and education*. New York: Teachers College Press, pp. 45–56.

Griffiths, R. (1935). *A study of imagination in early childhood*. London: Kegan Paul, Trench, Trubner.

Haley-Oliphant, A. E. (1987). Teacher thinking-in-action regarding the use of hypothetical questions in a science classroom. Paper presented at the annual meeting of the American Educational Research Association. Washington, D.C.

Hansen, K. (1988). Education and the perceptive imagination. In K. Egan and D. Nadaner (Eds.) *Imagination and education*. New York: Teachers College Press, pp. 128–149

Jagla, V. M. (1989). *In pursuit of the elusive image: An inquiry into teacher's everyday use of imagination and intuition*. Doctoral dissertation. Chicago: University of Illinois.

Noddings, N., and Shore, P. J. (1984). *Awakening the inner eye: Intuition in education*. New York: Teachers College Press.

Rubin, L. J. (1985). *Artistry in teaching*. New York: Random House.

Rugg, H. (1963). *Imagination*. New York: Harper and Row.

Ryle, G. (1949). *The concept of mind*. London: Hutchinson.

Schon, D. (1983). *The reflective practitioner*. New York: Basic Books.

Schubert, W. H. (1975). *Imaginative projection: A method of curriculum invention*. Doctoral dissertation. Urbana: University of Illinois.

Sutherland, M. B. (1971). *Everyday imagining and education*. London: Routledge and Kegan Paul.

Vaughan, F. E. (1979). *Awakening intuition*. Garden City, NY: Anchor/Doubleday.

Teaching occurs, of course, in a wide range of contexts. Schools are embedded in societies; they are institutions built in part to induct people into society, to reproduce social norms and relationships. It is impossible, then, to recommend or even understand schools without knowing, and perhaps warranting, the society served.

It is virtually impossible to become an outstanding teacher without becoming aware of the many contexts of teaching. In the next chapter Carol Melnick and a dozen other teachers examine the importance of context and of what she calls the out-of-school curriculum—the interests, perspectives, know-how, abilities, interests, hopes, dreams, life histories, aspirations, questions, activities, and experiences that students bring with them to school. Melnick and the others argue that teaching never occurs in a vacuum, and that exemplary teaching must be built in direct, explicit ways upon children's lives outside of school. The out-of-school curriculum is a rich, largely disregarded source of inspiration and knowledge for teachers.

The contexts of teaching vary, and they include politics, economics, racial and ethnic differences, culture, and more. The contexts of teaching can include oppression and privilege, poverty, homelessness, war, and the threat of nuclear annihilation. Knowing the world and seeing the students in as full a way as possible—this is an essential and ongoing challenge for teachers.

CHAPTER 6

The Out-of-School Curriculum:
An Invitation, Not an Inventory

Carol R. Melnick

Even the childhood experience itself becomes more vivid when it contains not one, but two clearly distinct modes of being: the one commonplace and familiar, compounded of home and school and street-corner and garden; the other abnormal and ecstatic, a "summer holiday self," moving in a magic dimension, far away amid the dunes and the forests, the towering grasses and the multicolored panoply of butterflies and unfamiliar birds. Mobility is of the very essence of the Childhood.

> Richard N. Coe, *When the Grass Was Taller:*
> *Autobiography and the Experience of Childhood* (1984)

When I began graduate studies, I had been working for twelve years as a speech-language pathologist with infants, children, and adolescents. Early on I encountered the progressive education literature, and it filled a vacuum for me, providing a unique context for my existing knowledge and experience. I was intrigued by the ideas of John Dewey (1897) in *My Pedagogic Creed*, Joseph J. Schwab (1970, 1971, 1973) in "Arts of the Practical and Eclectic," and a host of other curriculum theorists as outlined in William H. Schubert's (1980) *Curriculum Books: The First Eighty Years*. I was intent on knowing more.

I had been steeped in theories of linguistic development, child growth and development, theories of learning, as well as theories of diagnosis and therapeutic intervention for children with various medical, language, learning, emotional, social, and behavioral problems. These theories provided scientific and technological information that no longer satisfied. I was beginning to feel that technical theories and technocratic language were ill suited for addressing the complex social, economic, and ethical problems that beset us (Schwab, 1956, 1960; Bullough, Goldstein, and Holt, 1984).

I had encountered an escalating number of infants, saved by technological advances in neonatology, who were highly susceptible to multiple handicaps. I was faced with an increasing number of abused and neglected children who were at risk for physical, emotional, and learning problems. I was confronted by a rise in the number of single-parent families, physically abused women, unemployment, and drug and alcohol abuse. Nevertheless, there was a decrease in resources for children and their families with special needs. Finally, I was faced with teaching a generation of graduate students whose past education, for the most part, had been a highly technocratic endeavor.

I set out to read more by Dewey, Schwab, and Schubert. I began to develop a philosophical perspective and practical set of conceptual lenses to address some of my own dilemmas in my work with children, parents, teachers, therapists, administrators, physicians, and graduate students. Discovering principles of progressive education, practical inquiry, and curriculum theorizing through reading, reflecting, and writing helped mediate some of those dilemmas. My perspective on education grew and changed.

I was drawn to Dewey, Schwab, Schubert, and others, I believe, because their concepts were connected in some way with my own educational-therapeutic practices and ideals. My orientation toward intervention for children with language and learning problems, for example, is to begin "where the child is" developmentally, and to use intervention strategies based on diagnostic therapy. Dewey's belief that education must begin with "psychological insight into the child's capacities, interest, and habits" (Dewey, 1897, p. 631) was a powerful and strangely familiar statement. I delighted in Dewey's example of how an infant's instinctive babblings eventually develop into articulate speech and language through the process of stimulation and interaction. Proper stimulation of the child's powers was the "ability to see in the child's babblings the promise and potency of a future social intercourse and conversation which enables one to deal in the proper way with that instinct" (Dewey, 1897, p. 630).

Students who have problems learning are often blamed for their own difficulties. It is not unusual for a child who is unable to relate his or her wants, needs, and feelings verbally because of a speech-language problem to communicate in ways that label the child as bad, disruptive, and oppositional. Schwab argued that teachers' tendencies to blame students for lack of motivation, laziness, or a negative attitude was a myth to absolve themselves of failure as teachers. He believed this myth was reversible and urged that "education cannot, therefore, separate off the intellectual from feeling and action, whether in the interest of the one or the other. Training of the intellect must take place ('must' in the sense of 'unavoidably') in a milieu of feelings and must express itself in actions, either symbolic or actual" (Schwab, 1954, p. 106). Schwab's image of "the effect of a curriculum whose end was training of the intellect, pure and simple" as a "crippled intellect" (Schwab, 1954, p. 125) was striking given my daily contact with "crippled" bodies.

For too long, I considered the supervisory process of my graduate students as an either-or proposition. The students viewed the practicum with trepidation, while I looked upon my supervisory obligations as an albatross. I would not let the child/patient "suffer" for the mistakes of the student speech-language clinician. I justified jeopardizing the student's learning experiences by telling myself that the good of the patient came first.

I began to realize that neither the interests of the students nor those of the patients had to be sacrificed. Schubert conceived that curricula must first be *of* and *by* students in order for curricula to be truly *for* them, and proposed an interactive process of generating curricula that are *of, by,* and *for* students. Through this interactive process, Schubert intended to create curricular experiences that were:

(1) of students' experiences and perspective;
(2) by student as well as teacher design; and
(3) for students because they improved their perspectives about matters that held meaning for them.
(Schubert and Schubert, 1981, p. 244)

Schubert tried to help graduate students in education connect course content with personal meaning in their lives. One approach (Schubert and Schubert, 1981) I now use in my own graduate courses is to have students keep a journal in which they reflect upon the readings and ideas presented in class as well as upon the ways in which these ideas affect their personal and professional perspectives. This was merely one way in which Schubert tried to help his students find meaning in course content by connecting subject matter with their own particular concerns and interests. Finally, the Schuberts (1981) emphasized that if we want to teach students, whether they are in elementary school or graduate school, we must strive to know how students view their worlds, and "develop ways to form curricula with students so that learning activities come from within them as well as from without" (Schubert and Schubert, 1981, p. 250).

I decided to show my students faith in their ability to conduct speech-language evaluations with "our" rather than "my" patients. We became partners in interviewing parents and evaluating children. Through the students' journals, I learned that supervisors don't allow students to "bounce" their clinical impressions off one another. Instead, they are forced to give their clinical findings without benefit of such interaction. I realized how much my colleagues and I hashed over clinical findings in order to arrive at the most appropriate diagnosis and educational-therapeutic plan. My working *with* students helped them gain confidence in their own abilities, while I discarded my albatross.

"What knowledge is of most worth?" (Spencer, 1861, p. 5). "What is worth knowing and experiencing?" (Schubert, 1986, p. 411). What kind of study is most worthwhile for me? I gravitated toward studying the out-of-school curriculum for my doctoral dissertation. Schubert (1981) argues that the need for the study of the out-of-school curriculum is implicit in the single assumption that "the better we know children and youth, the more fully we can be in a position to provide good educational experiences for them" (p. 185). He suggests that educators must begin to view school curriculum in a "dynamic interdependent or ecological relationship with out-of-school curricula" (p. 185).

I decided to do a small piece of research at an after-school program. I discovered that the after-school program was perceived by children and staff as very different from school. They felt the quality of life at the program was characterized by freedom, fairness, respect, security, caring, acceptance of individuality, positive affective relationships, and fostering of self-worth. These qualities, alive in the culture of the after-school program, were almost nonexistent in the school. Paradoxically, the children felt that they were "getting a good education" in school, because "you have to be prepared." By the same token, the staff felt that school may be more worthwhile than the program because schools "prepare children for jobs."

How can educators be persuaded to use the insights of children and educators in nonschool settings to enhance education that takes place in school? Is a school curriculum rooted in a philosophy of experience and in harmony with democratic ideals possible? These are questions I began to consider more seriously.

MEANING OF THE OUT-OF-SCHOOL CURRICULUM AS THE LIFE HISTORY OF THE TEACHER

In my conversations with teachers, I set out to explore their knowledge of students' out-of-school lives, interests, and experiences; how they apprehended and put into practice this knowledge to enhance the school curriculum and their teaching; what constraints there were to attaining and putting it into practice; and what influenced them to apprehend and put into practice this knowledge. I was interested in the ideas and experiences that had influenced these teachers as well as their guiding beliefs today. Teachers' out-of-school curriculum may include their own childhood experiences, their experiences with their own children, their teaching experiences, and their experiences with a mentor.

Influence of One's Own Childhood Experiences

Maura Callahan's philosophy, "unless it was me in that work, what good was it," developed from negative experiences in her own childhood. She recalls her elementary school education as dreadful, dreary, bleak, and boring. "Nobody taught children," she says. "They taught subjects to children." As an art major, she realized that unless her work was tied to her own experiences in some way, she was not motivated to learn. "It would have no meaning for me," she says. All of Maura's curricular decisions and problem solving are guided by that one premise, that no matter what age the children, no matter what kind of classroom, something of that student's self had to be connected with the curriculum.

The "self" is related to individual talents. All the students in her elementary classroom are there to find themselves "in terms of what they're about, and what they're good at, and what they can do, and what's important to them." She has no set formula for helping students find themselves. Rather, she encourages them to follow their dreams. She tells them that "they could do and have things in life that they may not think are possible."

> There's no set formula for doing this. I think I pretty much started out believing in the fact that nothing could mean anything unless we tied it up to their lives. I guess I have a lot of the Horatio Alger in me, because of the way I grew up. I always tried to make it real clear to the children that they could do and have things in life that they may not think are possible. I'm not talking about material things. I'm talking about dreams, and not

ones that are unrealistic. That was very important to me, because I could have been that child sitting in that classroom.

Sensitivity to her students' needs is related to her own early school experiences. For example, every morning Maura has "talk time" with her students. She knows that unless she addresses their concerns, they will have difficulty getting on with the day. "Because I remember myself," she recalls, "coming from a rather stormy home, the lack of concentration, thinking about what went on at home. I could care less about the short 'i' business. So what I used to do in the morning was talk time." Talk time is a private invitation. Maura offers her students an opportunity to discuss in confidence anything they want to talk about, and only if they want to.

This caring approach toward her students is a remnant from negative experiences in her own childhood, when teachers talked to her in an intrusive, artificial manner. She makes a conscious effort in her own teaching not to relate to students in such a contrived way. This is how she sets the stage for each day of learning. What meaning will the curriculum have if the "self" is not involved?

Rob Wasserman arrived at his philosophy "that you teach students not subject matter" when he came close to flunking out of high school. He did not find out until two days before commencement that he would be allowed to graduate. After his negative high school experience, Rob decided to work for a year. In addition, he decided to "just start learning about stuff I was interested in." He went to the library daily and began reading books that interested him. For the first time he enjoyed reading, and began to discuss books with a few older people in the community. Rob concluded that "learning isn't so bad, and maybe it's teaching that's bad." He decided to "test this out."

Two of the things Rob was interested in were American history and political science. He taught himself as much as possible about these two subjects. At the end of two months he took the College Level Examination Program tests. He scored at the ninety-sixth percentile or above in all areas. "Maybe I'm not dumb," he thought. "Maybe I just haven't been well taught."

"The teachers I liked the best were the teachers that taught me the most," Rob said. He figured out for himself what his good teachers all had in common. First, they all knew their subject matter. Second, they had an enthusiasm for teaching. Third, they were able to communicate with students. Finally, they *liked* students:

And what I found was, when I first started my student teaching, I already had firmly set in my mind the kind of teacher that I wanted to be. I didn't know how to be it yet, because that just comes with experience. But I knew what approach I wanted to use with those kids.

One of Susan Oberman's guiding beliefs is that "being good is not enough when your dreams are great." This means "you can't settle for taking life as it is, getting by, or getting over. It isn't enough if you have dreams you want to fulfill . . . you have to go beyond, reach, and stretch":

I had grown up with problems. So I always had kind of a sympathy or an empathy for kids who just needed a little bit more attention than everybody else. The fact that I think

> I have a very positive view of life . . . I tend to be a scrapper, I tend to be someone who aggressively goes after what I want. And I tend to be someone who is not going to just sit down and take whatever the world gives me.

Guided by her philosophy and empathy for youngsters who need that special attention, Susan appreciates what she calls a student's "public self" and "private self." She understands and accepts the images or characters that her students, many of them gang members, portray in the classroom:

> Kids have what you could call the public self, and they have the private person. And the public self is the image that they like to project of themselves in school. There's another side to them, a very private self that focuses a lot on their fears, concerns, and frustrations. Very rarely do you find them feeling comfortable enough with a teacher to let that private self come out.

Even though the topic of gangs is a risky one to address, Susan uses the poem "Black Jackets" by Tom Gunn in her high school classes. The slogan of the gang in the poem is "Born to Lose." She chose the poem because so many of her students believed they were losers:

> They had no sense of themselves, they had no sense of their dreams, they had no sense of where they wanted to go with their lives, and they were really uncomfortable and afraid to talk about those things. Because it would prove that they were born to lose.

Ann Welles is guided by the belief that parents, students, and teachers need to work together. She is extensively involved with the parents of her fifth- and sixth-grade students, because of her own in- and out-of-school experiences as a child. Ann's mother is a retired public school teacher, and her father is a pediatrician. Both parents encouraged her participation in activities in and out of school:

> My parents believed in getting me into different activities. I found out when I was older that's a lifesaver. When you're busy and active, and you're a cheerleader, and you have Bible studies, and you're active in your church group, then you have very little time to get in trouble. Activities keep you very busy. They keep you right on task.

Ann's elementary school teachers encouraged interests outside of school. "They exposed me to ballet," she says, "and the fellowship with others who are not quite like ourselves." She learned about competition. In addition, she was able to see teachers interacting with her parents in contexts outside of school. "Teachers saw things that were going on in my life," she recalls. For example, her eighth-grade teacher knew that her mother was expecting a baby. Talking about her future brother or sister helped Ann feel closer to her teacher. She says, "We all shared in the birth of my sister." Ann appreciated her teacher's personal touch.

Today, Ann values the relationship between students' out-of-school and in-school lives. She extends her personal touch to all her students and their families by making home visits and participating in community activities:

What students do outside does make a difference as far as what they bring into school. Their ability, and what they've learned before they get in here, is enhanced. I try to build on what's there, and give them formal information.

Sean Murphy's philosophy that "children create knowledge" stems from his childhood. Fourth in a family of five, he recalls that he was always questioning the world around him:

> There's so much stimuli around you. I came to know my world by exploring. And after exploration, it was defined to me in words. My experiences were explained to me by my parents. I think that's how I came to know the world.

"There are three kinds of knowledge," Sean claims. The first is physical knowledge. Sean helps his preschool children know the world by seeing, hearing, touching, smelling, and tasting. The second is mathematical knowledge. He encourages his students to invent strategies to solve problems that arise in and out of the classroom. The third is social knowledge. He nurtures language development and social communication, and helps the children get along with one another:

> Children create knowledge. They are self-learners. They are self-initiated. As the teacher, I try to provide an environment for the children so that they are free and disposed to exploring and making relationships. Children are creating the world for themselves, and that's what learning is.

Sean enables his preschool students to create knowledge by developing a curriculum based on the individual needs of his students. In this way they are able to "live the life of a three- and four- and five-year-old":

> The classroom is developmental. We arrive to be twenty-one through a similar process. And for some of us it's at different speeds, and at a different level of intensity and quality. And in a developmental preschool, I accept the children at their own level. I try to know them at that level, what they do, and what has happened to them in the past. And we move on from there. I just take them at whatever stage they're at. There's a curriculum for each child. There are forty-four children in my class. I have forty-four curricula.

Influences of One's Own Childhood Experiences and Experiences with One's Own Children

Peter Cabot's belief that students' out-of-school lives should be valued is rooted in his own out-of-school experiences as a child:

> I felt good about my childhood. In terms of my out-of-school activities, I thought they were educative. I remember boasting in grade school about doing certain tasks and chores that I thought were magnificent. I prized my childhood. I think that's the necessary thing. If you don't feel your childhood was worthwhile, then I guess you have a real difficult time seeing that other people have valuable childhoods, or that it's important that kids have a good childhood. You see kids in a whole different perspective.

Peter is guided by the belief that students should be "invited to share their out-of-school curriculum." He is opposed to "investigating" students' out-of-school lives. During his first year of teaching, he was required to conduct two formal interviews with students. He asked about their life at school and home, and about their activities in and out of school. "It was like an out-of-school curriculum interview," he said. Peter felt he did not have any right to ask these questions: "They didn't know what I was going to use the information for. There was no trust relationship built up prior to that, in order to allow me to invade the kids' privacy." The interviews were discontinued at the end of the year, because students gave pat answers and, like Peter, people realized that this approach was not particularly worthwhile.

Inviting students to share their out-of-school lives, interests, and experiences is connected to Peter's respect for students as human beings. The births of his daughter in 1976 and his son in 1978 were "real humanizing," and positively affected the relationship with his students. His children eventually became part of the school community:

> So it probably was an important thing in terms of humanizing me to kids too. It was always a nice thing to bring my daughter to school too, because the boys always felt very awkward, and very vulnerable around her. She was in a faculty play we used to have every year. She was part of the school community after a couple of years.
>
> My son used to come every year for one or two days. The students would ask a lot of questions the next day about my son. And that would give me the opportunity to ask them questions. I'd ask if their fathers ever brought them to work. You'd find out what their fathers did, and you'd find out how they felt about that. If you make some kind of offering of vulnerability, sometimes they pick up on it. And you learn more about them if you're lucky.

Peter is guided by the firm belief that one has to "own the idea that children are valuable."

Marie Burdette's conviction that each child brings a "life history" to school that must be valued is connected with growing up as a "mascot" in a large extended family where she was respected and listened to. As early as six years of age, Marie could state and defend an opinion. She never felt out of place. "I was valued as a child," she says "and included in the adult world." In turn, she values her preschool students as fully human:

> I'm adamant about the fact that children are human beings, and that everyone learns and constructs knowledge in the same way. You can't devalue someone's past, albeit only three years have passed. You can't devalue that and expect the children to feel good about where they are in school. And you have to reconcile that. I don't think what a child brings to school can be ignored. You can't depend that the child comes in, and leaves all of his baggage at the front door any more than the teacher does.

Having her own children, Marie believes, enhanced her teaching. Because of experiences with her son and daughter, she values seeing the world from a child's point of view:

If you really put yourself in a child's place, then you're coming from where that child is into the strange environment of school. But if you're coming from your own perspective as a teacher, then *you* are comfortable.

I always try to get student teachers to explain from the child's point of view why he would be crying, or why he would be sad. Why would he be kicking? Why does the child always knock down blocks? It's not to irritate *you*. From your point of view it's because he wants to irritate *you*. He doesn't listen. He's disobedient. He's a behavior problem. But from his point of view why would a child do that?

Becoming a parent herself helped Marie develop a higher regard for other parents as well:

For ten years that I wasn't a classroom teacher, part of my education has been my own children. I respect parents more. It's made me figure out my role more clearly. I'm a secondary agent in a child's education. Parents are the primary agent. When you're dealing with very young children as in preschool, you're dealing with at least a duo, I mean the child and the parent. You can't separate the two. That child brings that parent into that classroom. And you have to deal with the parent. You cannot just deal with the child, and expect the child to learn.

The Teaching Experience Itself

Lynn Crosby is guided by the premise that "teaching is something that develops from the heart":

Children see through anything, and a child will know if this is something that comes from you . . . from your heart. You set the tempo for your own classroom. Teaching has to become part of your everyday life, and if you don't experience it, you just don't have it. Everybody doesn't have the knack.

Lynn says she did not have a feel for children when she first began teaching, but developed this over time. Lynn recalls her initial beliefs about students:

I didn't know that children have to be motivated. I just thought they knew that when they come in, and the work is there, and you talk about it, and you explain the work, that it's just something you do. I never thought children needed to have that time to feel that they're a part of the classroom, and that they have some input in what they're going to do.

Through experiences in the classroom, she discovered that "children basically are human beings who should be treated with respect." She finds that by respecting children, they in turn respect her.

Lynn describes herself as an "impromptu teacher" who is energized by the children:

The children keep me going. For example, one little boy entered an oratory contest. I gave him a black poem which was written in black dialect. I helped him practice. He won first place, and I was just so elated.

I worked with a little girl who was very quiet and subdued. She read exceptionally well, but had no self-esteem. I helped her with a poem in Spanish and English. She won second place. So it's basically the children who keep me going. It's not a special technique. It's more of an impromptu thing.

Eugene Meyers believes in "celebrating students, and celebrating education." He is troubled by people who enter the field of teaching for reasons "other than the fact they are excited by education," saying, "such people are afraid of education." For example, teachers intimidated by the process of education may view students who are "excited, exciting, and bright, as insubordination, as talking back, and getting off the point." He sees the children as center stage:

The interaction *is* students. I have an investment to believe that students are valuable, because my closest co-workers in this process are the children. I want to think that the people I'm spending my day with are valuable. If all the interaction with children is yelling at them, why are you there?

Eugene also believes that students' experiences outside the classroom are worthwhile. His unique strategies for connecting students' out-of-school experiences with writing assignments evolved slowly. "As I became more intelligent as a teacher, I became a better teacher, and I became more reflective," he says.

I randomly gave assignments. Some of them worked, and I began by seeing how certain kinds of assignments were more effective. To try and reflect why they were more effective, it always struck me that just as I liked to talk about myself, students are most involved when they're talking about themselves. And in fact, I always thought that writing was very vulnerable, and that the more involved the student was in the content of his writing, the more he'd be willing to do that.

Eugene recalls, "As a beginning teacher, I thought unless everyone was sitting behind a desk, there'd be cuisenaire rods flying all over the place." Through experience, he discovered he could have "sufficient control over dynamics in the classroom" and still be able to involve his students "in a much more real way."

Eugene's belief that students and the experiences students bring to school should be valued guide his teaching. "One cannot teach English as separate strands," he says.

I never thought of what I did with my students as using the out-of-school curriculum. I always thought I used the kids' lives, and it always occurred to me I was doing something no one else was doing. I always thought to myself that using the kids' lives was good, but it never occurred to me that anyone else would think it was good.

Paul Stewart believes in fairness and a democratic classroom. Initially he "taught by the book." He adds, "I felt I was fighting a losing battle." So Paul decided "to see other classrooms and different ways of doing things. I saw classrooms with some of the same problems that I had. And I thought, there's got to be a better way."

Paul's students had difficulty relating to one another and tended to solve problems by fighting, what he refers to as a "beat-your-butt mentality." He helped the youngsters in his classroom set up a student government: "I did this so that they could learn that the purpose of government is to have orderliness in society. So our little society, our little classroom, would become the place where we'd learn how to promote harmony."

Students decided to elect a president, spokesperson, and secretary. The role of the spokesperson was to intercede for classmates who felt they were being treated unfairly. The secretary's job was to record all the rules formulated by the class. The president was responsible for helping to identify problems and leading class meetings.

With Paul's guidance, students prepared rules such as these: You can't embarrass people intentionally and make fun of them in front of classmates; you can't solve anything by name calling; everyone has a right to private conversations; your desk is your business, and you have no right to go into someone else's desk without permission; it's wrong to interrupt a person who's talking; everyone has a right to speak.

Initially students wanted to severely punish anyone who broke a rule. Paul tried to present moderate alternatives:

> Why don't we work more toward working out the problem, and preventing it in the future? A lot of times they'll head for the punishment. That's how they're treated by a lot of teachers. They break a rule and they're punished. That's what they want to do a lot.

By asking himself what would be meaningful and relevant to his students, he began to develop his own curricular approaches. Paul explains how he decided to depart from the prescribed curriculum:

> By thinking of ways that would be relevant and useful to the students that I teach, I just kept searching my thoughts. I just kept thinking over and over: What could I do to make this relevant and interesting? How could I make the students see that this could be important to them?

Play acting is Paul's primary motivator for teaching reading. Students are interested in writing and reading their own plays about social situations (such as children arguing or how youngsters their age plan a party). They are motivated to read what they can understand and relate to.

Through student government and play writing, Paul helps youngsters in his classroom seek answers to problems on their own: "I would like them to find a better way to deal with their peers in their world without resorting to violence. I hope they have a desire to want to learn things on their own, and that I've sparked a curiosity in them."

A Mentor

Alan Stauffer credits his view that a foreign language should be taught stressing cultural rather than grammatical knowledge to his own mentor. He knows specifically how he became the kind of teacher he is. "It's one of those rare, key moments in life," he recalls. When studying science, math, and physics, he had no desire to become a teacher. A German professor learned that Alan grew up in Germany, and contacted him regarding a tutoring job. He helped three people translate German for their doctoral exams. The vocabulary in their German textbooks was scientific. The tutoring experience helped Alan realize how little he knew about his own language. He decided, for example, to "learn why certain grammar points were that way." "So I was supposed to be teaching somebody who really wanted to learn and suddenly I was learning myself," he says.

Alan studied German with the professor who had recommended him for the tutoring job. Eventually he dropped his science major, studied with the professor, and enrolled in education courses:

> Without thinking what I was doing, what I ended up doing was sort of copying him, Professor Reinhardt. He was very personable, and he really cared about his kids. He also knew about his students. He had met my wife . . . and he always talked about my son. And all the little things that normally, especially in a university setting, professors don't really pay attention to, he did. Now it was easier for him, because the German classes were small. But he still didn't have to do it. The tutoring experience, and then being with him, caused me to become a good teacher. I never had thoughts of going into teaching before that.

Rather than teaching technical grammar points in isolation, Alan stresses cultural knowledge with a "big C." He thinks it is more important for students to learn about a country and its people than particular bits of grammar.

Fred Smart was mesmerized by his mentor and high school teacher, Mrs. Gallagher. He attributes his empathetic regard for students to her. "She just had something about her that let you know she was alive," he says, "and I admired that in her then, and I still admire her today." Mrs. Gallagher comes alive through Fred's memories and his words:

> I had one teacher in high school, Mrs. Gallagher. She had to be, perhaps, one of the more classic, beautiful women that I have ever known. There was something about her that was so human, so beautiful, and so warm that she made literature and English just come alive for you. And you came to really enjoy every class, as really something exciting, or something different every day as you came into her classroom. She was the kind of person who would talk to you personally. You could enjoy things that she had to say. What I try to put in my classroom, that I got from her, is that sense of excitement about everything.

Fred tries to instill a sense of excitement and possibility in his classroom. He tells his students who have been stigmatized as slow learners that it is not too late to learn how to read:

> I tell them you are fifteen and you can't read. But we can't blame it on your mother or father or somebody else. Now you are at an age when you can think and reason for yourself. You can decide to put forth the effort that it takes. If it means going back to phonic sounds, or to a basic list of words, then that's what you have to do. You have *me*

a specialist who knows how to help you learn to read. And I find they have the desire to learn. I find success with them.

Fred thinks that fostering empathetic regard is more difficult for him than it had been for Mrs. Gallagher. His students have been abused, mistreated, or neglected for so long that they are suspicious of people who profess to care:

> You have to make them understand the extent of your caring. I tell students I care for you because you're a person like I am. I will care for you because you have an opportunity to do something. My caring is an extension of me. And the children come to understand that.

THE LIFE HISTORY OF THE STUDENT

What does it mean to view the out-of-school curriculum as the life history of the student? A youngster brings to the classroom a life history of likes and dislikes, interests, and experiences. And to view children's lives only "as the minute they walk into a room, and the minute they walk out of a room," explains Marie Burdette, "is destructive to the child, and makes the teacher's job more difficult." For Marie, it is critical to acknowledge, respect, and affirm the "baggage" students bring to school: "That child's life shouldn't and doesn't change just because he's coming to a school. And so you can't ignore that. And if you're a good teacher you don't ignore what the child brings."

If a student lives a life of poverty and fear outside of school, then that same fear and deprivation will spill into the classroom. Fred Smart is reminded daily of the poverty in his students' lives. He says he will not close his eyes to a child who is dirty, ragged, and does not have a decent coat to wear; Fred will find a warm coat for that youngster. "Unless we love and care, unless we're concerned and care," Fred says, "it's hard to say that you can't know or think the students have an outside life."

If a youngster knows what it means to emotionally commit to some activity out of school (a job, sport, or avocation), then that kind of energy and determination could be brought into the classroom. Eugene Meyers believes that his students are more keenly in touch with their own emotions, because of the emotional commitment given to an activity in their lives out of school. "And I think" Eugene says, "they tend to understand literature better, and in their own writing they portray emotions more vividly":

> The kind of energy and experiences and information that students bring is phenomenal. If you were to read the stories . . . their knowledge of material that is not taught in school, cultural things, like people in other countries, knowledge of what it's like to be a dancer, knowledge of what it's like to practice harp or something. I don't mean naturally be good at baseball, and pick up a team, but . . . I mean, their sense of commitment to activity is much more extensive than most children I taught at other places, because they have a lot of experience with what commitment means.

"There's no set formula," says Maura Callahan, for understanding the life history a student brings to the classroom. The life history of the student becomes less enigmatic when integration of that life with the curriculum in school is considered worthwhile. This has less to do with knowledge of specific details of a life, and more to do with teachers' willingness to "own" the idea that students have a life history that they bring to school. "And only if you can own that" Peter Cabot comments, "are you in the business then of [being] willing to take that out-of-school curriculum and begin to integrate that with the school curriculum." He adds, "I don't think most teachers, and most parents, are willing to own that."

Something of the youngster's "self" has to be an integral part of the in-school curriculum. Susan Oberman understands and accepts the images, or "characters," her students choose to portray in the classroom:

> And it's one of the things in a changing cultural background in a school that teachers have the hardest time tapping into. It's not [in] seeing the kids as you think they should be labeled, but in seeing the student as a person who is trying to let you know he or she is there . . . the private self.

Alan Stauffer expresses his concern about teachers who say they do not have time to get to know their students and their interests:

> First of all, I think it would actually make their job easier. It does involve more time, but then I think they would have an easier time in class. A lot of teachers I know have problems controlling their class. And I think because I know my kids in class, and I know their families, and brothers and sisters, I have an easier time with them in class.

When the "self" or life history of the student is connected with the educational process, then that youngster is able to live that life more fully in the classroom.

Students as Fellow Human Beings

Marie Burdette thinks that it is possible to bridge the gap between the two worlds of school and out of school for poor African-American children. A teacher can do this if children are viewed as human beings who basically learn in the same way:

> I'm adamant about the fact that children . . . are human beings. That everyone learns in the same way . . . constructs knowledge. Young children interact with the environment. The best motivation comes from teachers knowing they're interested in something, and that real life situations make the most sense.

During the first three years of teaching, Peter Cabot was so concerned with subject matter that he "didn't even have time to learn about kids." He did not see them as fully human, with emotions and needs: "I didn't even need kids. They got in the way of what I was trying to do." Once Peter got beyond his "authoritarianism," and by "recognizing their humanity," he gained insight into what it means to value children:

> But there's still this whole thing about owning kids as being human beings that is really a critical thing, and valuing that kids have important out-of-school lives. Maybe you've got

to have kids. Maybe that's what it takes. You've got to have kids to begin to understand how valuable their out-of-school lives are. Instead, we place them in contradiction to one another. We say what they're learning out of school is thwarting their education, and what they're learning out of school is deleterious to the process of their education. They can do that. They can spend time destroying themselves. And parents can do a lot in helping them have deleterious out-of-school experiences.

Lynn Crosby did not view children as "human" before she started teaching. She only fully recognized their humanity once she was in a classroom:

> I discovered that children basically are human beings, and they should be treated with respect. And I found that by giving the children respect, then that way it demands respect. They give me respect.

While Fred Smart, an African-American, chooses to teach in an all-black school in a poverty neighborhood, he knows that he can teach anywhere, because he accepts all children as human beings:

> It's not a racial thing. I feel that I can go to . . . any suburban school, and do just as well, because I accept them just as they are, human beings. And I say to them this is what I have that can help you to go from where you are to where you want to go.

Susan Oberman exemplifies her humanistic perspective of children through her favorite story of Michaelangelo's *David*. She tells her students that "Michaelangelo saw a beauty in the flaw (the unused piece of stone), a value to the shadow, a uniqueness, and individualism. He saw the potential of using that flaw and let *David* emerge from the stone." Her students are intrigued by this story:

> Because here was a stone that had been discarded, turned down by artists for thirty years because it was flawed. But Michaelangelo saw *David* in that stone. And I guess that's kind of my favorite story because I think of kids that way. I think if you can read the public self . . . this kid's a loser, this kid's a gang member, this kid's from an abused family, this kid's an alcoholic, this kid's a drug user, and so he's useless. Or you can see what you can do beyond the flaws.

Susan does not think of her students "in terms of just a body in a chair, or in terms of the books I had to cover, or the chapters I had to get through." She sees them as "kids" and "people."

Celebrating students as fully, completely human means that children are not foreigners, aliens, a thingified commodity, defective, handicapped adults, or nameless, faceless, cardboard bodies. By perceiving students in this holistic way, teachers can help to alleviate the sense of alienation youngsters feel when their lives are conceived as lacking, poor, isolated, and fearful. "I discovered," says Lynn Crosby, "that children basically are human beings, and they should be treated with respect." Just as teachers must "own" the fact that students' life histories must be valued, they must "own" the fact that students are whole human beings. "But there's still this whole thing about owning kids as being human beings that is really a critical thing," Peter

Cabot explains. When teachers see students as people who are valuable, they in turn enhance their own humanity. Eugene Meyers has an "investment to believe that students are valuable": "I want to think that the people I'm spending my day with are valuable." Viewing students as less than valuable demeans oneself as a teacher.

A CELEBRATION OF TEACHERS AS HUMAN

Integral to the pedagogic relationship is the willingness of teachers to reveal themselves as humans too, as "someone more than teacher." Fred Smart comments, "When [kids] come to find out that teachers are human with the same kinds of feelings, and the same kinds of desires that they do, they open up and become more vulnerable. Because they realize you're vulnerable also."

As part of the lived experience of her classroom, Maura Callahan tells students about her life as a child and as a commercial artist:

> So, I'd tell them a lot of things about myself. Mostly about my life before I was ever a teacher, my life as a child, my life as a commercial artist. Within that context, I would always tell them about the things I was good at, and the things that I liked to do, and the people who helped me. And the projects I did on my own, in hopes that the children would start to open up on their own.

Maura recalls that her elementary teachers were distant and impersonal. She does not want to "come off that way." In sharing her own experiences, Maura reveals her own human qualities. "I really wanted to let them know that I am a human being," she says, "and that I was a kid once too."

By letting students see her as a "real person," Susan Oberman makes the classroom a "safe place" for them to talk about their feelings and ideas. She tells them about her brother's death; she tells them about her husband going to Viet Nam a week and a half after they were married:

> And many times if they knew that teacher was a human being who had dreams that fell apart, and mistakes that were made, and concerns and frustrations . . . but also things that were realized, and joys that were felt, and things that were important that kind of grew and came to fruition. That somehow or another if you were willing to share the human part of you, it was that open door for them to share the human part of them. And so I could have done any number of things to get them going on a topic, or get them going on a book.

THE LIVED EXPERIENCE OF THE CLASSROOM

The lived experience of the classroom involves the coming together of the life history of the student with the life history of the teacher. "Somehow making an interaction was what's important," says Susan Oberman, "and there was more to life than just what they saw, there was more to life than just what I saw, and there was more to learning than what was in the textbooks." The lived experience of the classroom may be enhanced by this synergistic relationship, in which teachers and students combine their life histories and develop a shared trust.

The teacher, however, occupies a position of power in that classroom that determines the nature of the lived classroom experience. "The teacher has the potential of manipulating those children, and making them feel good or bad about themselves," says Eugene Meyers. Peter Cabot is fearful that knowledge of students' out-of-school experiences might be misused "in order to modify the in-school experiences for the purposes of transforming both." Such miseducation is "real scary stuff":

> You can utilize the out-of-school curriculum for the purpose of getting the specialized learning done. And that's a real scary thing. It's almost like modifying one's education, modifying the in-school stuff to match the out-of-school, with the purpose of inducing, or seducing the kids to learn. That's gimmickry though, that's not real education.

What differentiates a teacher who guides the learner through the process and content of educational experience and a teacher who manipulates them? Rob Wasserman speaks of teachers as judo instructors: "those who take students' momentum and throw them where they [teachers] want them [students] to go," characterize teachers who manipulate students to implement the existing curriculum. The lived experience of that classroom resembles the kind of classroom that Dewey (1916) described, in which each lesson is treated as an independent whole, with a teacher who does not attempt to help students find connections between other lessons in the same content area or with other subjects.

Teachers as judo instructors who use students' momentum to throw them where they [students] want to go, is closer to the idea of the teacher as a guide in the educational process. The lived experience of that classroom involves a teacher helping students use prior knowledge and experiences to connect to deeper and wider ways of learning, but "save by accident, out-of-school experience is left in its crude and comparatively irreflective state" (Dewey, 1916, p. 163). I propose the image of teachers as judo instructors who, with students, combine their energies to "throw students" where it is possible to go. The lived experience of this type of classroom resembles the classroom Dewey (1916) described, in which lessons are interconnected with the realities of everyday life by teachers helping students make these connections through conscious reflection and opportunity for discovery.

Dewey's definition of miseducative experiences seems straightforward and clearcut: "Any experience is miseducative that has the effect of arresting or distorting the growth of further experience" (Dewey, 1938, p. 25). Reflecting on the lived classroom experiences of the teachers in this study, the distinction between educative and miseducative experiences is more complex. There is a subtle distinction between creating classroom theatrics and genuinely sparking the interests of students. What is the difference between the teacher as a "magician who pulls a rabbit out of the hat," to use Maura Callahan's metaphor, or teaching as "all colorful and clowns," as Fred Smart says, and education that is appealing, worthwhile, and enduring? Maura Callahan explains that a genuine invitation to become involved in the learning process and theatrics could look the same: "But the emphasis is altogether different. You're starting with something that's meaningful within the context of your classroom, and the context of your children's lives."

James Henderson (1987, p. 5) writes that "it is difficult to separate the superficial and slick from the deep and enduring." He draws an analogy from the Sante Fe marketplace, which is "full of fake adobe, hot tubs, trinkets, and expensive boots and trivial art. This commercial junkiness has a kind of mindless "energy and appeal" (Henderson, 1987, p. 6). Henderson likens the educational "marketplace" to the Sante Fe marketplace. He suggests that in order to distinguish between the "enduring and the junk," "critical studies of elegant interpretations of teaching could be used to help educate the public on certain characteristics of the powerful and enduring in education" (Henderson, 1987, p. 6).

The lived experience of the classroom represents more than extracurricular activities, sports, and after-school jobs. The essence of the out-of-school curriculum is a classroom bonding between teachers and students, in order to enhance educative experiences. The out-of-school curriculum these teachers seek is the broader, total range of lived experience which we, as humans, have in common.

THE OUT-OF-SCHOOL CURRICULUM AS AN INVITATION

Whether teachers apprehend knowledge about students' out-of-school curriculum through informal conversations, writing assignments, or home visits, there is an element of trust and sharing involved in the invitation. Many teachers object to one-sided prying for information as something artificial and an invasion of privacy. During Maura Callahan's "talk time," the students come up to her desk only if they want to. She is sensitive about talking to students in a contrived manner, because "a lot of kids are not good in artificial situations." She encourages students to talk within a "regular time during the day," such as morning "talk time," or during an "irregular time," such as in the "context of a semiprivate situation during the day-to-day activities."

When Peter Cabot decided to become "much more casual" about the way he taught, he began to find out about his students' out-of-school interests and experiences informally and "unintentionally" within the context of a class discussion:

> Many times I can remember where we'd just wander off in thoughts. Something would spark a memory for me, or something I thought would be interesting to pursue, or a past experience I had, and I'd tell the kids about it. And then a kid would want to tell about it. And then a kid would want to tell us something that happened to him that wasn't all that dissimilar.

While these teachers do not deliberately investigate their students' out-of-school lives, they discover and connect in a variety of informal ways. When Eugene Meyers is on hallguard post "there's a circle of kids around me." The students know "I'm like an easy ear, and a kind of nonjudgmental ear." As a result, they "talk about themselves fairly openly, and they have assignments throughout that allow them to express themselves."

Alan Stauffer learns about his students' out-of-school lives from "general talk." It "ranges from lots of detail" to general kinds of things. He believes that students tend to "confide" in him and other teachers rather than school counselors or psychologists because "we just see them a lot more."

Marie Burdette sees how "hard" her students' out-of-school lives are from their informal conversations. They primarily talk about the "bad things that were happening in their life":

> I had one child who had been raped. I had another child who was abused. I had children who would come to school and talk about how there were shootings in the neighborhood last night. And that's mainly what they brought into school. That and young children watched TV shows, so there was a lot of talk about what they watched on TV. And music was real important in their culture, pop music stars, and popular TV shows.

Rob Wasserman's approach is more intentional and formal than Maura's, Peter's, Alan's, or Marie's, but it still involves students talking about themselves. He sets a "tone" within the classroom from the first day to convey to his students that each one is an "important part of this class." Rob's "written schedule" and classroom format help him find out about his students' interests and needs:

> Among the things that I do that is perhaps different from most classroom teachers is I prepare for [kids] a week at a time a written schedule. So they have time to prepare. And then we also have the classroom arranged a little differently. The students sit in large circles, rather than in rows, so it allows them normal interaction with each other.

Initially, Susan Oberman was faced with students who were "reticent" to talk in the classroom because it was "uncool and unmasculine to talk about your frustrations, your problems, your dreams, because that wasn't the manly thing to do." Susan understood their "need and their willingness . . . trying to let you know without coming right out and telling you . . . that they wanted interest in what they were doing":

> But they could, through a vehicle of either class projects, whether it be English or theology or history, sometimes do what I consider opening the door. Here's a little glimpse. And if you want to run with it, I'm kind of ready to share a little bit, but let's see how it goes. And you would get them very often, bringing in things of their personal lives.

Other teachers invite students to share their out-of-school experiences through writing assignments. Eugene Meyers' students write not only for class assignments but for themselves and for one another. He tells them that "those are life assignments." They will share their personal writings with Eugene because he "taps into something that makes them feel I care about them, which I do." Eugene's approach to creative writing "allows" the students to reveal their out-of-school experiences:

> As I define creative writing for them, . . . we talk about the way you fashion a story. I talk to them about how . . . one of my phrases is . . . you're the god of your own story. You create the entire atmosphere. You often create that atmosphere out of your own experiences and things that you've done. And of course a lot of the assignments are

autobiographical, so therefore it's going to bring in their own experiences. That's how I find out about trips and they talk about the activities that they've partcipated in.

In addition to "overhearing conversations," seeing how "they act to each other," and talking to parents at conference time, Paul Stewart uses writing assignments to help his students talk about their interests. He suggests topics, such as the best day they ever had, what they like to do on Saturdays, their vacations, or their best friends.

Several teachers learn about their students' lives outside of school through home visits. At the beginning of every school year, Ann Welles telephones parents and introduces herself to them. She sends letters home to each parent as a follow-up to the telephone call, and makes home visits as well. She feels that "it's not real easy to know what's going on with the children just by seeing them at school." Home visits enable Ann to determine what the individual "life style" of the family is like:

> I tell them about myself, and my expectations and my goals for my class as a teacher, what my program is all about. Then I ask them if there's anything that they would like me to know particularly about their child. What's their goal? What do they want? Is there something they feel I should watch out for, or they feel I should address? I always do that.

Sean Murphy not only visits his students' homes but has traveled to their parents' native homelands in three central states of Mexico: Michoacan, Jalisco, and Guanjuato. Sean thinks he has a deeper understanding of his students' cultural background, which differs from his own, by making the ultimate of home visits. He went to Mexico to study the culture, "certainly not to take the sun." He discovered that what he considers problems for the children in his classroom (for example, eating too much lard, which causes health problems, and not "speaking in conversations") are not necessarily problems in Mexico.

During her student-teaching experience, Susan Oberman found herself placed in a mobile vehicle outside the school, teaching thirteen high school youngsters whom nobody else wanted in their classroom. By the second week, Susan became "annoyed" because "something important was going on here, and I felt real distressed that no one had bothered to tell me." She began looking at school records and talking to people, and was able to "gather bits and pieces of the stories of these kids":

> And what I was able to learn from them themselves, and what I was able to piece together through the records in the school, and the fact that I was willing to take this different approach . . . here I am with all my mistakes, and all my foibles, and all my problems, and all the good things that I can recall in my life. Here I am, and I'll tell you, and whoever's brave enough you tell me.

Rather than determining students' interests, needs, and experiences through one-sided diagnostic inventories, teachers discovered students' out-of-school curriculum through a shared process that occurred "through reciprocal give-and-take, the teacher taking but not being afraid also to give" (Dewey, 1938, p. 72).

THE LORE OF THE OUT-OF-SCHOOL CURRICULUM

Teachers' insights generate a rich, multidimensional knowledge of the out-of-school curriculum. What emerges is a personalized construct, one that binds teachers and students in pursuit of knowledge that is worthwhile. The out-of-school curriculum is not a one-dimensional concept limited to out-of-school activities. As Marie Burdette simply but elegantly states, "The out-of-school curriculum has to do with the life history of the child that comes into the school." By the same token, it has to do with the life history of the teacher who comes into the school. The lives of the teacher and the students converge, and become the lived experience of the classroom. They "combine and recombine to reshape curriculum" (Schubert, 1986, p. 291).

The essence of that lived experience arises from a mélange of themes, metaphors, and guiding beliefs. The essence of the out-of-school curriculum involves teachers who acknowledge that students are fully human, and who are, in turn, willing to reveal themselves as human too. The essence of that lived experience is characterized by a mutual invitation for teachers and students to share each other's out-of-school curriculum. Students are co-workers in the educational process who are cared for, loved, and celebrated for their worth. Furthermore, that lived experience involves teachers with a vision, dedicated toward guiding students, and exposing them to a world of knowledge and possibilities, always mindful of connecting an unfamiliar world to more personal, meaningful contexts.

While having one's own children or a mentor may be missing from the lived experience of some teachers, one's own childhood and teaching experiences are available to all educators. Being able to identify with the child's way of knowing is an underlying dimension of the out-of-school curriculum. The teacher becomes a guiding example "who shows the child the way into a world. My world and yours. I know something about being a child. Because I have been there, where you are now. I was young once" (van Manen, 1982, p. 285). Maura Callahan conveys that sentiment to her students. " . . . I was a kid once too. And it's hard to be a kid. And I used to always tell them that." Recapturing a sense of one's own childhood makes it possible for the adult to experience the world from a child's point of view:

> I wish I could be young again but know what I know now. Many of us are nostalgic about our childhood, and not because we want to be children again. What we really want to do is be able to experience the world the way a child does. We long to recapture a sense of possibility and openness—a confidence that almost anything is possible. (van Manen, 1986, p. 29)

Teachers can always return to the life world of the classroom through reflection. All teachers are able to journey to this reflective world, and to recall experiential descriptions of interactions with students, parents, other teachers, and administrators. Teachers can "redeem, retrieve, regain, or recapture in the sense of recalling" (van Manen, 1982, p. 291). Teaching experiences in the classroom offer an opportunity for continuous reflection. "I view the educational experience" says Maura Callahan, "as somewhat of a psychoanalytic process." Furthermore, "When I read my interview, it looked to me like I present an opportunity for that same process to be possible for students." Eugene Meyers reiterates this theme: "If our job is to make a person feel [a sense of] worth and validity . . . the process of education is the process of revealing a person's self to himself."

Max van Manen (1982) has likened the adult's role as pedagogue to "an invitation, a beckoning to the child (*educare*: to lead into)."

> This is the meaning of leading: going first. And in the "going first" there is the "you can trust me" for I have tested the ice. I have lived. I now know something of the rewards as well as the trappings of growing toward adulthood and making a world for yourself. And although my going first is no guarantee of success (because the world is not without risks and dangers), in the pedagogic relationship there is a more fundamental guarantee: that, no matter what, I'm here. And you can count on me. (van Manen, 1982, p. 285)

Trust may be established when the invitation to share one's out-of-school curriculum is an integral part of the lived experience of the classroom. "If the invitation is made," explains Peter Cabot, "and it's made when people can see that they're living together, when they're spending part of their day together, and part of their lives have been intersected, then they can assume that posture of vulnerability." By sharing his or her own out-of-school experiences, the teacher makes it possible for the student to do the same. Both the teacher and the student have a right to accept or decline the invitation, which allows each of them to delineate and respect boundaries of privacy.

A PERSONAL MEANING

Writing about the influences that shaped the principles and beliefs of these teachers helped me think about influences on my life and educational practice. I have two outstanding images of my elementary school experience in the 1950s. The first image has to do with a fourth-grade homework assignment: Draw a floor plan of your house or apartment. Doing this homework assignment forced me to reveal parts of my life I wanted to keep private. I did not want anyone to know I lived in a one-bedroom apartment with my mother and grandmother. I did not want anyone to know that my bed was in the living room. I did not want anyone to know that my mother and grandmother shared the bedroom. I did not want anyone to know that my parents were divorced. I completed the assignment and felt ashamed. I believe strongly in an invitation and not an inventory.

The second image centers on a boy in my sixth-grade class. He was frequently punished by the teacher in front of me and my classmates. The form of punishment was always the same. The teacher would strategically place his finger on a sensitive nerve on the child's shoulder, apply pressure, and inflict pain. This boy was the only African-American in our class. He was the only student ever punished in this manner. I believe that we must view children as human, and have deep care and concern in our hearts for them.

Twenty years ago I began my professional life as an educator. I was a Head Start teacher in Boston. For seventeen years I worked as a speech-language pathologist. In that capacity, I was touched by the lives of the many children and parents with whom I worked. I value the out-of-school lives, interests, and experiences of students.

Like Alan Stauffer and Fred Smart, I too have been influenced by a mentor. Mine helped me to integrate the world of curriculum and the world of special education. Although called speech-language pathologist, I began to perceive myself as an educator. I have come full circle, and now have the opportunity to integrate my special education and curriculum backgrounds. I teach graduate students in regular and special education programs. They write journals. They consider what is most worthwhile for them to study. They bring to class their own lives, interests, and experiences. In turn, I encourage them to do the same with their own students or future students.

I believe we can use the voices of teachers who want to make a worthwhile contribution to their profession, to help students reflect on their current and long-term growth. I think that Maura Callahan's image of teachers signing their own death warrant is compelling. "When a teacher's own philosophy, which I believe should be the guiding force, is reduced to the definition of a mere attitude, we have a very serious problem," she says. "I've seen many good teachers put to death by an attitude." Through voices of experienced educators, other teachers can discover how others have faced the challenges of good teaching.

I began with stories, and I will end with a poem. I wrote this poem using the teachers' idiomatic expressions. It is written in the spirit of Max van Manen's concept of phenomenological research. He wrote that "phenomenology, like poetry, intends to be silent as it speaks. So, to read or write phenomenologically requires that we be sensitively attentive to the silence about the words by means of which we attempt to disclose the deep meaning of our world" (van Manen, 1982, p. 299).

THE METAPHORICAL LANGUAGE
OF THE OUT-OF-SCHOOL CURRICULUM: A POEM

An invitation, not an inventory
More than bringing a brain into school
More than hands or feet
There are the kids and me
And a hunk of paper and a bag of markers
Living the life of a three- or four- or five-year-old
We're all in this together
Part and parcel
One and the same
Co-workers
Happening in waves
Connected with other parts of the waves

Without eyes to see, we waltz around in a cloud of denial
Schizophrenic
Fragmented
A potter with no clay
Nameless, faceless children
Cardboard figures
Thingified

A rabbit pulled out of the hat . . . knowledge prostitutes
Enemy territory, it's close to war
Fighting a losing battle
Cuisenaire rods flying all over the place
Losing

Rip it all out, gut it all out, get down to the studs
Children unpacking your baggage . . . suddenly
You see stuff you never realized you had
The public self, the private self
You can own that
It's not magic, it's love
Giving witness
Making yourself vulnerable to a stranger
Sharing a gift
Prizing childhood
Celebrating students
Friends for life

REFERENCES

Bullough, R. V., Goldstein, S. L., and Holt, L. (1984). *Human interests in the curriculum: Teaching and learning in a technological society.* New York: Teachers College Press.

Dewey, J. (1897). My pedagogic creed. In R. Ulich (Ed.), *Three thousand years of educational wisdom.* Cambridge, MA: Harvard University Press, pp. 629–638.

Dewey, J. (1916). *Democracy and education.* New York: Macmillan.

Dewey, J. (1938). *Experience and education.* New York: Macmillan.

Henderson, J. G. (1987). Case knowledge of hermeneutical elegance: rationale and phenomenological quest. Paper presented at the annual meeting of the American Educational Research Association. Washington, D.C., April 1987.

Schubert, W. H. (1980). *Curriculum books: The first eighty years.* Lanham, MD: University Press of America.

Schubert, W. H: (1981). Knowledge about out-of-school curriculum. *Educational Forum, 45*(2): 185–199.

Schubert, W. H. (1986). *Curriculum: Perspective, paradigm, and possibility.* New York: Macmillan.

Schubert, W. H., and Schubert, A. L. (1981). Toward curricula that are of, by, and therefore for students. *Journal of Curriculum Theorizing, 3*(1): 239–251.

Schwab, J. J. (1954). Eros and education. *Journal of General Education, 8*: 54–71.

Schwab, J. J. (1956). Science and civil discourse: The uses of diversity. *Journal of General Education, 9*: 132–143.

Schwab, J. J. (1960). What do scientists do? *Behavioral Science, 5*: 1–27.

Schwab, J. J. (1970). *The practical: A language for curriculum.* Washington D.C.: National Education Association.

Schwab, J. J. (1971). The practical: Arts of eclectic. *School Review, 79*: 493–542.

Schwab, J. J. (1973). The practical 3: Translation into curriculum. *School Review, 81*: 501–522.

Spencer, H. (1861). *Education:. Intellectual, moral, and physical*. New York: D. Appleton.

van Manen, M. (1982). Phenomenological pedagogy. *Curriculum Inquiry*, *12*(3): 283–299.

van Manen, M. (1986). *The tone of teaching*. Ontario, Canada: Scholastic-TAB Publications Ltd.

A midwife we know describes a decisive moment in her own growth and education: She had delivered several hundred babies before she became pregnant and prepared for the delivery of her own child. During transition, the most difficult part of labor, she cried out, "I've told 300 women, 'You can do it,' and it can't be done!"

There is a lesson here. Teachers bring to classrooms certain professional knowledge and experience, an objective view—they are masters of certain ways of knowing. What they lack—and what parents often provide—is the insider's perspective, the sense of being there, the unabashedly subjective and fully invested view. Partnerships between teachers and parents can be a powerful force for education.

In the final chapter in this section, Pat Hulsebosch explores the dense and rugged terrain of parent-teacher relationships. She talks with two groups of teachers: those who value the involvement of parents in their classrooms, and those who scorn it. Comparing and contrasting the values and practices of these high-involvement and low-involvement teachers, Hulsebosch reflects on the potential power of partnerships.

Schools as we know them were, of course, created with a particular view of the family in mind. The school and the family were distinct venues with specific and complementary agendas and responsibilities. Whether or not the ideal American family ever existed, today only 7 percent of families fit the model "typical family"— breadwinning husband, homemaking mother, and two children. Only 10 percent of American schoolchildren have a parent at home full time. Teachers and others need to rethink the realities of schools and families, and to create new possibilities adjusted to the complex requirements of modern society.

CHAPTER 7

Significant Others:

Teachers' Perspectives on Relationships with Parents

Patricia L. Hulsebosch

AN EXAMINED LIFE

Teaching and Learning

As I look back, it seems inevitable that I would become interested in the connections between teaching and parenting. After all, I have been a teacher and a parent for the past twenty years of my life. Not only have I done the work of teaching and parenting, but teaching and parenting have both been at the core of my identity for all those years. Neither was a casual commitment. For me, parenting and teaching are so inextricably linked that it is sometimes difficult to tell which is which, each reinforcing and informing the other, each deeply embedded in and depending on the other.

My first four years as an adult were spent raising two toddlers while learning to become a teacher of young children. Although my formal education took place at a small commuter university in the South, I was also becoming a teacher by learning to parent. There were many nights when I fell into bed exhausted (sometimes only to be awakened a few hours later to the cries of a hungry baby), but what I remember most clearly of those years is excitement. It was wonderfully exciting to be learning and teaching, both at home and at school. That was my first taste of the energizing effect of watching a child's awareness of the world expand, bit by bit, in turn feeding my own expanding sense of the world. Even better, the children I taught were not just any children, but included my own children. I felt especially lucky, as the only mother in my teacher education classes to be able to test and explore the ideas and approaches that I was learning in university classrooms with my own sons.

The theory-practice split was never a problem for me because theory never remained theoretical for long. In my field experiences I talked and listened to, played with—taught—children in daycare centers, Head Start programs, and kindergartens. And each afternoon I could hardly wait to come home to be able to bring to life something new I had read or heard about. Sometimes my older son, Lonnie, and I would go for a walk and I would eagerly await a "teachable moment." On other days I would watch my second child, Sean, out of the corner of my eye, while I folded laundry, to see his reaction to his new set of blocks. I was keenly aware of the uniqueness of my own sons as they learned, and when I taught in school settings I would try to see my students through the eyes of their mothers to feel the passion of that perspective.

Maybe it was the challenge and excitement of being a mother, the connectedness and even the intellectual stimulation I experienced with my own children that prompted me to consider foregoing the search for a teaching job in favor of devoting my energies to full-time parenting. As it happened, a first-grade teaching job in a new open classroom school was offered to me through a friend of a friend, and it was too good an opportunity to turn down. Thus I joined the ranks of double-duty mothers in teaching other people's children by day, and my own at night.

A Home Away from Home

Although, at twenty-one, I was "leaving home" to work, there was much about my first teaching job at Shady Grove Elementary School that kept in- and out-of-school life tied together for me. In fact, those early years of teaching reinforced in me an even deeper belief in the importance of connections in people's lives. For one thing, I was fortunate enough to work with a team of three other teachers in the school's first-grade "pod." And, because I was joining the school as it was preparing to open its doors for the first time, I had a chance to work with faculty and staff members, to create a learning environment from the ground up, to spend some time thinking through just what it was we wanted the school to be. I remember long days and evenings spent thinking and talking, moving furniture, cutting and pasting, planning and questioning, and talking to parents who wandered in to see what was happening. The school community was developing into a kind of family of its own.

Unfortunately, few of the faculty lived in the community immediately beyond the school grounds. Most of us drove an hour or more through sleepy, cow-lined roads to get to Shady Grove each morning. Most of us, it seemed, had little in common with the parents of our students, who were mainly "country folk" or migrant workers. As our work progressed, we began to see that teachers and parents shared a great deal. All of us were excited about the prospects of education in the new school building, rising like a modern football stadium in the midst of orange groves. The school was designed to enable teachers and students to move more freely within its walls so that interests could be supported and pursued and so that children were at the center of the action. We were all eager to make this new learning environment a success. Finally, new-found feminist stirrings were awakening in me a keen awareness of how much the mothers of my students and I shared: as women, as parents, and as working mothers with multiple demands on our energies and our time, demands that often conflicted with an ardent desire to do what was best for our children.

Maybe because most of us were so far from our own homes, or maybe because most of us were women, the teachers at Shady Grove seemed to want to build a sense of community there at the school. Much of what happened at school was intriguing to the community members, adults and children alike, and the school took on aspects of a community center and neighborhood hub. We opened up the school on Saturday mornings for movies ($.50 for the show and $.25 for popcorn) and for a chance to raise money, bring our own families to school, and meet some mothers who might not be able to come in during the week. This was a year-round district, which, I believe, contributed to the community's ownership of the school and our own investment in the community. There was less of a sense of "getting through the school year" to be home with our own families, and more of a sense of ongoing contact with "neighbors" throughout the year.

Through social activities and informal events I began to see the value of blurring the boundaries between home and school. Once I had a face to go with a name, I was much more likely to jot a note to a mother letting her know of a child's accomplishment or asking for a "second opinion" on some new twist in progress or behavior. And in turn she was able to approach me with concerns and interests. I was finding that the more contact I had with these parents the more I was likely to have, and the more able I was to know the children I taught.

Blurred Boundaries

When I started teaching, my own children were still preschoolers. Over the course of my three years as a first-grade teacher at Shady Grove one of my sons, Lonnie, became a first grader himself at a small school close to home called Learning Space, while the other, Sean, was fast approaching school age. I was again at a magic point where the lines between teaching at home and teaching in my classroom became fuzzy, and I was able to intermingle my teaching and learning experiences with my students and children. I often found that what Lonnie was doing in first grade was a stimulus for my work with children in school, and that what I was discovering in teaching was also worth bringing home.

Over time several of my closest colleagues and friends from Shady Grove moved on to other schools, to other states, to other roles. The distance between home and work began to feel greater in the absence of my fellow pioneers, and, having just come through a divorce, I was longing for a school community closer to the community in which I lived.

Meanwhile, Learning Space was expanding what had been a preschool through first grade to include a new first–second grade classroom and the school was looking for a teacher. The "catch" was that my son Lonnie would be in that class next year, and, if I were to take the position, not only would I be Lonnie's mother, I would also be his teacher. Although I was intrigued by this chance to fold together the two roles, mother and teacher, I was also cautious. Would I feel pressed to respond to the needs and demands of one child in the midst of an entire classroom of children? But then, isn't that, to some extent, the dilemma of every good teacher? I was drawn to the position by the prospect of team-teaching again, this time with the woman I'd gotten to know as Lonnie's first-grade teacher. I was excited about cross-age grouping, and I thought Lonnie and I were both up to the challenge. I accepted the job.

Learning Space had for years been a childcare center with a commitment to progressive education and to an antisexist, antiracist approach to curriculum. Because its roots were in daycare, it drew a diverse population, including children whose parents were college students, working-class families from an adjacent apartment complex, and professionals, including faculty from the nearby university. As a parent, I had valued the staff's efforts to make Learning Space a warm and inviting place for all children and for all parents as well. I was excited at the prospect of joining yet another community of teachers and learners, this time one that was just down the block from where my sons and I lived.

At Learning Space I discovered for the first time what it means to teach without the constraints of state-mandated scope-and-sequence charts and achievement tests. I learned about the joys and benefits, as well as the difficulties and effort, when parenting and teaching are literally combined. Although I had always seen the ways in which I had infused my parenting with teaching, I was coming to realize more clearly the ways in which parenting influenced my teaching. At the most obvious level I was now trying to juggle both roles simultaneously in the classroom with my own child. But, more subtly and more importantly, I could now see that the parental sense of investment, and the inclination to perceive the particular needs of each child, always an important part of my teaching, was affirmed and given space to grow and develop.

While I had always experienced commonalities between the parents of my students and myself, at Learning Space the connections were magnified as I became close friends with many of these women and men, and more than just passing acquaintances with all. I would find myself showcasing Brooke's accomplishments to her parents, comparing notes on Jimmy's behavior with his mother, or listening to Maya's father describe an idea for our current unit on reproduction. At times, the discussions were heated—as, for example, when a parent and I would each try to make the other see why we believed so strongly in our convictions. (Why *did* Steve have to complete an activity requiring scissors when it was frustrating for him? Was Michelle's mom right when she pointed out to me that a reward system distracts from the intrinsic value of class activities? And what potentials and problems did our unit on cemeteries hold for Charlie?) I was learning a great deal from these parents, not only about the individual children but also about the larger meaning of education, both for me and for my students.

Learning Space epitomized a family orientation to schooling, not only in the way in which it invited parent-teacher interactions, but also in the environment it created for its students and faculty. Children worked together in multiage groupings, acting sometimes as learners and sometimes as teachers to their peers. Often students remained with the same teacher over a span of several years. For each of the next six years the school grew by tiny increments, in parallel development with the growth of its oldest students: second, third, fourth, fifth, sixth, and finally a seventh grade. When I left Learning Space there were three children who had been my students for six years. The opportunity to know my students in extraordinarily intense and intimate ways was exhilarating, challenging, and often humbling as well, for I came to realize that whatever I knew about these children as their teacher was insignificant compared with what I knew about my own sons, and what each of their parents knew about them.

Distance and Disconnection

It's hard to say exactly why I finally chose to move on from Learning Space. There were both external and internal influences: "Graduating" our first students after six years, a consensus decision that my sons should live with their father, a job offer from another state, and the accompanying lure of graduate school all played a part in the leaving. But leave I did, from Florida to Chicago, and from firsthand to long-distance parenting, to take a position at a residential school for deaf adolescents who had been labeled "emotionally disturbed."

The stark contrast of these years to the earlier ones in my life again emphasized for me the importance of home-school interaction. My new students' lack of connection—to families, to peers, and to society—was dramatic. Their hearing impairment had isolated them from much of the "hearing" world, and, for most of them, an added emotional problem, as defined by school systems, had served to alienate them from relationships with their family and the deaf community. Support and sustenance were difficult to come by for these students, and my own disconnectedness to home mirrored internally the alienation I experienced around me. Teaching, removed from family and community, was more difficult for me, as was learning for my students. Although I worked simultaneously to find niches in the community that these kids could plug into, and to rebuild a sense of family for myself, I continued to see and feel the impact of living a fragmented life.

Lessons Learned

Over these years I had experienced a spectrum of home-school interactions. On the one hand, I had tried combining the roles of parent and teacher; on the other, I had distanced myself from my own home and attempted to work with students for whom connection to home and community was virtually nonexistent. Under the best circumstances I had seen that collaboration between a teacher and a parent can offer a resource for these two people, people who are usually women, with jobs that are often isolated, devalued, and overwhelming. A view that "we're in this together" had often helped me assuage the frustration, guilt, and discouragement that frequently accompanied these highly complex and demanding roles. Rather than seeing each other as adversaries vying for control of the education of a child, a teacher and a parent working in partnership can gain both personal and professional rewards that are unavailable when working in isolation.

My experiences had also shown me that parents and teachers are not the only beneficiaries of a positive home-school relationship. When I was able to have a dialogue with parents regarding both the in- and out-of-school curriculum, we were able to convey to the child a sense of wholeness and connection, and an image of education as an ongoing process larger and richer than the confines of schooling. And so, Steve's mother and I worked out a plan in which he would have alternatives to using scissors in school coupled with opportunities to use scissors at home, and I spoke frequently with Charlie and his mom as I thought through where to go next with the cemetery unit. These resolutions also provided a much-needed model of adults working together collaboratively in common interest.

Finally, the linkages I had helped to forge between school and community brought my democratic goals for education into the forefront of a conversation about the mission of schooling. I advocate parent involvement in schools because I think it is better for kids, but also because I believe that schools belong to citizens, not as clients but as owners of public institutions. It was equally important to me that the parents of Shady Grove, a public school, and Learning Space, where parents paid tuition, felt an ownership of their school. Both schools belonged to the children, parents, and staff, and these communities of people belonged to the schools.

Woman to Woman

As a teacher, I had been profoundly affected by my many and diverse relationships with parents, and I had often wondered how other teachers perceived similar contacts. When I returned to graduate study, I returned as well to this question. I was surprised to find that despite discussions, definitions, and prescriptions on home-school relationships, there have been few formal attempts to understand teachers' conceptions of their interactions with parents (Lightfoot's *Worlds Apart* being a particularly wonderful exception to this). I decided to address that gap by looking into the experiences, thoughts, and conceptualizations of elementary school teachers regarding the parents of their students.

Since my early days as an undergraduate, feminism had been a particularly compelling lens through which I had come to view the world. Through feminism I was able to see the points of intersection between my experiences and those of other women, and to realize that the commonalities we had were more than just coincidence. Realizing that most teachers are women, and that it is women who are still the primary care givers in most families, I looked to feminist theory to help me understand and interpret teachers' relationships with parents.

RE-SEARCHING HOME-SCHOOL CONNECTIONS

I had seen that teachers and parents can have a profound influence on the lives of children. Yet I also knew that a teacher and a parent may have only the most fleeting contact with each other. Never mind that each has something unique to offer the other in their respective experiences with the child. And never mind that they may even have similar hopes and dreams, and almost certainly, each in her own way wants "the best" for the child. In fact, parents and teachers often maintain an uncomfortable relationship with one another. At times this relationship erupts into all-out warfare between parent groups and school personnel, but more commonly it is characterized by mutual hostility and cool indifference.

Because any life is an intricate and complex web of interwoven connections, what occurs in the home life of a child cannot and should not be isolated and separated from the child's school life. When the web is broken there is pain, loss, and alienation—all of which are essentially disconnectedness (Bronfenbrenner, 1986). We are confronted daily by the most overt signs of alienation in our children: suicide, drug abuse, teen pregnancy, and violence. Stark contrasts between different components of life can have profound affects on a child's psychosocial development, in turn affecting school performance (Comer, 1986, 1988). The obvious and most hopeful way to counteract alienation is through the creation of links in a child's life. This is why many educators focus on a holistic "community-based system" rather than a narrow and constrained "school-based system" (Fantini, 1985). This "community-based system" is one comprised of school curriculum as well as "out-of-school curriculum," including families, museums, peers, media, and work.

If disconnection is to be repaired, if alienation is to be addressed, there must be teacher awareness of students' out-of-school experiences, and this awareness can be achieved in part through relationship with parents. Yet in the lives of many children the connection between home life and school life is slight at best. For many, school and home are hostile, warring worlds with sharply distinct cultures. Parents and teachers often say they want contact with one another, and researchers confirm what is already intuitive knowledge to many: that there are benefits of parent involvement in schooling. Still, in virtually any discussion of home-school relationships a discrepancy emerges between warranted and actual practices of parent involvement. "Why is this?" I wonder. I am not naive or unaware of the many obstacles to meaningful contact between parents and teachers. So, at other times, I think about the question in a different way and ask myself, "What moves some teachers to develop strong positive relationships with the parents of their students?"

With nearly two decades of firsthand experience in teaching and mothering as my foundation, I set out to explore why elementary school teachers working in similar settings (in this case, schools in a predominantly middle-class, suburban community) might make different decisions about their interactions with parents. To do so I talked to teachers who had established and maintained a range of relationships with parents: teachers who made choices that brought parents into their teaching on a daily basis, and teachers who felt they were most effective when they put distance between the school curriculum and the home. I asked these high-involvement and low-involvement teachers to talk about their work, the role of mothers, and their thoughts on the payoffs, problems, and puzzles of teacher-parent relations. Comparing teachers at the extremes of parent involvement, some of whom were teaching in the same grade level at the same school, I hoped to glean some insights into the elements that contribute to a robust teacher-parent relationship.

The Landscape of Teaching

At the heart of a teacher's relationship with parents is the way in which she conceives of teaching. One way of categorizing the goals that teachers describe for their curriculum is along a continuum that ranges from child- to adult-centered. Child-centered implies a focus on people and a practice that puts the learner at the heart of the curriculum and teaching decisions, in contrast to adult-centered, which is oriented more to procedures, compliance, departmentalization, content, and control. Although elements of both child- and adult-centered teaching appeared in most interviews, the high-involvement teachers tended to emphasize the more affective, child-centered aspects of teaching than did the "low involvers."

Monica, a "high involver," sums up her priority in teaching: "First thing, I think you *care* for the kids. I mean, that really sounds pie in the sky, but I do. . . . You know, I really do think you have to have a care and concern for the kids."

Fran, another "high involver," says she wants her students to know that learning is fun, that she likes to "transfer her enthusiasm to them," while Katia talks of trying "to instill a sense of confidence in each one of my kids." High-involvement teachers say they "do an awful lot of counseling," "help to develop a healthy personality," and "teach the whole child." When "high involvers" describe their teaching, they acknowledge that children are in school to learn, but describe teaching as rooted in children's feelings, interests, needs, and desires. Monica again:

> I mean, you can have all the head knowledge and book knowledge, as far as teaching your subjects. But, at least in the elementary—I think it must be true all the way, to some degree, but certainly in the elementary level—I think that you want the kids to do their best and you care for them as a person.

For the low-involvement teachers, those who prefer limited contact with parents, the roots of teaching lie in academic achievement and students' responsibility to society. Barb, a "low involver," says she tries "to help the kids to be good citizens" and Lisa says she tries to "develop them academically." For all of the "low involvers," responsibility and related themes like self-reliance and independence come up repeatedly as they describe what they want to accomplish. Lisa says of her students:

> This is the end of the elementary experience and I think that one of the most important things I can do is give them a good academic base, give them very good study habits, and also get some intrinsic motivation and some preparation for the junior high experience. And that has to be self-reliance.

Barb adds: "Lack of responsibility is a big thing. [The students] don't care about the responsibility of it. And they figure that if they don't get the work done the teacher will sit there and get it done for them."

Barb and Katia exemplify the curricular emphases of low- and high-involvement teachers, and the influence of those perspectives on their relationships with mothers. Barb, a low-involvement teacher, says she has little in common with parents in the middle-class community in which she lives and teaches. She portrays her students as sorely deficient in the qualities that are most important, and so, in the interest of being "protective of her community," sees her job as compensating for the deficiencies that children and parents alike possess:

> As an educator, I will tell you I think my job is to give [my students] an academic base: good study habits, good interpersonal skills, and even though we're not supposed to, maybe some values. But, they have to be in agreement with the child's home life. And so, a full circle is *for the family to cooperate with the teacher*, with the child in the center of this in agreement with both entities. (emphasis added)

Although she says that the values of the educational enterprise must be in agreement with the home, with the "child in the center," Barb is actually describing an agreement of home and child with what she, the teacher, believes to be most appropriate. She sees the relationship as a one-way street, with the family cooperating with the teacher. She portrays herself as the translator of the needs of the community via her work in the classroom. In this view, it is the teacher who functions as the community's trustee, who knows what's best for students and for their families.

Katia, a high-involvement teacher, also talks about responsibility as a teaching goal. But, in doing so, she shifts her focus back and forth between child-centered goals, such as "feeling ten feet taller," and adult-centered goals, such as being "prepared for the next year":

> I try to instill responsibility and pride in [my students] and what they know their capabilities are, how far they've come, that they should be proud of themselves, of their work. The responsibility part as far as participating, what their job is, . . . [is] to come to school, to learn as much as they can, to cooperate with one another. It's not an academic goal. It's a personal goal. I want them to leave my room ten feet taller than they came and I want them to feel good about themselves, the bottom line, you know, and in their abilities as a fourth grader so they're prepared for the next year. So they feel competent and ready for what's ahead of them. I don't want them afraid.

Although Katia emphasizes adult-centered goals, she conveys a view that these goals can be accomplished only through an awareness of and response to child-centered needs. Katia says she finds it difficult, if not impossible, to do a good job of knowing what the child's needs are without a great deal of "back and forth" between home and school:

> I think it's real important for the child to understand that I'm working with their parents. And I tell this to the parents at open house and at the beginning of the year. I say, "My job is to educate your child for one year. Yours is a lifetime job. I will do whatever I can to make this one year as beneficial as possible, but, really, the main job is yours."

For the low-involvement teachers, the goals of education and the path of the curriculum are not just adult-centered, but are, more specifically, teacher-centered, thereby situating the locus of control for achieving the goals solidly with the teacher. For the high-involvement teachers, on the other hand, a dialogue between child- and adult-centered goals holds the potential for a broader coalition of influence in achieving goals. A teacher who sets out to make students self-reliant and more responsible may approach her job differently from one whose focus is on "caring for the kids" and guiding them. These differences may, in turn, become exacerbated depending upon how the teacher views the influence of parents on her goals.

Parents: Assets or Liabilities?

As my inquiry progressed, I knew that parent involvement was taken for granted in the particular schools I was studying. Teachers had contact with parents on formal occasions (PTO meetings and report card pickup days) and when there were problems. Most of the teachers felt they could depend on parents to support their work in some basic ways, such as encouraging children to do homework. But in each school there were a few teachers for whom parent involvement was broader and deeper. These teachers, the "high involvers," interacted with parents more frequently when the child was doing well in school, on informal occasions, and in the context of the parent making suggestions or providing feedback. I was curious about these differences and what the teachers' interpretations of their various experiences were.

For the high-involvement' teachers, parents are a resource, both to them and to the child's education. One of these teachers says, "[Parent involvement] helps to get a total picture of what's going on," while another says, "When I'm having problems and I don't relate well to a child, or the child isn't relating well to me . . . I like to go to a group of people who can give me the most help." The same affirming tone is conveyed whether it is the parent or the teacher who initiates the contact. One "high involver," Fran, describes a mother (who herself was a teacher) who came in after her daughter had failed a social studies test:

> [The mother] came in and we talked about it. And she said she has worked with this girl, and she has applied all the study skills that she teaches. . . . We decided that maybe she hadn't read the questions carefully. . . . And we talked a lot about it and I got a note from her later in the week and she asked if the girl's seat could be changed because she sits in the back of the room and she felt that maybe she was distracted back there, so we changed her seat. So now we'll see how all that works.

At times it's a matter of the teacher reaching out for another "expert" opinion. Patty:

> I feel badly when I'm not getting along well with the student. . . . Things are going bad and I can't seem to pull myself out of it or the child out of it. If I call the parent and I say, "You know, we are having problems. I don't know who's fault it is." And the parent says to me, "Oh, I'm so glad you called. He's impossible at home! I don't know what's going on!" And I think to myself, "Well, the child is going through something!" And knowing that helps me deal with the child and sometimes together we can pull this kid out of whatever is bothering him. So, I like to communicate with the parents a great deal.

According to Karen, contact with parents can add deep, affective dimensions to a teacher's work:

> I think of parent involvement as parent input, as far as sharing ideas, getting background from where the kid comes from, what his experience has been . . . a lot of feedback. Sometimes if the parent will jot me a note in the morning if something happens at home or other environments, I can understand. Because Maria . . . her aunt's lost a baby . . . she had no reaction at home, but she came to school and she's writing a journal and tears are streaming down her face. And I said, "Maria, what's wrong?" So she showed me her journal. So I talked to the mom and touched base with her. So the involvement is kind of like a pre-, during, and post-, ongoing thing.

For the high-involvement teachers the detailing of the child's world extends both ways between classroom and home. For Fran it is a way to bring the parent's particular experience of a child in contact with the teacher's more global experience of one child among many:

Sometimes you have parents who don't really understand that their children aren't doing that well because to them they are. They only see their work. But some of the parents who get in the classroom can see, "Oh, somebody else wrote this story, but look at my child's story. It's not as good in comparison." And so when you try to tell them something they'll understand more.

Others want the parents to know what the classroom world is like, not only for the children, but also for the teacher. Sally notes:

If every parent could spend, not just an hour or so, if they could spend a whole day in a classroom and they would really see what it's like from morning until night. And how busy you really are! . . . Then they would understand how you just don't have time to think of everything.

For these teachers involvement with parents is folded into their very definition of themselves as professionals. Fran again: "I mean, we want our doctors to defend their actions . . . and . . . almost anybody we deal with in a professional way. We want explanations for what they do. Why not in teaching?"

When high-involvement teachers describe interactions with parents, they tend to welcome and include parents as partners in the education of the child. They describe parent involvement as a "relationship among the three of us," and say, "We made a good team" and "We had an honest exchange." "High involvers" say they want to draw the parent in in any way they can. For help, yes, but also for feedback, information, affirmation, and commiseration in order to understand and be understood by parents.

"Low involvers" are more likely to view parents with reservation, doubt, and distrust. "Problems" with parents and their involvement in schools weave their way through many of the descriptions by "low involvers." Parents are problematic for children when there are "bad" situations in the home, such as divorce, or when parents act in indulgent ways, such as "running to their room and picking up after them or bringing a forgotten thing to school." Parents are problematic to teachers when they come up with "silly" ideas at PTO meetings, or interfere with schooling by taking the child out of school for vacations, or by stopping by the classroom during the school day. Lisa comments: "That's a disadvantage, the parents dropping by all the time. That's a nuisance. It's probably one of the biggest nuisances that I can think of, is the parents constantly dropping by and bothering you."

Disruptions are, of course, commonplace in schools. But, while all teachers face disruptions, and the "low involvers" are often teaching in the same schools as the "high involvers," it is only the low-involvement teachers who talk about disruptions. High-involvement teachers describe occasions when people and events change the course of their teaching, but rather than perceiving these as detracting from their students' learning, they describe them as "opportunities" that "add" to their teaching.

Although both high- and low-involvement teachers perceive time and effort as a "cost" of parent involvement, there is a qualitative difference in the perception of that cost. The "high involvers" acknowledge the extra work it may take to have parents involved, but they often accompany such acknowledgments with an additional statement indicating their acceptance of this effort as a necessary and important part of their work. Low-involvement teachers, on the other hand, are more likely to imply that the effort is an unnecessary add-on to the real work of teaching. Katia believes "there is a benefit to using parents in that way [as volunteers], but I have just found for my own . . . I guess I'm more of a self-reliant type of person where I want to do it myself rather than delegating."

Other "low involvers" tell of ways in which they direct their full attention toward their students, even in situations in which collaborating with others might be more appropriate. Katia tells of the time when she tutored a child at home in order to strengthen her ties with the student, but had little interaction with his mother. Barb longs for the days when teachers could keep students after school when there were problems.

Barb describes the frustration she feels when the school year comes to an end and she must face the unmet goals she has had for a child. She says that her principal reminded her that "there's somebody next year." Barb says," It's like I want to . . . I have to do this *all* for this kid so he's gonna be OK—forever." Laura is clear and direct in describing her ideal of teaching:

> You try to keep things under control and manage things on your own. But sometimes you *have* to resort to talking to the parents to see if you can get a better grip of the situation through them. You know, you *feel* like you want to keep control on your own. It's nice to know that you can go through your day or lessons or whatever it may be, and fulfill yourself in completing what you want to complete with the children and have the satisfaction of knowing that they're getting what they should be getting out of the lesson, and things are running smoothly, without any major disruptions. It's a personal satisfaction right there.

While Laura talks about the satisfaction of maintaining control without having to "resort" to reaching beyond the school walls, other low-involvement teachers are more critical of parents who enter into classroom life. Barb feels that parents

> are self-serving. I think they want for themselves without looking around to see what's good for a school district. Oh they wouldn't admit to that, but I think many of them really want . . . something *they* want!

Nina adds:

> Nowadays parents question—every teacher is questioned and put up against the wall no matter what they do. *Everything*! Doesn't matter whether it's behavior, doesn't matter whether it's academics. . . . It's getting more and more and more the parents controlling what goes on in the school.

If parents are seldom an asset to the educational enterprise, then, as the low-involvement teacher sees it, the solution is to concentrate their own efforts on working directly and exclusively with the child. According to the "lore" of the low-involvement teacher, the best way to respond to these out-of-school experiences is to attempt to minimize their impact on what happens within the school. Laura, for example, responds to kids who are "having a rough go of it at home" by "making sure that they keep on target and focus in on what we're doing academically instead of having their mind wander on to the personal family problems." She then clarifies her approach: "By getting them focusing in on this stuff, it eliminates the outside situation."

For these teachers, education seems to take place in the crucible formed by teachers in their classrooms, a crucible that acts to "protect" students from influences, such as parents, that are "outside" the correct and fitting path they have constructed. The crucible is safe and protective for teachers as well. And so, while teachers who are characterized by high involvement with parents seek ways to strengthen their links with their students' out-of-school lives, "low involvers" attempt to minimize the influence of the connection between home and school.

GENDER-BASED CONSTRUCTIONS OF TEACHING

How is it that teachers in the same district, in the same school, often even at the same grade level can have such different perspectives on schooling and on the interactions they have with parents about schooling? Of course, when we talk about parent-teacher relations we are talking, for the most part, about interactions between women. I therefore bring feminism back into the conversation as a perspective that places women at the center in order to directly consider the influence of gender on the relationships between teachers and mothers. Gender plays a decisive role in how teachers define their profession in at least two ways: first, in its influence upon their choice to become teachers, and second, in its influence in establishing the criteria that define a "professional" teacher.

The Choice to Teach

Teaching has long been women's work. Not only has it been argued that women are better suited than men to "begin the first work in the Temple of education" (Horace Mann, cited in Hoffman, 1981, p. xvi), but teaching has also been one of the few careers regarded as suitable for middle-class women. It comes as no surprise to find teachers referring to the ways in which gender has influenced their career choice.

An interesting difference between high- and low-involvement teachers is the path they took to teaching. For the low-involvement teachers, teaching was the only career they had ever considered. Many spoke about how they had "always" wanted to be a teacher. Some "low involvers" had had a teacher in the family, and each had spent time in that relative's classrooms during childhood. Barb and Katia remembered thinking of teaching as a profession that was accorded a great deal of respect by the community. When asked to talk further about the decision to enter teaching, most of the "low involvers" explained their choice as linked to the limited career options available to them as women.

Low-involvement teachers also spoke of the limitations and drawbacks of being a teacher nowadays. They reminisced about the freedom from nonprofessional "interference" and the concomitant status accorded teachers in the past. Barb recalls that people would "sign their letters, 'Respectfully yours.' They figure you're a teacher, you know what you're doing. They don't care if you're young or what. I'm saying thirty years ago there was this attitude, I can tell you."

All but one of the "low involvers" said she would not choose teaching again; each had second thoughts about her decision to become a teacher. Patty said she eagerly awaits her time to retire, while Katia recalled the period of time when she felt, "I just can't do this [teach]. I want something else." Although Katia attributed that period of doubt to events in her personal rather than professional life, she went on to say that she envies the prestige that businesswomen have, and has considered the possibility of financial work as a sideline to teaching. Thus, although all the low-involvement teachers said that teaching was the only career they had considered, they also expressed major reservations about their career choices.

The "low involvers" seem to have chosen teaching as their life's work, not freely from among all possible options that might have suited them, but from within a set of choices limited by social and family expectations of appropriate career choices for women. Paradoxically, for at least some of the "low involvers," their perception of what teaching had to offer them was also biased by an idealized view of the profession.

High-involvement teachers made the decision to become teachers after considering, studying for, or working in other jobs. For the "high involvers," teaching had *not* been the realization of a long-held dream, as it had for most of the low-involvement teachers. Only one of the high-involvement teachers mentioned the limited options available to her for career choice. When the high-involvement teachers described their route to teaching, they referred to a twisting and turning path with multiple decision points along the way. Karen recalls:

> I decided that business . . . it was enjoyable, but my heart wasn't in it. Then I took an education class, and I loved it so much and I knew that's what I wanted to do. . . . It's the kids. I don't think there's anything other than the kids that would draw you to this, because, let's face it, it's not a well-paid field!

Several "high involvers" had completed certification programs while raising young children, often with little or no intention of teaching professionally but with a desire to learn more about education. All of these teachers now value their work, and say that they believe teaching was the right choice for them. Having come to teaching circuitously, the high-involvement teachers seem to see the choice to become a teacher as one freely made, with eyes wide open, then and now. In addition, there is the implication that each decided to become a teacher because it was what she felt best suited her.

The satisfaction of the high-involvement teachers with their work may be partially based on their ability to compare it firsthand with other careers. Having worked at other jobs, they feel they can now more realistically evaluate the merits and drawbacks of teaching. Some explicitly speak of the benefits of their previous experience in other professions, or in raising children. Most often, they say things like, "*I* understand because I worked in the food field" or "I *know* because I remember how I felt when *I* was at home and my kids were in school."

Although the high-involvement teachers acknowledge that teaching is not without problems, they say that neither are other jobs. Like the "low involvers," they feel that teachers are not valued by parents and the community as much as they deserve to be, but rather than experiencing the lack of status as a personal affront, the high-involvement teachers see it as inherent in the teaching role.

There are differences between high- and low-involvement teachers in both their initial and their current perspectives on teaching as a career choice. The present-day attitudes of the low-involvement teachers reflect a disappointment in the difference between the idealistic expectations they held for teaching and the realities of the profession. There is a hint that these teachers were hoping for more of the satisfactions that have historically been associated with male-dominated professions—respect, status, deference—a movement "up and away" from their origins; satisfactions that teaching does not seem to provide. In contrast, the high-involvement teachers seem to have come to teaching more freely, with eyes wide open. Possibly because what they anticipated were rewards intrinsic to the work of teaching—those that come from understanding, working with, and emotionally supporting children—"high involvers" express greater satisfaction with their career choice than do "low involvers."

Male and Female Perspectives

If a teacher's vision of her profession lays the foundation for her interactions with parents, then the architectural design for that foundation is developed along gender lines. In other words, the high-involvement teachers are embedded in a female-identified vision of teaching, while for the "low involvers," the vision of teaching is decidedly male-oriented.

Popular notions, as well as theorists in a variety of fields, refer to masculine and feminine attitudes, traits, and behaviors (Miller, 1976; Biklen, 1982, 1986, 1988; Gilligan, 1982). This categorization of characteristics along gender lines has more to do with custom, history, and politics, of course, than with biology. Irene Claremont de Castillejo (1973) addresses this issue when she talks about a "feminine consciousness," adding, "It is not a question of sex at all, but rather of a masculine or feminine attitude of mind, the possibilities of both being latent in every individual. Artists and poets of necessity have both" (p. 62). Bearing that caveat in mind, we can describe a number of life's dimensions along a continuum that ranges from masculine to feminine.

In her empirically based exploration of the moral development of men and women, Carol Gilligan labels the ideological perspective in which relationships are subordinated to "rights" as distinctively "male," while the conception of morality as concerned with relationships and interdependence is "female." Gilligan contrasts the male perspective on relationships as hierarchical with that of the female image of a web of connections.

There are other dimensions that reflect a gender-based tension for women in education. Biklen (1986, 1988) calls our attention to the fact that traditional definitions of career professionals emphasize the need to separate work and family. And so typically, for a man, doing a good job at work is a way of showing commitment to family, while for women the need is to balance commitment to work and commitment to family. Shakeshaft (1986) talks about the way in which "the very nature of schooling is shaped in a male image" (p. 500). Among other things, she points to the ways in which schools support a male-oriented ideology of competition. Shakeshaft contrasts this with a female ideology of cooperation which, she says, is not ". . .highly valued nor is it the basis of many teaching and learning strategies in schools" (p. 500).

Historically "profession" has been a male-dominated concept based on the medical model (Biklen, 1988). In this tradition, the more professional a career, the more abstract and objective it is, the more distance it maintains from its clientele, and the more it is hierarchically authoritarian. The more of these attributes that the occupant of a job role possesses, the more "professional" that person has become and the more status that person is accorded. Many of the recent efforts of the reform movement to enhance the status of teaching have, in fact, emphasized those aspects of teaching that are most male-identified: the cognitive, intellectual, and technical aspects of teaching to the exclusion of the affective, intuitive, and artistic aspects of teaching (Comer, 1988).

Female-Identified Teachers

The high-involvement teacher could be described as female in her perception of continuity and interrelatedness in her teaching. Often the boundaries between home and school, parent and teacher, are softened or erased. Monica remarks: "I might say to a parent, 'I know firsthand it's not easy as a parent. We love our kids so much and it hurts and we want to help our children.' . . . I'm talking to them on the level of a parent, as well as a teacher."

Patty adds: "They want you to know how special their child is. A child is an extension of them. And there's no other way for them to look at it. You know, they are so emotionally involved and rightly so. How else are we supposed to be with an eight-year-old?"

And when Fran says, "The mother and I got the student organized and we established this daily routine," she makes no attempt to specify whose problem this was or where the responsibility belongs. The "high involver" relates to a child in a complex, multidimensional way. Fran, in talking about the value of firsthand information from parents, says, "It helps, you know, to get a total picture of what's going on."

The "high involvers" ' approach to parent involvement places emphasis on the feminine values of relationship between teacher and parent rather than on the parameters that govern parent involvement for "low involvers." For these teachers, mutuality and honesty are important components of their interactions with parents. Monica says that "I would like [parents] to tell me when they see the child is having trouble, and is maybe afraid of me, or afraid of asking me for help. I know my feelings won't be hurt. I'd like to know that. I would like them to be honest with me."

Sally expresses similar feelings:

[I like to know] if they sleep at night. If parents read to the kids. Do they go to the library? Do they travel? If they like school. If they ever say, "No, I don't want to come to school." If they talk about what they do in school. If they're satisfied with their learning. The kids themselves. You know, what's their opinion. Do the kids say anything about what they learned or do they say, "I'm not learning anything."

For the "high involver," the mother is not simply a parent but also a woman, a member of the community, maybe a divorcee, perhaps a person with common interests and experiences. When a parent comes into the classroom, she is not simply fulfilling a role as a volunteer, but she too is a person with thoughts, ideas, and feelings. Sally, for example, worries about what it must be like for a mother to be in the classroom when her child is being reprimanded. To the "high involver," the parent is not just a vehicle to enable her to fulfill her teaching goals, but another human being working side by side with the teacher: Patty remembers that she and the parents of a child were helping him "and he never felt put down, and he never felt punished. But he was constantly being guided. Nobody was letting him slip through their fingers."

In addition to more often making positive statements about parents, high-involvement teachers also were more likely to draw parallels between the mothers' feelings and experiences and their own. Fran says: "I can understand it because I've been divorced myself. I feel—I know that—I mean I can understand their—how upset [parents] are. That's a terribly hard time to go through."

Karen adds:

I think it's finding something in common. People like what you're doing, they're more apt to help you out. I think they like just the way that you deal with them, and they deal with you in the same way. I don't know how to explain. it, but there are people you hit it off with. And you meet people, and you talk a common language and there's no façade, and there's no ulterior motive—other than what's best for the kid. They see that you're concerned. It's genuine. And they like you!

Hand in hand with the interweaving of mothering and teaching is an empathetic regard for the parents. Fran comments: "I know it's difficult to work with your own child. I understand that myself. I know it's true. And particularly for teachers." Sally also understands that parents can be too tired to help their children with homework: "If you work all day long you're sometimes too tired to spend it with the kids." Patty epitomizes this feeling when she says, "As I look back over my career I think that's one of my biggest strengths. I *know* how important children are to their parents."

High-involvement teachers hold a view of their work that values the role of the teacher, but, in its child-centeredness, also acknowledges the significance of out-of-school experiences in a child's life. In order to do the work necessary to achieve their goals, high-involvement teachers rely on the multiple relationships that both they and the child bring into the classroom. High-involvement teachers remain connected to the homes of the children and to the personal, the emotional, and the spontaneous aspects of themselves, despite the fact that such qualities continue to be associated with lowered professional status (Freedman, 1989).

Karen is particularly interesting to me in her empathy with parents. She is single and has no children and is, therefore, the only one of the high-involvement teachers who is not herself a mother. But Karen grew up in a large family with which she continues to maintain steady contact. Karen says she spends a great deal of time "mothering" her nieces, nephews, and godchildren. And Karen herself infers a causal relationship between mothering and being a good teacher. About a colleague she says:

> I do think that some of the teachers in the building are scared of parent contact. There was one instance last year [when] the teacher said, "What are you doing?" I was on the phone. And I said, "Well, I'm talking to parents." And she says, "Well, I don't think that's right because if you're having a problem at school, you should deal with it at school. And as a parent, I would see that as a sign of incompetence." . . .She was a single girl. She wasn't a parent too, so that might have made a difference.

When I asked Karen about her description of her colleague, she said:

> She didn't have any nieces or nephews. She was insecure and yet very self-centered. . . . I think I looked at her circumstances maybe a little bit closer and tried to project what I thought part of the problem was. I think part of the problem was that most teachers like kids. . . . I said *most*. . . . I hope I have kids someday. I know I have nieces and nephews and talk about them a lot. We have a close family. I see them frequently. . . . So she didn't have this. Maybe I just don't think of myself as single. Maybe I don't look at myself as a nonparent. But I just feel very close to [my nieces and nephews] and see them a lot. I don't think she had as much personal time with them away from school— kids that age.

Karen is talking about and affirming the care-giving, nurturing component of teaching and links it to parenting when she says, "I just don't think of myself as a nonparent."

But for Karen the direction of the relationship between mothering and teaching is not always the same. Although at some points Karen implies that not being a mother can have a negative influence on teachers, about herself she seems to feel the opposite. In her case she hypothesizes that, as the youngest in a family of five, not having enough opportunities to take care of younger siblings left her hungry for interactions with children, and thereby motivated her to become a teacher. Furthermore, she describes herself as a teacher who gets emotionally involved with her students. In comparing herself with the teacher who supervised her as a student, Karen says she purposefully emulated the experienced teacher in most ways. But Karen goes on:

> I think she stood back a little from the kids, which would be good, but I wanted to get a little closer. And I think she might have stood back a bit more because she maybe had— we get back to this—had children of her own. And so it was much more of a, I suppose, teacher-pupil relationship should be ideally. But I like to get in there and get my hands dirty. I roll up my sleeves. It's more of a—it's not draining me to touch the kids and talk to them and put my arm around them and things like that. Where she was maybe a little more standoffish and the kids didn't approach her.

Again Karen says she wants to "get closer" and "to touch the kids." She also worries that this is not quite the way a "teacher-pupil" relationship should be ideally. When she does so she alludes to the dichotomy that has been created between love and labor in popular definitions of professionalism.

When the high-involvement teachers talk about their roles, they mention the unique contributions that they make by virtue of their knowledge of children in classrooms. Their priorities lie in doing the job well, which includes the ability to inform and be informed by parents. Parent involvement allows them to open the system to input and negotiation, thereby also allowing both them and the parents to fulfill their responsibilities by responding to the needs of the child. Because the educative needs of the child are seen as broad and far-reaching, the power and control over the education of the child is seen as appropriately belonging to an array of involved adults.

"High involvers" have constructed a vision of teaching that contradicts the detached, isolated view often held up as a professional goal. "High involvers," with their focus on the affective, child- and family-centered aspects of teaching, have kept what can be considered female qualities alive in their work, despite the fact that these qualities are devalued in more conventional definitions of profession (Biklen, 1988).

Male-Identified Teachers

For low-involvement teachers, adopting a traditional male-oriented definition of teaching means basing their feelings of accomplishment as professionals on autonomy, on doing the work themselves, rather than collaborating with others. They value independence and self-reliance in their students and in themselves. Barb says: "I make school important and I make school serious. I take my job seriously and I'll tell them [the kids] that, and I expect them to. And if they do, they'll be successful students because they'll learn more."

Some low-involvement teachers implied that they felt the necessity for assuming sole responsibility because others (parents, community, colleagues) would not maintain the appropriate standards. Nina, for example, is critical in describing the younger generation of teachers as "a little looser, a little freer with a lot of things. They would go along with a lot more things than the older teachers would . . . with parents." Katia simply did not see value in what parents might have to say to teachers: "I don't feel like I see some of these parents real often. But I don't feel a need for it, and I don't feel I have the time for it."

Sometimes low-involvement teachers felt they would rather focus their attention on their own teaching instead of relying on parents or aides who were "undependable" or "inconsistent," or who did not know as much as they about their students. Katia says, "I feel I'd rather just be teaching myself than to have mothers in there helping."

"Low involvers" also portray their interactions with parents as ideally flowing one way, with the parents supporting their work with the student. For Lisa, parent involvement is "the willingness to cooperate in whatever way I might feel . . . that if I needed some help from them that they would give it, or that they would be willing to listen to me." Betty adds: "To me a complete education is a full circle. . . .And so, a full circle is for the family to cooperate with the teacher, with the child in the center of this in agreement with both entities."

Rather than looking for, or at least remaining open to, shared experiences and common ground, "low involvers" intentionally maintain a distance from parents. Relationships are limited, one way, top down. For Betty, this reflects a view of low-involvement teachers as dissimilar to parents: "I don't think they've had the kinds of responsibilities or the values that I do. And I think we've probably raised our children differently. No, I don't think [they and] I have a lot in common."

Although some low-involvement teachers bring their beliefs about parenting into their teaching, rather than using their beliefs and experiences with mothering as a basis for an empathic identification with parents, low-involvement teachers tend to use them as a standard against which to make critical comparisons. In doing so they establish a barrier between school and home. Rather than describing interactions with parents as flowing two ways, the low-involvement teachers deal with parents hierarchically, as though the parents were not as smart, not as moral, not as worthwhile. Both Nina, a single parent with no children, and Barb, a mother of two, emphasize their values and beliefs concerning good parenting. Both find the parents of their students lacking in this regard. Nina:

> The parent should take an interest in the child's work at school and be involved with the child at home, either working with things that the child is having problems with— correcting things that they've done at school. To me this is the parent taking an interest in the child and the child knows that the parent is interested and is very much aware that the parent is going to be checking on things. It is a much closer relationship between the parent and the child and they get to know each other. And it gives the parent time to be with the child. Because so many of the parents do not bother to take any time with the child or children. They don't bother.

Barb concurs:

> I find that many of the children in this community, maybe everywhere, are quite dependent. . . . I don't approve of that because I don't think this is what makes for good life skills. I raised three children of my own. I taught for most all of those years, I did. . . . This is my twenty-ninth year of teaching—this with three children. I asked them, I said, "What do you think about mother having worked?" And they said, "Mother, the reason we're self-reliant today is because you made us. It was important and necessary."

Barb is unique to the low-involvement teachers in her constant use of mothering images in her discussion of teaching. Unlike the high-involvement teachers, however, her strong identification *as* a mother was not accompanied by an identification or empathy *with* the mothers of her students. Instead, Barb says she has little in common with these mothers because "we've probably raised our children differently." Barb's attitude toward most mothers is patronizing. For example, Barb discusses Open House, the point at which she talks at length to the parents about what her goals and expectations are for the upcoming year. Sandwiched between statements about how cooperative parents are, she provides a tidy depiction of parents:

> They feel our goals are good. This I describe for parents at Open House. This much goes over the head while they're looking to see whether their slip is showing—I don't know

what they're doing! But whatever—wishing they were home watching television. I don't know. But I explain this, hopefully.

In this description Barb paints a picture of herself, the teacher, patiently, hopefully explaining the goals to parents who, like children, are so busy worrying about their "slip" or "watching television" that her words go "over the head."

The attitude with which Barb approaches not only her students but also their parents is one that leaves no room for question or challenge, much less collaboration. On several occasions she responded to questions on how accepting parents are of her decisions by saying things like, "I'm not a person people try to tell how to teach," "They usually back down," "I've never had anybody dare [complain]," and "I think they're afraid of me."

"Low involvers" may also keep parents distant by making them the last recourse when there is a problem. In addition to being likely to contact parents for a more limited type of problem, and to dealing with them in a more constrained way, these teachers often made the contact to parents after having consulted with other people within the school. They then reached out to parents, either to inform them of what was occurring or at the suggestion of their principal. In doing so, they once again kept parents at the periphery of the problem. Nina recalls:

> We all felt that this boy was very capable and he was just kind of sliding down, and we all wanted to work together. And we brought the child in and sat him down with all of us and the guidance counselor, and we discussed the problems he was having, and he came up with certain things too, himself. His parents were phoned and told that there was something that was going to be happening, and he was going to be confronted by the teachers. [The mother] wanted to wangle out of it and not let the kid do it.

While high-involvement teachers convey a sense of parent and teacher as reciprocally interested in one another, for "low involvers" contacts with parents are serious occasions that require careful planning and preparation on the part of the teacher. Perhaps that's part of the reason that Katia advocates involving parents only "if you feel comfortable," while Nina says that parent involvement should be "up to your discretion."

Furthermore, to the "low involver," there is a superior status that rightfully belongs to teaching—a sense of entitlement that the "low involvers" often convey when they talk about teaching: entitlement to respect, trust, and irreproachability. When mothers "dare" to question the teachers' authority, the teachers are unequivocal in their anger, implying that they have lost something in the process of losing power or control over their students. Nina continues:

> It's like any kind of relationship. Like take the medical field, with doctors. They say they should not have anything to do with their patients. Say government work, not having anything to do with people at one level that are at another level. I think there can be a lot of problems caused by having a closeness to parents in that they can suddenly turn on you and really do you in. . . . It's a lot easier to support the professional role if you maintain distance. And I think you gain perhaps a bit more respect in the community too.

For the low-involvement teachers, being a professional means being beyond approach in relation to parents. These teachers have a sharply delineated, central place for themselves in the educational enterprise. They are holding back and fending off the intruders while working valiantly to instill responsibility in their young charges. In the end, it is they, the professionals, who should control education.

The manner in which these teachers define their roles has implications for the way in which they define their relationships with parents. For the high-involvement teachers, the definition of teacher includes a morality of response and care that includes provisions for interacting with others who can and do have influence on a child. But for "high involvers" there is still room for autonomy—autonomy within the community of people who care about and know the child. For low-involvement teachers, however, being a professional means relying on an ethic of rights and responsibilities that places the teacher in a position of authority in relation to parents, and ensures an autonomy based on isolation and distance.

Teaching in Patriarchy

When a teacher's own uncertain sense of efficacy is coupled with the low regard with which any work considered to be female (such as mothering and teaching) is held by virtually all societies (Mead, 1953) a particularly painful combination may result. As Lightfoot (1975) says:

> Even though our idealized vision of the teacher demands the impossible, asks that she be superwoman, mother earth, mind reader, and soothsayer, the teacher's real-life status in the social and occupational hierarchy is dramatically low. There is a great contrast between the great expectations of our idealized images and the negative qualities of the teacher's real experience. (p. 116)

This combination is likely to be exacerbated if, as is likely in the case of these low-involvement teachers, a woman enters teaching with idealized expectations of what the profession has to offer, both to her and to the world. A teacher in such a position may attempt to cope with the realities of her work as a teacher by minimizing her exposure to contradictory elements. She may, in fact, do just what the low-involvement teachers I talked to seem to do: (1) protect herself from negative input from mothers; (2) attempt to maintain her idealized self-image as a teacher by elevating her importance to the child; and (3) repress connections between home and school in order to bolster a particular conception of professionalism for teachers.

Protecting, elevating, and repressing all have in common a distancing and detachment from relationships that have been subordinated to rights, rules, and responsibility. Both popular and academic literature have addressed the issue of the pressure exerted on women to distance themselves from their female tendencies and to adopt male perspectives in order to "get ahead' and be valued in the professional world. Lightfoot (1975) says: "It is evident that the womanly qualities linked with teaching are not only of low status in the literature, but they are also considered to be nonprofessional and lacking in maturity and humanity" (p. 118). Lightfoot wonders whether the tensions between mothering and working may not "lead to teachers having to magnify their separateness in order not to succumb to their biological, female tendencies to be mothers" (1978, p. 69).

Perhaps in their attempts to bolster their self-esteem and to justify and earn the superior status that they so ardently seek, low-involvement teachers *disassociate* themselves from connections to the female. One way they might do so is by adopting the images of the sex that is associated with status and strength, and embodies the popular ideal. Indeed, not only do low-involvement teachers show signs of having incorporated and integrated male perspectives into their vision of what it means to be a teacher, but in addition, there are signs that they do emphasize the split between mothering and teaching.

The dichotomy that "low involvers" set up between themselves and their students' mothers extends even beyond the typical role of classroom teacher to encompass the teacher-as-mother. The low-involvement teacher creates a paradox in which she, on the one hand, separates and alienates school and home, while at the same time attempts to fold the roles of teacher and mother into one, with the one being this penultimate teacher-mother. But perhaps the teacher-mother is not the paradox it at first appears to be. It is startling to see the low-involvement teacher reflected in Grumet's 1988 description of early common school teachers:

> Fleeing the isolation of households which were, following industrialization, no longer vital, productive units, young women flooded into the common schools where they promoted Horace Mann's vision of a national character. The authority and morality of the common school would supplant the slack and unpredictable parenting provided by the immigrant and agrarian mothers and fathers trying to make a place in the cities for their families. The new school marms were expected to *model the rationalized maternal ethos* of Catherine Beecher, whose arguments supporting the education of women and their employment as teachers were *based on an assertion of their spiritual purity and moral superiority*. These arguments made them prime candidates to promote a curriculum devoted to inculcating obedience and social cohesion, an ability to break children to the yoke, so gently that they would not balk under its weight. (emphasis added) (p. 9)

The elevated isolation of the low-involvement teacher carries through into her perception of her relationship to the community as a whole. Even while stating that she is a member of the community in which she teaches, the "low involver" sees herself distinctly different in values from other community members. Of course, the differences that exist favor her, the "low involver." She is, in contrast to the parents, not materialistic or "spoiled" like they are. She is an idealistic island of traditional values and life style within a community of modern-day philistines.

The high-involvement teachers, who perhaps went into teaching because they were aware of the centrality of care giving—women's work—in their lives, seem to have remained in touch with their female selves. Furthermore, they have found ways to infuse their work with affect—the personal, the spontaneous, the instinctual, the private and therefore the secretive—through ties to home and family.

AFFAIRS OF THE HEART

Others who have written in hopes of improving parent-teacher relationships have looked to teacher education in order to help teachers communicate or to learn techniques for dealing with parents. The teachers in this study suggest that differences between teachers are not so much differences in skills or techniques, but are more the result of divergent purposes and visions of what it means to be a "professional" teacher.

One way to categorize these differences is through gender-based categories. Although these categories, like all categories, are overly simple, they can help us look beyond the classrooms and schools of individual teachers. They can help us reflect upon the ways gender-based definitions of teaching influence the way a teacher defines her profession and her use of parent involvement, and the possibilities for altering and enhancing parent-teacher relationships.

In educational reform movements that have aimed to raise the relative attractiveness of the profession by increasing the status of teaching, there has been a strong tendency to emphasize the male-identified approach to professionalization. Reform efforts have been geared toward emulating the medical model: to envision teachers as "transformative intellectuals" while finding someone else to do the "dirty work" (Biklen, 1988) of teaching, to exclude outsiders from educational decisions, and to add hierarchical levels to the profession. As Biklen points out, the reform reports often address "problems" in teaching that are a result of women's ties to family life and the career path that is particular to women. When they do, the reports portray women's careers through a deficit model.

What has been lacking in these discussions is a valuing of those things characteristically associated with females, including nurturing, intuition, connectedness, caring, and the personal. Comer (1988) maintains that there is significant overlap between parenting and good teaching, while Epstein (1986) describes schoollike homes and homelike schools. Biklen asks why, instead of utilizing a male-identified medical model as a basis for improving teaching, female-identified experiences such as "mothering," cooperation, integration, and balance cannot be used.

An awareness of these predispositions in preservice teacher education programs is a starting place. Unless female-identified values, models, and systems can be brought into teacher education programs, preservice teachers will continue to adopt idealized versions of teaching that lead them to enact roles cut off from the many connections and complexities that could play a part, both for them and for their students.

An alternative for preservice teachers would be an approach that acknowledges the richness and complexity of schooling—for teachers, parents, and students. An inquiry-oriented approach to teacher education (Tom, 1985; Ayers, 1988), which might include autobiographical, critical, and reflective elements, could enable preservice teachers to probe the connection between self and work in much the same manner as other helping professionals, such as psychologists and social workers do. Utilizing an approach that moves students from the psychological (self) to the logical (others) in teacher education programs would support women in trusting their own perceptions, and feeling safe in expressing them, rather than adopting dominant, male-oriented definitions. It could also encourage preservice teachers to examine the assumptions with which they are entering teaching, and to explore contextual forces that impinge on those assumptions.

Preservice teachers might also benefit by exploring their motivations for choosing teaching, along with some honest discussion with people who are already immersed in the educational system (namely, parents, teachers, and even students) on how accurate their expectations of teaching are. It may be, in fact, that in the course of such discussions teacher candidates may discover that what they desire from their work can best be obtained in professions other than teaching.

Teacher education programs should also demonstrate a valuing of aspects of a female-oriented model such as collaboration, and the ways in which one can be an autonomous, thinking professional within an educational community that values all participants. Rather than downplaying or minimizing the love of children and caregiving aspects of teaching that often draw women to the profession in the first place, programs could emphasize the "affairs of the heart" that are so central to teaching. Rather than adopting a pathological perspective on the overlap between mothering and teaching, teacher education programs could seek to capitalize upon and respond to the dialogue that takes place within teacher-mothers.

PARTING GLANCES

I wonder if my life has been one long serendipitous accident, or whether my desire for connectedness is so strong as to continuously influence the decisions that I make. Once more I am teaching, this time adults in a teacher education program. My sons are now young adults (or so they would like me to believe), nineteen and sixteen years old. Again I feel lucky because I can learn from my students and my sons about the "other half" of my life. Sean complains about his physics teacher who responds impatiently to student inquiries, and I guiltily recall my own impatience at a student's question about a seemingly obvious piece of information. I try to explain my perspective, as a teacher, to this son of mine who is also someone's student, and he, in turn, tells me what it feels like to take risks and ask questions in a classroom.

The nine teachers who gave form to this study have, in the truest sense, enabled me to re-search the connections in my own life. What I see in that search is that the mother voice within me has always been the wellspring from which my teaching has flowed, and that teaching has, in turn, seeped back into and fed that source. Like the teachers who form rich relationships with parents, I see teaching as both rich and complicated and therefore turn to a variety of sources in establishing the kind of learning environment that I believe in. Intermingled with language arts, science, and social studies in my teacher education curriculum are themes of integration, collaboration, and the personal.

Moving from elementary teacher to university teacher, I have found it increasingly difficult to stay loyal to my female self. At times I become so removed from the mother in me that she can find voice only in dream sequences that are a swirl of students tucked into the warmth of a Learning Space classroom and babies at breast. If elementary classrooms are unfriendly to the personal, the emotional, the spontaneous, and the instinctual, then university classrooms are even more so. And so I rely once more on connections—to the women's community, to friends and family, to colleagues who see the world as I do—and encourage my students to do the same.

REFERENCES

Ayers, W. (1988). Fact or fancy: The knowledge base quest in teacher education. *Journal of Teacher Education*, *39*(5): 24–29.

Bastian, A., Fruchter, N., Gittell, M., Greer, G., and Haskins, K. (1985). Choosing equality: The case for democratic schooling. *Social Policy*, *15*: 34–51.

Biklen, S. K. (1982). *Autonomy in the lives of women elementary schoolteachers*. ERIC Document Reproduction Service No. ED 215 964.

Biklen, S. K. (1986). "I have always worked": Elementary schoolteaching as a career. *Phi Delta Kappan*, *67*(7): 504–508.

Biklen, S. K. (April, 1988). *Is there a feminist view of career and what are its implications for educational reform?* Paper presented at the Annual Meeting of the American Educational Research Association. New Orleans.

Bronfenbrenner, U. (1986). Alienation: The four worlds of childhood. *Phi Delta Kappan*, *67*(6): 430–436.

deCastillejo, I. C. (1973). *Knowing women*. New York: Harper and Row.

Comer, J. P. (1986). Parent participation in the schools. *Phi Delta Kappan*, *67*(6): 442–446.

Comer, J. P. (1988). Is "parenting" essential to good teaching? *Today's Education*, National Education Association, *1*: 34–40.

Epstein, J. L. (1986). *Toward an integrated theory of school and family connections* (Report No. 3). Baltimore, MD: Johns Hopkins University, Center for Social Organization of Schools.

Fantini, M. D. (1985). Stages of linking school and nonschool learning environments. In M. D. Fantini and R. L. Sinclair, (Eds.) *Eighty-fourth yearbook of the National Society for The Study of Education—Part I: Education in school and nonschool settings*. Chicago: University of Chicago Press, pp. 46–63.

Gilligan, C. (1982). *In a different voice: Psychological theory and women's development*. Cambridge, MA: Harvard University Press.

Grumet, M. R. (1988). *Bitter milk: Women and teaching*. Amherst: University of Massachusetts Press, pp. 164–182.

Hoffman, N. (1981). *Women's true profession: Voices from the history of teaching*. Old Westbury, NY: Feminist Press.

Lightfoot, S. L. (1975). Sociology of education: Perspectives on women. In M. Millman and R. Moss-Kanter (Eds.), *Another voice*. New York: Anchor Books, pp. 106–143.

Lightfoot, S. L. (1978). *Worlds apart: Relationships between families and schools*. New York: Basic Books.

Mead, M. (1953). The contemporary American family as an anthropologist sees it. In J. Landis (Ed.), *Readings in marriage and the family*, Englewood Cliffs, NJ: Prentice-Hall.

Miller, Jean Baker (1976). *Toward a new psychology of women*. Boston: Beacon.

Schubert, W. H. (1981). Knowledge about out-of-school curriculum. *The Educational Forum*, *45*(1): 185–198.

Schubert, W. H. (1986). *Curriculum: Perspective, paradigm, and possibility*. New York: Macmillan.

Shakeshaft, C. (1986). A gender at risk. *Phi Delta Kappan*, *67*(7): 499–503.

Tom, A. (1985). Inquiring into inquiry-oriented teacher education. *Journal of Teacher Education*, *36*(5): 35–44.

PART III

Learning from Teacher Lore

CHAPTER 8

Extending the Dialogue:
Resources for Expanding
the Natural History of Teaching

William Ayers

When I began teaching in 1965, I consumed all the teacher autobiographies I could find. I was deeply influenced in my thinking and practice by the stories of Sylvia Ashton-Warner, Herb Kohl, John Holt, Jonathan Kozol, and Paul Goodman. Each story filled me with practical insights, and each described a process I was experiencing personally: teaching as an act of opposition to the given world, to much of the machinery of schooling. Sylvia Ashton-Warner's innovative approach to teaching reading to Maori children in New Zealand, for example, was in part a conscious resistance to the oppressive colonial British system of education. Herb Kohl's open classroom, his laboratory for learning for thirty-six Harlem children, was also a struggle against the monumental indifference of the school system to the lives of these particular kids. And so on. Each story became for me a source of nourishment, air, life itself, as I struggled in my own classroom to interpret critically and to invent anew. Each story strengthened my own attempts to choose for children, to choose for families—to resist and even to rebel.

James Herndon's autobiography is the account of one rebel teacher. Herndon's story is in turn funny, gripping, and vivid. When he is fired at the end of his first year, the principal tries to explain why the dismissal is necessary. The principal knows that Herndon works hard and cares deeply, that he has character, intelligence, and dedication. The problem, it seems, centers around opposing ideas of order and control:

> This is a problem school, I do remember his saying. His job, and the job of the teachers, was to make it into something that was no longer a problem school. He was certain that was possible. It is the belief in this goal that counts, he told me. . . . No one is perfect, so a teacher may lose control once, twice, a hundred

times, but if he believes in that control himself, that order, he will eventually win through. (p. 173)

Herndon's big sin, by all accounts, is that he doesn't seem to understand the way things are supposed to be run. He does not begin lessons on time, for example, nor does he inculcate good study habits. There is too much discussion of irrelevant (unofficial) issues, and there is too much noise and motion. He may see some pattern and method in the class, he may perceive some orderly intent in the classroom confusion, but the principal remains unimpressed. Even the kids can defend every convention, rule, and commonplace—no matter how idiotic—explaining that each is justified simply as "the way it spozed to be."

Outstanding teaching can begin with a genuine regard for and understanding of the learner, a reaching out to students with care and respect, avoiding the negative judgments and implied superiority that characterize too much of teaching and that lead inevitably to failure. One teacher who describes learning this lesson in vivid detail is Eliot Wigginton (1985). His account of his first year teaching high school in Rabun Gap, Georgia, is painfully familiar:

> I had never been in a situation before where I was so completely confused by all that was going on around me. . . . It was a through-the-looking-glass world where the friendlier I was . . . the more liberties the students took and the harder it became to accomplish anything . . . I'd crack down . . . and the mood would turn sullen and resentful and no sharing and learning would take place. It was impossible. I began to regard them collectively as the enemy and I became the prisoner. . . . (p. 31)

On one particularly gloomy morning Wigginton confessed his disappointment to his students, and admitted the obvious: His classes were a failure both for him and for them. He asked his students what they thought they should do together, not in order to accomplish *his* goals, but simply to make it through the year. The honesty of the question, perhaps, or the unexpectedness of it broke the pattern of failure, and an initially hesitant, awkward conversation began.

Wigginton nurtured the dialogue, and he let it guide him in curriculum decisions and the style of his teaching. The conversation grew, springing off project ideas, readings, and assignments along the way. He asked students to write a composition, for example, describing positive and negative school experiences that stood out in their minds. The student responses awakened his own memories, and his personal list of positive experiences included times when visitors from the outside world brought their interests and projects into the classroom, times when students were given real responsibility and work to do, and times when their efforts were projected to an audience beyond the class itself.

One day a student—"one of my sixth-period losers"—said he'd be out of class for four days because he was going into the woods to collect "sang" for a "sang bed." Secretly relieved that he would have a break from this student, Wigginton asked as an afterthought, "What's sang?" Over the next several days he learned more than he thought there was to know about ginseng, how to grow and cultivate and market it, about the biology of it and the economics of it. The experience also transformed his relationship with the "sixth-period loser" into one of mutual respect and under-standing. He was seeing this student as he had never seen him before. No longer merely a collection of bad behaviors and little intellectual promise, he was now connected to ginseng, and his concerns, experiences, intelligence, and know-how were suddenly less obscure.

Wigginton became the student of his students' lives as a step toward becoming their teacher. He began to think of teaching as a bridge-building activity, a process that spans from the intelligences and experiences of his students to other ways of thinking and knowing. He found that when their lives were treated with respect, students responded with respect, and when engaged in work that they thought to be of value, they treated it valuably. *Foxfire*, initially conceived as an extracurricular literary magazine, became the central classroom focus, a journal of culture and history, filled with students' projects and interests, primarily photographs, interviews, and essays on the lives and work of their own relatives and neighbors. It became the medium through which Wigginton challenged his students, and it became the vehicle in which they stretched themselves to learn things like grammar and composition as well. At its center *Foxfire* remains an affirmation of the students' heritage, and an active search for their own voices.

Vivian Gussin Paley is another teacher who documents the importance of teach-ing from the perspective of an empathetic regard for students. A schoolteacher for over thirty years, in the past ten years Paley has chronicled her own teaching in a series of books. Her vivid accounts of children at work and play are the result of her attentive eye, her relentless reflective mind, and her tape recorder with a single tape, her "disciplinarian," which forces her to transcribe and reconsider the talk and events of each day soon after they occur.

Paley understands the importance of fantasy play for young children, demon-strates the power of watching and listening to children with care and respect, and eloquently describes her own search for self-understanding as part of her larger quest for a common ground with children. In *Mollie Is Three* (1986) we hear the delightful sounds of three-year-old discourse. Paley's precise recording of what she sees and hears and her own reflective sense making combine to rescue the dialogue of the threes from adult judgment or dismissal. In Paley's account this talk is at bottom neither cute nor confused, although it can be both of these, but rather is an attempt to connect, construct, and make sense. What may look to a more casual observer like a chaotic, upside-down world is to Paley a genuine and exciting search. This perspec-tive is the source of a continuing challenge to her teaching.

When she flirts, for example, with applying a straightforward, technical solution to a messy, human problem, she steps back and rethinks the affair in larger terms.

Is something wrong with Christopher? The question is as unavoidable as it is nonproductive. The moment I decide his condition has a name, my vision becomes blurred and whatever he does or says will be prejudged. "This is the way children with his problem behave," I am bound to think. But of Mollie I say, "This is the way three-year-olds act." (p. 20)

Another time she attempts to teach her students a game:

"I have a game," I say at snack time. "Try to guess what animal I'm talking about. It flies around outside and does not fly into our classroom."

"A bird!"

"And it does not bother our blocks."

"A bird!" (p. 66)

When she invites the children to make up their own animal riddles, Mollie shouts, "A wolf! Mine goes fast as a wolf. It's a wolf." Barney says, "Mine goes down the side of a long nose called an elephant."

Again and again, as in most classrooms that are alive and breathing, lesson plans and curricular content are unraveled and left in a heap on the floor as children push past in pursuing their own purposes, dreams, and interests. After several hilarious and futile attempts to teach the riddle game, Paley gives up: "*My* games consistently miss the point of *their* games" (p. 68), she acknowledges.

There are, of course, more stories to read, more lives to consider as we pursue a growing understanding of what teaching is and might be. There are heroic teachers— not celebrities, but people of real and sustained accomplishment—almost everywhere. Teachers like Lucy Matos and Yvonne Smith in New York, Paddy O'Reilly, Alice Brent, and Sarah Cohen in Chicago, Bob Peterson and Rita Tenario in Milwaukee, Susan Kilbane in Seattle, and Jessica Howard in Vermont have each built a practice on a base of dialogue, respect, and efficacy. Each has found a way to do what any teacher can do now: validate the dignity and worth of students, build bridges of mutual respect and caring, and create curriculum that nurtures personal visions as well as collective achievement. These teachers' stories are unwritten, and so they are mainly a source of knowledge and inspiration locally. But teachers like them can be sought out, observed, and interviewed. They, too, contribute to an enlarged sense of what teaching can become.

Of course some will argue that the accomplishments of these teachers are not generalizable to others, that they are the result of extraordinary personalities and superhuman efforts. This, it seems to me, begs the question. Before there were published autobiographies, before there were awards or recognition, before anyone came to visit, there was, in every case, a confused and sometimes despairing teacher alone in a classroom. What each teacher did differs in detail, but follows an essential rhythm of empowerment. Each resisted the temptation to sink into the conventional, becoming merely a clerk in a system. In this sense each was a resistant teacher, perhaps a subversive teacher. Each looked unblinkingly at students as people with intentions, needs, hopes, dreams, aspirations, and agendas, students as whole human beings, and each struggled to build bridges of meaning from the knowledge and experiences of each to broader ways of thinking and knowing. Each conceived of teaching as an improvisation of judgment and action played in an arena as mysterious as it is familiar. Each goes on learning and teaching and living with uncertainty but also with a sense of purposeful commitment. What else can they do?

NETWORKS OF TEACHERS

There are a number of formal and informal networks of teachers striving to develop a more learner-centered practice. Following are **nine** centers readers may find worth-while.

Among Teachers
JCTD Publishing Group
252 Bloor Street West
Suite 10-138
Toronto, Ontario
Canada M5S 1V6
416-923-6641 ext. 2630

Center for Collaborative Education
1573 Madison Ave.
New York, NY 10029
212-860-5876

Hands On
Foxfire Fund
Rabun Gap, GA 30568
404-746-5319

The Institute for Democracy in
Education
1241 McCracken Hall
Ohio University
Athens, OH 45701-2979

The Network of Progressive Educators
P.O. Box 6028
Evanston, IL 60204

North Dakota Study Group
Center for Teaching and Learning
University of North Dakota
Grand Forks, ND 58201

Rethinking Schools
P.O. Box 93371
Milwaukee, WI 53202
414-546-5506

The Workshop Center
City College of New York
North Academic Center 4-220
New York, NY 10031
212-690-4162

Herb and Judy Kohl
40561 Eureka Hill Rd.
Pt. Arena, CA 95468
707-882-2615

REFERENCES

Herndon, J. (1969). *The way it spozed to be*. New York: Bantam Books.
Paley, V. G. (1986). *Mollie is three*. Chicago: University of Chicago Press.
Wigginton, E. (1986). *Sometimes a shining moment*. Garden City, NY: Anchor Books.

CHAPTER 9

Readings as Resources
for Teacher Lore

William H. Schubert

Rather than simply write a bibliography (which may be obtained from chapter citations), and rather than providing an annotated bibliography, I have opted for the less
formal presentation of an essay about writings that relate to teacher lore. That seems
more in harmony with the autobiographical character of the book. So, I will be a
teacher talking briefly with you about readings that have had an impact on the idea of
teacher lore as I have tried to develop it here. The sharing of books is, itself, a form
of teacher lore worth promoting.

I still recall sitting glued to a living room chair as I read Herb Kohl's *36
Children* (New York: Signet, 1968) as an elementary school teacher in suburbia. I
profited from vicarious experience with Kohl's inner-city students. I was especially
impressed by his tales of having students write books about their own experiences. I
tried it with my own students and liked the results. It helped me know them better
and learn from their lives; one thing I learned was that suburban students don't fit the
TV family show stereotype. They have many different backgrounds, a rich variety. I
have followed Kohl's writing, more than twenty books from his experiences in teaching, over the years, and consider his *Growing Minds: On Becoming a Teacher* (New
York: Harper, 1984) to be one of the best introductions to teaching.

John Holt is another. I recall being enthralled with *How Children Fail* (New
York: Delta, 1964), and through it how Holt taught me to empathize with children
who did not do well in school-expected requirements. I saw clearly that blaming the
child was blaming the victim, and that worthwhile reform was to overcome adult
oppression of children. His other books also had an influential impact on my outlook,
particularly one of his last books, *Teach Your Own* (New York: Dell, 1981), which
inspired my wife (Ann Lopez) and myself to take charge of the education of our own

young children and use society's institutions (including school) as resources to that process.

The work of Holt and Kohl illustrates a genre of literature on education that has had great appeal to teachers—namely, the writing of first-person accounts by teachers. Clearly, these have been the most popular of writings on education—the only ones, in fact, that seem to make it out of specialized, intellectual bookstores and into regular bookstores. Some intellectuals would see this as evidence of the low-calibre character of these books, but I think the fact that teachers have chosen them indicates that they speak to teachers' needs and interests. They are clearly a form of teacher lore. From early writings such as Edward Eggleston's *The Hoosier School Master* (New York: Hill & Wang, 1957; orig. pub. 1871) to A. S. Neill's *Summerhill* (New York: Hart, 1960) and Sylvia Ashton-Warner's *Teacher* (New York: Simon & Schuster, 1963) in the 1960s, to the more recent accounts of such teachers as Eliot Wigginton, *Sometimes a Shining Moment* (Garden City, NY: Anchor Books, 1986); Vivian Gussin Paley, *Boys and Girls* (Chicago: University of Chicago Press, 1984); James Nehring, *"Why do we gotta do this stuff Mr. Nehring?": Notes from a Teacher's Day in School* (New York: Fawcett Columbine, 1989); Ray Raphael, *The Teacher's Voice: A Sense of Who We Are* (Portsmouth, NH: Heinemann, 1985); and Stuart Palonsky, *900 Shows a Year: Looking at Teaching from the Teacher's Side of the Desk* (New York: Random House, 1986). Teachers turn to these sources for good reason. The lives of other teachers help them understand themselves better. They learn of other teachers' guiding ideas, of ways they dealt with problems, of their hopes and aspirations, and of concrete teaching approaches that they can add to their own repertoires.

A more scholarly set of sources can be found in the works of John Dewey. I see Dewey, a (some say *the*) major American philosopher, as a source of justification for engaging in teacher lore. Dewey says we learn from reflecting on experience; such reflection gives meaning and direction to our lives. As we encounter dilemmas (and life is a series of dilemmas), we shape them into problems so that they can be articulated. As we articulate them, make them public to significant others, we learn that others have experienced similar problems, and as we probe them more deeply we see that our dilemmas are part of the great human dilemmas about life, death, love, freedom, justice, goodness, beauty, contribution, and so on. When these topics emerge for educators, and they often do, they can gain strength and insight from other teachers, people from all walks of life, and from the great ideas in the great books, and even from research studies. I therefore suggest that the philosophically inclined turn to Dewey—*Democracy and Education* (New York: Macmillan, 1916); *Experience and Education* (New York: Macmillan, 1938); and his many other writings. Further, I suggest that the less philosophically inclined try to be more philosophically inclined and read these sources, too.

Books about memorable teachers are of considerable worth, too. Here, I highlight just three: William Ayers, *The Good Preschool Teacher* (New York: Teachers College Press, 1989); Joseph Epstein, Ed., *Masters: Portraits of Great Teachers* (New York: Basic Books, 1981); and Ken MacCrorie, *20 Teachers* (New York: Oxford University Press, 1984). Similarly, fictional accounts of teachers are important contributions; if the fictional is illuminating it matters little that it has not been lived. I think of the impact on my life and teaching of stories and film (biographic, based on fact, and fiction). I reflect on many Dickens' books and vivid portrayals of horrendous teachers and school situations that all too often creep into our experience today in subtle ways. I think of being riveted to the PBS film versions (film, theatrical, and book) of *Goodbye, Mr. Chips* (written by James Hilton in 1935), and to movies such as *Fame, Stand and Deliver, Educating Rita, Conrack, To Sir with Love,* and *Blackboard Jungle.* All are susceptible to criticism, of course, but all are inspiring and offer insights about teaching and being a teacher. I think, too, of great moments of learning in books and films and plays—how in these instances of conversion to a new way of thinking or being (Scrooge in *A Christmas Carol,* for example) I feel the power of education from story more fully than I can from discursive presentations.

Teachers are often good storytellers; they relate the essence of their experience, their best teacher lore, through anecdote rather than by trying to explain the essence directly. Story has always been a major means of passing on the understanding from earlier cultures over the centuries, from the storyteller around the prehistoric campfire to the revered elder figure in many so-called less developed cultures today to more highly developed ones (though, apart from technology, I contend that they are not more highly developed in significant ways). Perhaps, like it or not, television, movies, and popular music are our significant storytellers today. Despite negative comment, there is much to learn about ourselves, and ourselves as teachers, from television (I think of *The Wonder Years*), and movies *(The Breakfast Club* and *Pump Up the Volume*), and pop music (how it speaks to the inner questioning of children and youth). Stories are teachers and teachers convey their understanding by story. Robert Coles' book title, *The Call of Stories: Teaching and the Moral Imagination* (Boston: Houghton Mifflin, 1989), says it well. The stories of life that help teachers teach emerge from a deep human calling to cultivate the moral imagination that fashions the lives they lead. In a similar vein, Kieran Egan, in *Teaching as Story Telling* (Chicago: University of Chicago Press, 1986), calls for the reinstitution of stories as the basis of pedagogy—rather than the more dominant expanding horizons, logical, or chronological presentations of curricular content.

Speaking of curriculum, about which I have been deeply concerned since my elementary teaching days, I have found it ironic that teaching has so often been omitted from the writings on curriculum. As a teacher, I turned to curriculum writing because it was there that I found the deepest and most serious thought about what I considered the most important curriculum question: What is most worthwhile to know and experience? Or expressed somewhat less academically: How can I decide what to think, do, and be? This kind of questioning, for me, was the mainstay of my work as a teacher. It was not that I thought a once-and-for-all answer would come; rather, I wanted to keep these curricular questions alive—in myself, my colleagues, and my students. I am still convinced that the most important outcome of educational experience is to ask in new ways what it means to grow into a better human being, to make that a lifetime assignment or project, and to act on increasingly better answers to questions about the kinds of contributions that can be made to others, life generally, and the planet that is our context.

I was convinced that teachers played a big part in curriculum, understood as embedded in the foregoing questions. I thought, and still do, that teachers create the curriculum (even are the curriculum) as they reflect on such questions and imagine what to do next with students. As I began to pursue doctoral studies, however, I was astounded at the lack of mention given to teachers in curriculum books. Therefore, I resolved to do my small part and devote a doctoral dissertation to the study of how teachers imagine curriculum in light of their assumptions. I searched the literature, finding a few books that directly addressed the teacher's place the curriculum development, such as George Sharp, *Curriculum Development as the Reeducation of the Teacher* (New York: Teachers College Press, 1951); Joseph Lease, K. Frasure, and Mauritz Johnson, *The Teacher in Curriculum Making* (New York: Harper & Row, 1961); and Dale Brubaker, *The Teacher as a Decision Maker* (Dubuque, IA: William C. Brown, 1970). Just coming out at the time was the work of Joseph Schwab, *The Practical: A Language for Curriculum* (Washington, D.C.: National Education Association, 1970), which characterized curriculum as made up of four commonplaces—subject matter, milieu or environment, learner, and of greatest significance for our consideration of teacher lore, *teacher*. At about the same time, Lawrence Stenhouse, in his *Introduction to Curriculum Research and Development* (London: Heinemann, 1975), coined the phrase "teacher as researcher," which acknowledged the significance of teachers' systematic inquiry and reflection as viable knowledge.

My explorations took me to books that inspired teachers in earlier days; while these books did not indicate in the title that they were about curriculum, they did indeed reveal insight into questions that I considered curricular: Harry S. Broudy and John R. Palmer, *Exemplars of Teaching Method* (Chicago: Rand McNally, 1965), which insightfully examines the teaching of some of the great teachers throughout history (Socrates, Alcuin, Abelard, Ascham, Comenius, Pestalozzi, Froebel, Herbart, and Kilpatrick); Gilbert Highet's *The Art of Teaching* (New York: Vintage, 1950), in which he relies on exemplars such as Socrates, Plato, Aristotle, and Jesus, as well as those in everyday life such as parents, spouses, doctors, psychiatrists, advertisers, executives, clergy, and authors; Caroline Pratt's accounts of progressive teaching as founder of The City and Country School in New York City in 1914, in *I Learn from Children* (New York: Simon & Schuster, 1948); *Tolstoy on Education*, translated by Leo Wiener (Chicago: University of Chicago Press, 1967), which consists of essays by the renowned novelist interpreting his experientially derived philosophy and practices of teaching—containing more than a hint of progressive education that would not appear until the next century; *How Teachers Taught*, Larry Cuban's historical reconstruction of the ways teachers taught from 1890 to 1980 (New York: Longman, 1984); *The Emerging Self* by L. Thomas Hopkins (New York: Harper & Brothers, 1954), one of the too seldom remembered classics of the progressive era; *When Teachers Face Themselves*, a psychological talk with teachers about their ideas and feelings by Arthur T. Jersild (New York: Teachers College Press, 1955); Marie I. Rasey's *This Is Teaching* (New York: Harper & Brothers, 1950), a set of dramatic dialogues illustrating the progressive methods of Rasey, an exemplary teacher of students of education; Julia Weber Gordon's tale of experience in the one-room country school, *My Country School Diary* (New York: Dell, 1970, orig. pub. 1946); and William Van Til's autobiography of a career in teaching in many settings, *My Way of Looking at It* (Terre Haute, IN: Lake Lure Press, 1983). These are a sample of historical sources that help provide insight into the larger idea of teacher lore, beyond our project.

Sociology of education studies also help create broader perspective on the larger idea of teacher lore. For example, Willard Waller's *The Sociology of Teaching* (New York: John Wiley & Sons, 1932) and Dan C. Lortie's *Schoolteacher: A Sociological Study* (Chicago: University of Chicago Press, 1975) are classics in the field, as is Jacques Barzun's *Teacher in America* (New York: Atlantic-Little Brown, 1945), although Barzun writes from somewhat outside the field. A recent example is Martin Lawn and G. Grace, Eds., *Teachers: The Culture and Politics of Work* (London: Falmer, 1987).

In 1968 Philip W. Jackson published the now classic *Life in Classrooms* (New York: Holt, Rinehart, Winston). I well remember an address he gave based on the book to the Downers Grove teachers in the early 1970s. I was impressed in his presentation by what would become a basis for study of what is now known as the "hidden curriculum"—see Henry Giroux and David Purpel, Eds., *The Hidden Curriculum and Moral Education* (Berkeley, CA: McCutchan, 1982)—or the idea that teachers' mannerisms, institutional factors of schools, and societal structures subtly teach students a great deal. Among other observations from Jackson's perceptive look at classrooms, one can glean that children learn much from being in a crowd of agemates for a good part of the day, from living under conditions of power, authority, and hierarchy, and from incurring frequent evaluation that creates an image of their place in a "pecking order." Given this background, I was interested in again listening to Philip Jackson when opportunity arose; therefore, at the 1976 Annual Meeting of AERA (the American Educational Research Association) in San Francisco (having recently finished my Ph.D. and embarked on a career that involved teaching teachers about curriculum) I attended Jackson's critique of a session on research about teacher judgment, presented by Bruce Joyce and a team of researchers. I recall that Jackson was quite critical, noting that teaching was too busy and complicated an endeavor to expect judgment to be carried out in any reasonable way, especially during the course of action. Having taught and felt that I exercised reasonably good judgment for a decade, I was taken aback by his remarks. However, I did remember that in Jackson's *Life in Classrooms* (New York: Holt Rinehart and Winston, 1968), he noted John Dewey's admonition to learn about teaching by studying what gifted teachers do intuitively—see Dewey's *The Sources of a Science of Education* (New York: Liveright, 1929, pp. 10–12), and that he was critical of the possibility of doing this.

Despite the cautions of Jackson and others, the study of teacher judgment, thinking, reflection, beliefs, and so forth has continued to develop since the mid-1970s. In fact, Penelope Peterson, one of the graduate students on Bruce Joyce's AERA symposium (noted above) continued work in the area of teacher judgment and, in fact, joined with Christopher Clark to write a widely cited review of a research article entitled "Teachers' Thought Processes," in Merlin Wittrock, Ed., *Handbook of Research on Teaching* (New York: Macmillan, 1986, pp. 255–296). More than any other book, it was likely that Donald Schön's *The Reflective Practitioner* (New York: Basic Books, 1983), was the landmark that gave legitimacy to a huge range of writing on different aspects of a broad image of "teacher lore," an image that of course extends far beyond the teacher lore project presented in this book. The range extends from results of quantitative studies of teachers via classroom interaction, expectation, motivation, student cognition, instruction, and testing, and the advice derived from such studies for teachers (see David C. Berliner and Barak V. Rosenshine, Eds., *Talks to Teachers* (New York: Random House, 1987); to phenomenological, such as Max van Manen, *The Tone of Teaching* (London: Heinemann, 1986); and critical theory such as Henry A. Giroux, *Teachers-as-Intellectuals:. Towards a Critical Pedagogy of Learning* (South Hadley, MA: Bergin & Garvey, 1988). Remaining central to many citation lists was the aforementioned instant classic by Donald Schön, *The Reflective Practitioner*, which provided support for professionals from different fields reflecting seriously about their work *and* in the course of their work. Schön also explained ways to enhance reflective practice in *Educating the Reflective Practitioner* (San Francisco: Jossey-Bass, 1987). I was pleased by this emphasis in the 1980s and its steady growth to the present, since I had hoped for such a movement ever since doing this kind of research for my dissertation in the early 1970s titled *Imaginative Projection: A Method of Curriculum Invention* (University of Illinois, Urbana, 1975).

In the 1980s, therefore, the focus on reflective practice in teaching became very popular, leading into the 1990s. I will highlight some of the work in different subareas of educational writing. The curriculum area has vigorously moved toward emphasis on teachers as paramount developers of curriculum, through what they plan and do and who they are. While Schwab and Stenhouse have already been mentioned in this regard, others should be noted. F. Michael Connelly (a student of Schwab) spearheaded the study of teachers as creators of personal/practical knowledge for a decade, and together with his former student D. Jean Clandinin demonstrated the power of narratives about teachers' inquiry in *Teachers as Curriculum Planners* (New York: Teachers College Press, 1988). More recently Connelly and Clandinin have summarized the research on narrative inquiry of teachers' experience in an article entitled "Stories of Experience and Narrative Inquiry" in *Educational Researcher (19* (4): 2–14, 1990). The review, of course, cited others who do related work, such as Freema Elbaz, Antoinette Oberg, and Hugh Munby.

Those whose interests and concerns are more political in the sense that they question the values and practices that are the basis of an ideology provide another dimension of curriculum discourse—for example, Michael W. Apple and Lois Weis in *Ideology and Practice in Schooling* (Philadelphia: Temple University Press, 1983); Apple, more recently, in *Teachers and Texts (*London: Routledge and Kegan Paul, 1986); Linda McNeil in *Contradictions of Control* (New York and London: Routledge and Kegan Paul, 1986); Shirley Grundy in *Curriculum: Product or Praxis* (London: Falmer, 1987), Ivor F. Goodson in *Teachers' Lives and Careers* (London: Falmer, 1985); Robert Connell in *Teachers' Work* (Winchester, MA: Allen and Unwin, 1985); and in a large sense the parent of many of the works that encourage critical questioning of the ways in which matters of race, class, and gender affect access to knowledge, Paulo Freire's *Pedagogy of the Oppressed* (New York: Seabury, 1970).

Some curriculum writings focus on one of these crucial dimensions, such as gender. For example, *Bitter Milk: Women and Teaching* (Amherst: University of Massachusetts Press, 1988) by Madeleine R. Grumet, *Creating Spaces and Finding Voices (*Albany: State University of New York Press, 1990) by Janet L. Miller, and *Exiles and Communities: Teaching in the Patriarchal Wilderness* by Jo Anne Pagano (Albany: State University of New York Press, 1990) all situate curriculum within a larger sphere of teaching from a feminist perspective.

The whole realm of school improvement literature and supervision has moved in recent years from a mainly autocratic focus (what experts can offer for practitioners) to a more democratic posture (let's cooperate to tap our mutual expertise), and is exemplified by John Smyth's *Critical Perspectives on Educational Leadership* (London: Falmer, 1989), Andrew Gitlin and John Smyth's *Teacher Evaluation: Educative Alternatives* (London: Falmer, 1989), Ann Lieberman's *Building a Professional Culture in Schools* (New York: Teachers College Press, 1988), and Noreen Garman's perceptive article "Clinical Supervision: Quackery or Remedy for Professional Development?" in *Journal of Curriculum and Supervision* (*1*(2): 148–157, 1986).

Teachers' stories (both autobiographic and those told by others) continue to carry considerable influence. I think again of Herb Kohl and John Holt, discussed earlier, and how they and James Herndon—from *The Way It Spozed to Be* (New York: Bantam, 1969) to *Notes from a School Teacher* (New York: Simon & Schuster, 1984) —spanned several decades with their insights from practical educational situations. Teachers sometimes tell about only small features of their learning from experience, such as the collection of teachers' best teaching approaches by Beatrice Gross and Ronald Gross, Eds., *Will It Grow in a Classroom?* (New York: Delta, 1974). Much more oriented to philosophical and psychoanalytic understanding of self is the journey of two college teachers as they sought to make meaning in the present through careful, phenomenological reflection on themselves as actors in a complex social situation by William F. Pinar and Madeleine R. Grumet in *Toward a Poor Curriculum* (Dubuque, IA: Kendall/Hunt, 1976). Those who write about teachers' reflection on experience often immerse themselves in the situations of those teachers for considerable periods of time; they do what Richard L. Butt and Danielle Raymond call for in "Arguments for Using Qualitative Approaches in Understanding Teacher Thinking: The Case for Biography," in *Journal of Curriculum Theorizing* (*7*(1): 62–93, 1987). Examples include William Ayers, *The Good Pre-school Teacher* (New York: Teachers College Press, 1989); Robert V. Bullough, *First-Year Teacher* (New York: Teachers College Press, 1989), *What's Going On,* a portrayal of several episodes in the learning of language by Mary Barr, Pat D'Arcy, and Mary K. Healy (Montclair, NJ: Boynton/Cook, 1982); and Eleanor Duckworth, *The Having of Wonderful Ideas* (New York: Teachers College Press, 1987). Work under way by Stephen Smith and others at Simon Fraser University shows much promise in developing understanding of the essence of teaching through a situation in which several university faculty members and teachers meet regularly over dinner to discuss meanings of their being with children. I also look forward to Rob Traver's dissertation at Harvard, which involves a search for central themes in a range of published, first-person books on teaching by teachers.

Finally, books that provide perspective from philosophy and the arts on teaching include Alan Tom's *Teaching as a Moral Craft* (New York: Longman, 1984), Maxine Greene's *Teacher as Stranger* (New York: Wadsworth, 1973), Nel Noddings' *Caring* (Berkeley: University of California Press, 1984), and Louis J. Rubin's *Artistry in Teaching* (New York: Random House, 1984).

These are books that have had an influence on my perspective on teaching. At the time of this writing I look forward to the publication of the following books: *Stories Lives Tell: Narrative and Dialogue in Education,* edited by Carol Witherell and Nel Noddings (New York: Teachers College Press, 1991); *Teacher Personal*

Theorizing, edited by E. Wayne Ross, Jeffrey Cornett, and Gail McCutcheon (Albany: State University of New York Press, 1992); and *Reflections from the Heart of Educational Inquiry: Understanding Curriculum and Teaching through the Arts*, edited by George Willis and William H. Schubert (Albany: State University of New York Press, 1991).

While most of the sources noted above pertain to teaching generally or at secondary, elementary, and/or preschool levels, it is important to note that recent attention has been given to college teaching, specifically portrayals of teaching about education. Teacher educators and curriculum scholars tell about their perspective on teacher education and relate their approaches to teaching about curriculum in *Teaching and Thinking About Curriculum*, edited by James T. Sears and J. Dan Marshall (New York: Teachers College Press, 1990). Former students of influential educational scholars (now noted contributors to educational theory and practice) interpret the teaching of their mentors and also share descriptions of ways in which they teach about education in *Teaching Education*, a relatively new journal founded by Craig Kridel, its first editor, and now edited by James T. Sears. The understanding of teaching cannot progress far without a complementary understanding of ways in which education itself is taught.

I speak for all the contributors to this book when I say that we continue to seek new books, articles, and other resources to help us understand teachers and teaching more fully. We encourage you to do the same.

CHAPTER 10

Keeping Them Variously:
Learning from the Bees Themselves

William Ayers

Over the years many people have struggled to "neatinize" teaching, to simplify and
define it, and to somehow get control of it. For the past thirty years educational
researchers have made large claims for the value of research on teaching. Scientific
approaches and process-product designs would herald a new day of understanding and
enlightened practice. The fanfare has faded, the results turn out to be small. Recently
the efforts to define teaching summatively have coalesced around an ambitious project
of developing and codifying a "knowledge base" for teaching. Teachers' organizations, colleges of education, scholars and researchers alike have been abuzz in constructing a teachers' knowledge base. It is, of course, a big job. Lee Shulman (1987),
for example, argues that teacher knowledge "organized into a handbook, an encyclo-
pedia, or some other format for arranging knowledge" would necessarily include the
following items at a minimum:

- content knowledge;
- general pedagogical knowledge, with special reference to those broad principles
  and strategies of classroom management and organization that appear to transcend
  subject matter;
- curriculum knowledge, with particular grasp of the materials and programs that
  serve as "tools of the trade" for teachers;
- pedagogical content knowledge, that special amalgam of content and *pedagogy* that
  is uniquely the province of teachers, their own special form of professional understanding;
- knowledge of learners and their characteristics;
- knowledge of educational contexts, ranging from the workings of the group or

classroom, the governance and financing of school districts, to the character of communities and cultures; and

- knowledge of educational ends, purposes, and values, and their philosophical and historical grounds (p. 302).

Like most attempts of this type, Shulman's list is exhausting if not exhaustive. The impetus to make such a list is clear enough: It offers some organization and clarity in the often messy business of teaching; it promises to consolidate and make sense of all the fragmented and detached bits and pieces of knowledge about teaching, and it elevates research on teaching while it forms the basis for the argument that teaching has become a more fully developed profession.

But the list also intimidates. It implies that teacher knowledge is extremely rational and highly technical—or that it ought to aspire to be so—rather than being essentially multidimensional and intersubjective. The list constructs teaching as orderly, systematic, and generalizable, rather than person-specific and circumstantial. It casts teacher knowledge as arcane and inaccessible, something that is primarily generated by outside researchers and experts and then transferred more or less successfully to practitioners. Even if one believes, as I do, that schoolteachers are the ultimate generalists and must, therefore, have revolving access to knowledge of an infinite range of disciplines and literacies, the list may be unhelpful. No one would argue for less knowledge, of course, or less skill or less intellectual rigor in teachers' backgrounds; yet the list, perhaps intentionally, perhaps inadvertently, limits what teachers need to know even as it bullies them with its hugeness. Shulman acknowledges as much in a humorous footnote: "I have attempted this list in other publications, though admittedly, not with great cross-article consistency" (p. 320).

Any choices made in a list like this will demean or exclude something: Where, for example, do we find knowledge of self, something central to good teaching, or knowledge of human development, knowledge of the hidden curriculum, knowledge of racism and its impact on all students, knowledge of gender differences and gender oppression, or knowledge of classroom survival skills like creative insubordination? If teaching involves the complex synthesizing of the kinds of knowledge on Shulman's list, and the effective application of this knowledge in practice, then self-awareness may be indispensable. If teaching is in part the effort to create opportunities for children to choose to learn, if it is in part guiding children to make sense and to become competent, powerful, and ethical in a world that is at least in some ways limiting and unjust, then awareness of race and gender differences, for example, may be critical.

Furthermore, any list of teacher knowledge ignores or obscures another, perhaps more urgent consideration: the dispositions of mind that may be required to be an effective or outstanding teacher, dispositions that may be difficult or impossible to teach in a straightforward way but are still somehow indispensable. Who would deny, for example, that a compassionate and caring attitude is essential in good teaching? Who would not hope for teachers who are curious and inquiring? But the search for the "knowledge base," noble in some ways, is unhelpful to us as we pursue these attributes, as we uncover and understand the heart of teaching.

Teachers, like other people, make sense of their experiences as stories, and listening to the stories teachers tell can be a useful step in the process of understanding teaching. Of course, teachers' stories are various. There are funny stories and sad stories, accounts of accomplishment as well as combat, descriptions of heroism and parables of disaster. The stories are mostly informal, fragments brought home from the field for friends and family. These short and unfinished stories are often about exhaustion, about too many children and too few resources, about the seemingly intractable structural problems of formal schooling, or the elusive difficulties presented by this or that child. Sometimes the stories are about the absurd, the weird, the ridiculous revelations students share in classrooms. And they can also be about moments of real accomplishment and satisfaction, stories with hidden subtexts of passion and commitment.

Unfortunately teachers' stories are hard to find. They are generally dismissed, even by teachers, even by the storytellers themselves, as personal and unimportant. They are in the main uncollected and unexamined, and they become, then, irrelevant as a source of knowledge about teaching. Teacher lore is largely a lost treasure, and the natural history of teaching is subsequently diminished. Happily this general trend has been increasingly challenged in recent years. There has been a resurgence of interest in the voice, perspective, and insight of teachers. Perhaps this is the result of confronting the failure, the rather puny results of decades of expensive and highly touted research on teaching. Perhaps it is part of a general movement toward recovering and strengthening the voices of individuals as they name their own situations and wrestle with their own problems in contexts that are often impersonal, and always somehow resistant. Perhaps it is part of a general movement in science in which paradigms are shifting.

Walker Percy (1990) notes that the "physical sciences are converging whereas the psychic 'sciences' are diverging—and getting nuttier as they do" (p. 12). In any case, the interest in the voice of the teacher is a welcome development, for it is a process with promise for building greater confidence, consciousness, and power among teachers themselves.

One example of this direction is an autobiographical project I undertook with a group of colleagues and friends, each a preschool teacher (Ayers, 1989). This project was an attempt to understand preschool teaching from the inside, as it were, as these teachers themselves understood it. Instead of aggregating teachers in a search for the common teacher, the point here was to understand concrete situations, to hear the particular voices of specific teachers. The choice was to discover a lot about a few teachers rather than a little about a lot of teachers, to give full voice to a relative handful of teachers. The goal of the work was for these teachers to say what was significant for them about teaching, and in the process to become more reflective themselves, more intentional—freer—more able to endorse or reject aspects of their own teaching that they found hopeful or contrary, more able to author their own teaching scripts. The project was a partnership—if I was a participant observer, then each of these teachers was an observant participator—and the results were textured portraits of teachers teaching and then reflecting on their own lives. I cannot claim to have arrived at any lawlike propositions or even to have achieved a testable hypothesis though these narratives. More modestly, we have, I believe, together created credible accounts, and contributed to an expanded natural history of teaching.

Part of what we learned is summed up by Sue Hubbell (1988) in a lovely account of her journey as a beekeeper:

> Beekeepers are an opinionated lot, each sure that his methods, and his methods alone, are the proper ones. When I first began keeping bees, the diversity of passionately held opinion bewildered me, but now that I have hives in locations scattered over a thousand-square-mile area I think I understand it. . . . Frosts come earlier in some places than in others. Spring comes later. Rainfall is not the same. The soils, and the flowering plants they support, are unlike. Through the years, I have learned that as a result of all these variations I must keep the bees variously. Most people who keep bees have only a few hives, and have them all in one place. They find it difficult to understand why practices that have proved successful for them do not work for others. But I have learned that I must treat the bees in one yard quite differently from the way I do those even thirty miles away. The thing to do, I have discovered, is to learn from the bees themselves.
> (p. 45)

Being aware of oneself as the instrument of one's teaching, aware of details and distinctions—aware, that is, of the bees themselves, and aware of the story that makes one's life sensible—allows for thoughtful change and growth. Steady, empathic scrutiny can help in this sense making, and may even improve teaching. Teacher autobiographies can offer the kind of detail from which one can fruitfully interpret practice, value, and belief in light of an unfolding story. They can provide a means of stretching contexts. Autobiographical projects have potential for creating greater questioning, critique, and intentionality in teaching choices, because autobiography highlights the experimental, improvisational nature of constructing a life. Alice Walker's (1970) comment about her narrative-gathering work among African-American women in Mississippi in the 1960s applies in this way to teachers:

> Slowly I am getting these stories together. Not for the public, but for the ladies who wrote them. Will seeing each other's lives make any of the past clearer to them? I don't know. I hope so. I hope contradictions will show, but also the faith and grace of a people under continuous pressures. So much of the satisfying work of life begins as an experiment; having learned this, no experiment is ever quite a failure.
> (p. 17)

There are other approaches, of course, to understanding teaching and teachers from the inside. While researchers who follow a positivistic paradigm search for truths and facts that are somehow "out there," interpretive researchers are concerned with the personal and social meaning that human beings construct beneath all the observable behaviors. And while the "scientific," quantitative folks are justifying their work by pointing to methods and procedures, their "loose" qualitative counterparts are concerned chiefly with the content of the story: Is it credible? Does it contribute to the larger sense-making conversation? Qualitative researchers tend to be comfortable with Vaclev Havel's comment that because of "the miracle of speech, we know probably better than the other animals that we actually know very little, in other words we are conscious of the existence of mystery" (Havel, 1990).

Increasingly researchers are becoming conscious of mystery, conscious too of the power relationships inherent in any research paradigm, especially when mystery is denied. These researchers are searching for ways to build a collaborative process of inquiry, one that serves the needs of teachers and students rather than the more abstract goal of "knowledge production" disembodied from conduct and practice. They are dissatisfied with the conventional notion of knowledge as something to be divided up and transferred to the uninitiated. They are interested in empowering people through a kind of research linked to practice, in people defining solutions and actions for themselves. Nel Noddings (1986) argues that we

> have perhaps too often made *persons* (teachers and students) the objects of research. An alternative is to choose *problems* that interest and concern researchers, students, and teachers. . . . Such research would be genuine research *for* teaching instead of simply research on teaching. (p. 394)

This book, *Teacher Lore*, is one attempt to systematically collect the stories, insights, knowledge—the lore—of experienced classroom teachers. The project is a search (perhaps this is a better word choice than "research," pointing as it does to the singular quest and the specific challenge) for detail, for the unique signature of each teacher. The book is based on the idea that it is in the lived situations of actual children and teachers—rather than in, for example, the educational commissions, policy panels, or sanctified research reports—that the teaching enterprise exists and can best be understood. Teaching is found in the actions of everyday practice, the very stuff that is washed away in most attempts to generalize about teaching. To unlock the reality of teaching is to move beyond the distanced and sanitized language of the social scientist, the bloodless objectivity of the technician and the expert—the official language of research, and increasingly the only acceptable language of public life—and to enter the messy, subjective world of teachers where the talk is idiosyncratic and particular, infused with immediacy and urgently linked to conduct. It is to pierce the veil of facts, and to partake of value-talk and feeling-talk, talk of the ordinary and the mundane, and yet talk that is frequently eloquent, consistently thoughtful, and almost always characterized by an abiding sense of care and connection. It is to willingly enter Havel's world of mystery.

REFERENCES

Ayers, W. C. (1989). *The good preschool teacher: Six teachers reflect on their lives.* New York: Teachers College Press.

Havel, V. (1990). Words on words. *The New York Review of Books*, 26(21–22): 5–7.

Hubbell, S. (1988). The sweet bees. *The New Yorker*, May 9, 1988, pp. 45–76.

Noddings, N. (1986). Fidelity in teaching, teacher education, and research for teaching. *Harvard Educational Review*, 56(4): 384–389.

Percy, W.A. (1990). The divided creature. *Teaching and Learning*, 4(2): 9–19.

Shulman, L. S. (1987). Knowledge and teaching: Foundations of the new reform. In Margo Okazawa-Rey, James Anderson, and Rob Traver (Eds.), *Teachers, teaching, and teacher education*. Cambridge, MA: Harvard Educational Review.

Walker, A. (1970). But yet and still the cotton gin kept on working. *The Black Scholar*, *1*(3–4): 13–17.

CHAPTER 11

In the Country of the Blind:

Telling Our Stories

William Ayers

Research on teaching is still dominated by what Clifford Geertz (1983) has called a "laws-and-causes social physics" (p. 3), still suffering from what Patti Lather (1988) calls "physics envy," that perverse phenomenon of striving anxiously to be like the Big Guys who we imagine are doing all manner of classy things with all sorts of fancy equipment. Never mind that the work of physicists is quite different from what we believe, that many physicists are, for example, necessarily dreamy and imaginative. The tragedy lies in what we obscure and what we distort when we move from a study of high-energy particles, say, to one of human interactions, from planets to people, from quarks to kids. The positivistic frame, which rumbles along, some would say uneasily, in the natural domain, proves to be entirely too thin, too narrow, altogether inappropriate when superimposed on the fuzzy, fugitive world of human beings. We need a different frame, an altered angle, if understanding people is our aim. Abraham Maslow pointed out long ago that when the only tool one has is a hammer, one treats everything as if it were a nail. A laboratory experiment may enlighten us in regard to the properties of a virus; to get a joke, to understand a poem, to comprehend a mystery requires a different sort of tool.

The concept of teacher lore offers a different sort of tool. It offers a parallax view, an alternative way in, not by criticizing or confronting the dominant research paradigms so much as by ignoring them. The idea is still in its infancy—more promise than design, more possibility than dogma—and shaping what it is to be is still an open invitation. For some this rawness and newness, this lack of definite shape, represents a weakness; for others it is its singular strength. Teacher lore may yet become embodied in a diversity of approaches, a range of people and places. With some luck and a bit of consciousness, a sense of wonder, acceptance, and invitation may survive.

At its heart, teacher lore, as its name implies, is a storytelling and a story-hearing activity. We are, each of us, grounded in a context, embodied in a physical, cultural, historical world not of our own creation. What we make of that world, and what we make of ourselves in that world, is what our stories are all about.

There is, of course, not a single story to tell, but a kaleidoscope of stories, changing, flowing, crashing against one another, each one playing, light and shadow, off the others in an infinity of pure and crazy patterns. There are moral myths and heroic accounts, subversive parables and standard homilies, women's stories as well as men's stories, black and white narratives, tales of humiliation and of triumph, tragedy and transcendence, the sad story of the slow and silent erosion of passion or concern. The key is that teaching and teachers are never quite summed up, never easily reducible to a simple story. The storytellers are various, and the stories themselves infinite.

Most often, the stories teachers tell are partial and uneven, anecdotes exchanged in the teachers' lounge, jokes passed in the hallway. I take teacher lore to be in part an attempt to apprehend the ragged tales teachers tell, an exercise in making them accessible to teachers themselves as well as to others who care what teaching is, what teachers do. To the extent that teacher lore is involved in a larger project of creating a public space for teachers, it is the voice of the teacher that must at last be heard, the action of the teacher that must finally come nearer center stage. The more this occurs, the more accomplished, the more difficult, elusive, complex, as well as rich and meaningful, our portrait of teaching may become. And in a way, the more troubling, the more problematic becomes our view of the researcher. I am reminded, then, of the old Chinese caution to the anthropologist: If you stay in China for two weeks, you will write a book about all you have learned; if you stay for two years, you will have nothing to say. As we mine the fields of teacher lore, we should, at the very least, remain clear regarding the relationship of researcher and researched, and Geertz's (1983) caveat may help: "In the country of the blind, who are not as unobservant as they look, the one-eyed is not king, he is spectator" (p. 58).

I taught school for nearly a dozen years, mainly in preschool, always in early childhood education. For me, teaching was much more than a job, more even than a career, more than a contingent activity with neat boundaries separating it from the rest of my life. I began teaching as what seemed a natural part of my involvement in the peace and freedom movements; after several years away from school but engaged in related activities, I reentered teaching, again in what seemed a holistic, instinctive act, following the birth of our oldest child. The reason to teach was, for me, bound up with an interpenetrating sense of the political and the personal: engaged in the world enough to want to change it (and to share it, or parts of it) and loving children enough to want to be with them, to care for them (or, perhaps, loving what became of me when I was caring for them). In any case, teaching was part of a project of social change, of critique and transformation, as well as what I hoped would be a humane, person-affirming activity, a collection of tiny deeds and small achievements, each heavy with significance and pointing beyond itself to something larger, something yet to come.

In my years in classrooms I learned many things, not the least this: Teaching is a deeply personal experience, but it is at its heart a social activity, even a political act.

This is in part because of the collection of lives gathered together in a shared space, sometimes a common pursuit, more often now a remarkable and irregular struggle. Teaching and learning occur increasingly in spite of or in resistance to the institutions of education with their reliance on rule, order, procedure, and compliance. More to the point, teaching is typically embedded in schooling, and schooling in the larger historical, economic, and social structures that shape every other institution. School systems serve social systems in all kinds of direct and indirect ways. The schools of South Africa, for example, whatever else they teach, teach apartheid and each person's place in it. How could it be otherwise? Here, too, teaching cannot be divorced from social and cultural contexts.

While context sets the stage for what will occur, it cannot determine every outcome. Teachers are certainly shaped by their relationship to power and their role in a vast bureaucracy bent on reproducing social relations, but teachers also decide much of what goes on in classrooms. Teaching can be conscious or unconscious, reflexive or reflective, insipid or insurgent. Teachers, like others, can choose to satisfy distant demands or not, accommodate established expectations or not, embrace the narrowest self-interest or not. Teachers can decide to pass on the lessons of conformity, mindlessness, and obedience, or they can decide to rebel when necessary, to interpret and invent when possible, to join with others, with students and parents perhaps, in creating something new and hopeful. Teaching can be miserable and cowardly, and teaching can also be noble and heroic. It all depends.

Shortly after I returned to graduate school I was confronted with the problem of doing an independent research project. I had reentered school for a credential only, and had been surprised to find much of deeper value and greater importance in the experience—the good fortune of having stumbled into Bank Street College, I think. In any case, I now looked toward the project with dread, assuming that "research" meant either a controlled experiment complete with dependent and independent variables or counting some observable phenomena and then analyzing to death some data set—neither a prospect to delight. As I considered the problem, I came upon Clifford Geertz's *The Interpretation of Cultures* (1973) and was jolted with a new (for me) idea: I could look closely at actual cases of teachers at work, and my goal could be rendering lives or interpreting work rather than testing hypotheses or generating laws.

Reading Geertz was the right thing at the right time: He said what I thought, articulated what was still unformed and in search of a frame, nurtured my instinct and challenged my developing thought. Liberation. Soon my "research" was under way: I was working in classrooms of teachers I admired—observing, participating, recording what went on, noting everything of significance that I could note. I was also interviewing teachers: How did you come to take on that idea? Why did you make that decision? Working with teachers as conscious collaborators in telling the larger story of teaching—this became my research project.

Teacher lore covers a lot of ground (a multitude of sins? a range of dimensions? a host of possibilities?). From my point of view, teacher lore, or each particular piece of teacher lore, whatever else it does, must grapple with certain core assumptions about teaching and about research. In teacher lore, teaching is assumed to be a voluntary, intelligent, collective activity that occurs in contexts that are often coercive, ignorant, and individualizing. Good teachers are too often turned into turkeys because they work for the most part on turkey farms, and yet teaching remains intellectual and ethical work, person-specific and situationally grounded, an activity like swimming or riding a bike, practically impossible to describe in an intelligible way outside of the doing of it. All of this fuels a view that teachers are a key source of knowledge about teaching.

In teacher lore, research is not didactic, intimidating, or oppressive, but is allowed to be interpreted, shared, and creative, and always in the service of teachers and students. All the pseudoscientific baggage—the authoritative third-person voice, for example, the blizzard of propositions, scholarly citations, expert conclusions—can give way to some sort of autobiographical style, some honest accounting of how the author-researcher got where she or he was going. This invitation to the reader into the researcher's head, this personal, close-in approach, is risky because it flaunts tradition, making the process public and the conclusions open to greater scrutiny. It can also be, for some, more satisfying because it gets at teaching in a way that is more holistic, perhaps more complete. It is no longer sanctified as "real research," so perhaps we can just call it search.

While teacher lore coheres around certain propositions, it does not solve many difficulties, and it in fact opens problems (explicitly or not) in practically every instance. All the pitfalls of qualitative inquiry are questions here as well: problems of reliability and validity (were phenomena observed? were informants plentiful or at least believable? was sufficient time allowed for the inquiry to progress?); problems concerning the relationship of researcher to researched (is the position of the researcher stipulated? are disturbances in the field noted?); analytical problems (is material overinterpreted or underinterpreted? does analysis choke on too much detail or starve on abstraction?). In addition, there are problems particular to biographical or autobiographical methods: the problem of self-knowledge, of personal biases and beliefs in both gathering information and making sense of findings; the problem of "good faith" in creating rapport with another person in what is essentially an interactive, collaborative enterprise; the problem of subjective responsibility, of personal implication in the research report. The fundamental problem common to this work is an interpretive (and not a scholarly) one: how to simultaneously convey a sense of individual life and collective design, how to move between local detail and universal structure, how to grasp both personal integrity and social dimension, how to balance being both within the research project and outside of it. The value in meeting these problems (apparent whenever successfully done) lies in the fact that autobiography— personal life as cultural window—is an act of self-definition, of self-creation, and is, then, potentially an act of transformation. Only human beings, after all, are capable of creating a public, conscious life history; only human beings, then, can sift through, shape and reshape that history and thereby create a purposeful tomorrow. Imagination—that distinctly human capacity—allows us to reflect on our lives and to project a future different from today, to focus, not on an indelible past or an immutable present, but rather on something to live for.

People outside of natural history may find it quaint, as Stephen Jay Gould contends, that naturalists study chimpanzees, for example, case by case, constructing elaborate accounts of a single individual. Gould argues that it is far from quaint—that it is in fact essential science. This is because there is no essence of chimpness; there are, instead, endless details and possibilities, the study of which expands our understanding, enriches our knowledge, complicates as well as makes truer our conclusions.

Teacher lore can help expand the natural history of teaching. We need more details, more instances, more cases. Teacher lore can be an antidote to arid research, to prescriptive policy, to empty promises. It can be a force for combatting the culture of cynicism—that pervasive sense of powerlessness and meaninglessness flourishing in so many schools—and it can be a means of supporting accomplishment (a quality grossly devalued in our society in favor of celebrity) and collective action (equally diminished today in favor of individual wish or will).

I am left with questions:

- Can teacher lore be taught? Can it be nurtured in schools? What would have to change to allow teacher lore a foothold?

- Does teacher lore imply a reconceptualized structure or content for teacher education? For supervision?

- Does teacher lore inform the discussion of equity, of social justice, of emancipation? Does an awareness of teacher lore have implications for the larger project of reform?

- Is teacher lore a helpful frame for all teachers? Does it serve the interest of teachers? Does it serve the interest of school systems? Of families and children?

- Is teacher lore the province of university-based researchers? Can it be a project of teachers themselves?

- Does teacher lore isolate or organize? Does it contribute to teachers seeing the common—collectivizing, rebelling—or could it promote preciousness and elitism?

And on and on. This conclusion, like teacher lore itself, is no conclusion at all. It remains unfinished; it, too, awaits the next utterance. It is up to many of us, including you, the reader, to take the next steps. Your insights, experiences, and contributions can become a central part of this ongoing project. Once again I am reminded of an ancient admonition: She who thinks she knows does not know; she who knows she does not know, knows.

REFERENCES

Geertz, C. (1973). *The interpretation of cultures.* New York: Basic Books.

Geertz, C. (1983). *Local knowledge: Further essays in interpretive anthropology.* New York: Basic Books.

Lather, P. (1988). Informal talk at Bergamo Curriculum Conference. Dayton, Ohio.

Postscript

We are interested quite naturally in your response to the idea of teacher lore as developed in this book. Therefore, we would be grateful for comments that you might send us. Our address is below. In addition, the larger outcome of this book could be found in teachers and other educators who do teacher lore—perhaps even inventing their own versions. Sometimes this might take the form of written accounts and at other times it might take the form of communities of sharing wherein educators reflect together about what, how, and why they do what they do. We are most interested in this, as well, and extend our good wishes to you.

William H. Schubert or
William Ayers
University of Illinois at Chicago (m/c 147)
College of Education
Box 4348
Chicago, Illinois 60680

Index